HUMAN RESOURCE DEVELOPMENT IN HOTEL INDUSTRY

By

Prof. Basant Mehta

Ph.D.

Ex-Professor

Deptt. of Banking & Financial Management

Ex - PG Dean (Research)

Janardan Rai Nagar Rajasthan

Vidyapeeth (Deemed) University

Udaipur (Rajasthan) (INDIA)

&

Dr. Priyanka Daya Choudhary

Post-graduate

Ph.D.

D P H

DISCOVERY PUBLISHING HOUSE PVT. LTD.

NEW DELHI-110 002

Published by:
Tilak Wasan

DISCOVERY PUBLISHING HOUSE PVT. LTD.
4383/4B, Ansari Road, Darya Ganj
New Delhi-110 002 (India)
Phone : +91-11-23279245, 43596064-65
Fax : +91-11-23253475
E-mail : discoverypublishinghouse@gmail.com
sales@discoverypublishinggroup.com
parul.wasan@gmail.com
web : www.discoverypublishinggroup.com

***First Edition:* 2014**

ISBN: 978-93-5056-396-0

Human Resource Development in Hotel Industry

Printed at:
Dynamic Printers
Delhi

Preface

HOTEL INDUSTRY is one of the core industries of the country. It is the main pillar of Tourism Industry. It plays vital role in the development of the country. Historically viewed as an industry providing a luxury service valuable to the economy only as a foreign exchange earner, the industry today contributes directly to employment and indirectly facilitates tourism and commerce. The Success of any hotel depends on the synergy created by its human resources. The human resources appreciated in value through increase knowledge, experience and efficiency. Therefore Human Resource Development has become very popular in the recent years. Many Hotels spend considerable effort and skill in planning the purchase, installation and maintenance of machinery and often pay little attention to the need for planning their manpower requirements. New Hotels and restaurants are built and almost as an afterthought, management applies itself to the recruitment and training of human resources. There are some Hotels where future needs to various categories of human resource are considered and plans are set in hand for their training and development.

The present investigation is an attempt to study the Human Resource Development in five star hotel industry. This book has been divided into five chapters. The first chapter deals with 'Development and Growth of Tourism and Hotel Industry.' In the second chapter 'Human Resource Development in Hotel Industry' has been discussed. The third chapter 'Review of Literature and Research Methodology' deals with the review of work already done on the subject, importance and objectives of study, hypothesis framing, methods of data collection, sampling design and profile of the respondents. Analysis of field work has been done in chapter fourth 'A Case Study of Five Star Hotels'. Finally in chapter fifth 'Research Findings and Suggestions' gives a brief summary of the whole study and findings of the investigation. It's also highlights the problems faced by employees in the hotel industries and offers possible solutions. Suggestions for further improvement have been also incorporated so as to provide suitable guidelines for the successful development of human resource in the hotel industries.

This book would not have been completed without the support of various generous and intellectual people. Author is thankful to Discovery Publishing House Pvt. Ltd., New Delhi and all those who have contributed in successful realization of this book.

—Authors

Contents

CHAPTER

1 Growth and Development of Tourism and Hotel Industry

INTRODUCTION

Hotels and the catering industry started late in the 19th century, with the development of the major cities, easier sea travel and the coming of the railways. In ancient times, travelers were a rarity, but they could always rely on a meal while passing through. As the centuries progressed, travelers, mostly pilgrims, would be cared for in the temples or in monasteries. During the Moghul rule, the fort and the surrounds would cater to the needs of the traveler– often in exchange of no more than the story of their adventures during their travel or any news from other towns or villages.

Tourism has the potential to stimulate other economic sectors through its backward and forward linkages and cross-sectoral synergies with sectors like agriculture, horticulture, poultry, handicrafts, transport, construction, etc. Expenditure on tourism induces a chain of transactions requiring supply of goods and services from these related sectors. The consumption demand, emanating from tourist expenditure, also induces more employment and generates a multiplier effect on the economy. As a result, additional income and employment opportunities are generated through such linkages. Thus, the expansion of the tourism sector can lead to large scale employment generation and poverty alleviation. The economic benefits that flow into the economy through growth of tourism in the shape of increased national and State revenues, business receipts, employment, wages and salary, buoyancy in Central, State and local tax receipts can contribute towards overall socio-economic improvement and accelerated growth in the economy.

Ellsworth M. Statler — The Henry Ford of the modern hotel — once said, "The guest is always right." [1] "The hotel Industry is a part of larger enterprise known as the travel and tourism industry. The travel and tourism industry is a vast group of business with one goal in common: providing necessary or desired product and services to travelers." [2]

Table 1.1: Overview of the Travel and Tourism Industry

Lodging Operations	Transport Activities	F and B Operations	Retail Store	Activities
Hotels Motels	Aeroplane Ships	Restaurants lodging properties	Gift Shops Souvenir	Recreation Business
Resorts Time Share hotels Conference Centers	Autos Buses Trains	Vending Shops Catering Malls Snack bars Cruise ship	Arts/Crafts Shopping Markets Miscellaneous Stores	Meeting Study trip Sporting events
Camps Parks Bed and Breakfast Casinos Convention Centers Cruise Ships	Limousines	Bars/taverns Banquets contract food service	—	Ethnic festivals cultural events seasonal festival gaming

Source: Kasavana, M.L., and Brooks, R.M., Front office Procedures 4th E.D., Educational Institute of American Hotel and Motel Association, Michigan, 1996.

Table 1.1 divides the Travel and Tourism Industry into five parts and shows some of the components of each part. Among five parts of travel and tourism industry lodging operations includes hotels and motels, resorts and time share hotels, conference centers, camps and parks, bed and breakfast, casinos, convention centers and cruise ships. Among transport segment aero plane ships, autos and buses, trains and limousines are included. Further restaurants and lodging properties, vending shops and catering malls, snack bars and cruise ships, bars/taverns, banquets and contract food services included in F and B operations. Tourism industry also operates as retail store such as gift shops and souvenir, arts/crafts and shopping markets and miscellaneous stores. Various recreational business activities, gaming, meeting study trip, sporting events, ethnic festivals and cultural events and seasonal festivals are organized by travel and tourism industry.

"The Hotel and Operations stand apart from other travel and tourism business since they offer overnight accommodation to their guests. Many hotel properties provide Food and Beverage service, recreation service and more such facilities. There are, as estimated 10 millions guest rooms available to tourists around the world." [3] "According to World Tourism Organization (WTO) Madrid, Tourism has now become the world's largest Industry, ahead of automobiles and petroleum products." [4] "Further, with regard to employment, as per the World Tourism and Travel council report, Travel and Tourism Industry is the largest civilian industry in the world, employing one out of every ten persons worldwide." [5] "Besides the Tourism sector provides direct employment to 80 lacs people and indirect employment to two crores people." [6] "The Indian Tourism Industry has been defined to include the following segments." [7] Hotels, restaurants, resorts and other tourist complexes providing accommodation food and catering services to tourists.

1. Travel and agencies and tour operators.
2. Units, providing facilities to tourists on culture, adventure wild-life experiences.
3. Surface water and air transport facilities to the tourists.
4. Leisure, entertainment, amusement sports and health units for tourists.
5. Convention and Seminar units.

Hotels are the vital and essential parts of tourism industry. Without an adequate development of hotel resources, all the national scenery, all the climate virtues and all sporting and recreational facilities will not suffice to sustain a good volume of tourist's trade. While considering the importance of the hotel within tourism industry the report of the estimate committee of Lok Sabha (1975-76) says, "Since the hotel constitutes the most important and in fact, a basic element of tourism promotion will not produce the desired results if the hotel accommodation in the country lags behind." [8] *Dr. Negi* writes, "It has been rightly said, 'No hotels, No tourism.' The expansion of tourism will inevitably bring about the development of the hotel industry. "Hotel Industry is so closely linked with the tourism industry — that it is responsible for about 50 per cent of the foreign exchange earnings from tourism." [9] "The employment avenues in the services — oriented hotel industry are quite large. The significant feature of the employment in the hotel sector is that it employs a large number of women — a need of present times. Then, it employs, the educated, uneducated, skilled and semi-skilled and even unskilled also - again, a need of a country. As regards the direct employment it is estimated that the room to staff ratio for a hotel varies between 1:5 to 1:3, whereas the committee on unemployed for 2.5 persons." [10] "On an average, the visit of each foreign tourist provides employment to one person and 6.5 domestic tourists generate one job." [11] Further, with regard to indirect employment there are a number of other employment avenues connected to the hotel industry — *viz.*, supply of food items, various machinery items, from kitchen to air conditioning, laundry equipments, computers, furniture fixtures, cutlery, crockery etc. "The Bhagwati committee said, it would (indirect) offer nine times employment to the number of persons directly employed in hotels." [12] Moreover, hotel industry seems more effective than industries in generating employment.

The hotel industry has a direct impact on regional and rural development. The industry has encouraged cottage industries in many ways — handlooms for furnishings, carpets, handicrafts etc. "In Keeping with the philosophy of self-reliance through indigenous sources, the hotel industry has relied predominantly on getting the supplies and equipments fabricated in the country." [13] "The hotel industry also provides an opportunity to the guests to know the regional or a country's way of life and culture. In overall terms it has multiple economic benefits which are an urgent requirement for a developing country like India." [14]

Tourism in the World

Tourism is travel for recreational, leisure or business purposes. The World Tourism Organization defines tourists as people who "travel to and stay in places outside their usual environment for more than twenty-four hours and not more than one consecutive year for leisure, business and other purposes not related to the exercise of an activity remunerated from within the place visited." [15]

"Tourism has become a popular global leisure activity. In 2008, there were over 922 millions international tourist arrivals, with a growth of 1.9 per cent as compared to 2007. International tourism receipts grew to US$ 944 billion in 2008, corresponding to an increase in real terms of 1.8 per cent." [16] "As a result of the late-2000s recession, international travel demand suffered a strong slowdown beginning in June 2008, with growth in international tourism arrivals worldwide falling to 2 per cent during the boreal summer months." [17] "This negative trend intensified during 2009, exacerbated in some countries due to the outbreak of the H_1N_1 influenza virus, resulting in a worldwide decline of 4 per cent in 2009 to 880 million international tourists arrivals, and an estimated 6 per cent decline in international tourism receipts." [18]

Tourism is vital for many countries, such as Egypt, Greece, Lebanon, Spain, Malaysia and Thailand, and many island nations, such as The Bahamas, Fiji, Maldives, Philippines and the Seychelles, due to the large intake of money for businesses with their goods and services and the opportunity for employment in the service industries associated with tourism. These service industries include transportation services, such as airlines, cruise ships and taxicabs, hospitality services, such as accommodations, including hotels and resorts, and entertainment venues, such as amusement parks, casinos, shopping malls, music venues and theatres.

Table 1.2 revealed the growth rate of foreign tourist arrivals in top ten countries of the world during 2006 to 2010. The table 1.2 showed that in 2006 highest number of FTA was recorded in France (77.90 Mn) whereas Malaysia (17.50 Mn) ranked last in this context. However in terms of FTA growth rate during 2006-07 Malaysia ranked first with 20 per cent growth rate and United Kingdom with the least growth rate of 0.65 per cent only. Number of foreign tourist arrivals increased from 22.20 Mn to 25 Mn with the growth rate of 12.61 per cent in Turkey during 2007-08. Turkey scored highest growth rate during that period. The year 2010 showed that number of FTA was highest in France (76.80 Mn) followed by United States (59.70 Mn), Spain (55.70 Mn) and China (52.70Mn). It is noticeable that FTA growth rate was negative in France, China, Spain and United Kingdom in 2008 and 2009; in U.S.A, Germany and Mexico in 2009 and in Italy in 2008. Turkey and Malaysia were two countries where FTA was positive during 2006 to 2010.

Tourism in the Country

"The tourism industry in India is substantial and vibrant, and the country is fast becoming a major global destination. India's travel and tourism industry is one of the most profitable industries in the country, and also credited with contributing a substantial amount of foreign exchange. This is illustrated by the fact that during 2006, four millions tourists visited India and spent US $8.9 billion. Several reasons are cited for the growth and prosperity of India's travel and tourism industry. Economic growth has added millions annually to the ranks of India's middle class, a group that is driving domestic tourism growth. Disposable income in India has grown by 10.11 per cent annually from 2001-2006, and much of that is being spent on travel." [19]

Table 1.2: Most Visited Countries by International Tourist Arrivals (In Millions)

Year	France		United States		Spain		China		Italy	
	Arrivals	GR %	Arrivals	GR %	Arrivals	GR %	Arrivals	GR %	Arrivals	GR %
2006	77.90	—	51.00	—	58.00	—	49.90	—	41.10	—
2007	80.90	3.85	56.00	9.80	58.70	1.21	54.70	9.62	43.70	6.33
2008	79.20	-2.10	57.90	3.39	57.20	-2.55	53.00	-3.10	42.70	-2.28
2009	74.20	-6.31	54.90	-5.18	52.20	-8.74	50.90	-3.96	43.20	1.17
2010	76.80	3.50	59.70	8.74	55.70	6.70	52.70	3.53	43.60	0.92

Contd..

Year	United Kingdom		Turkey		Germany		Malaysia		Mexico	
	Arrivals	GR %	Arrivals	GR %	Arrivals	GR %	Arrivals	GR %	Arrivals	GR %
2006	30.70	—	18.90	—	23.60	—	17.50	—	21.40	—
2007	30.90	0.65	22.20	17.46	24.40	3.39	21.00	20.00	21.40	0.00
2008	30.10	-2.95	25.00	12.61	24.90	2.05	22.10	54.24	22.60	5.61
2009	28.00	-6.97	25.50	2.00	24.20	-2.81	23.60	6.78	21.50	-4.86
2010	28.10	0.35	27.00	5.88	26.90	11.16	24.60	4.23	22.40	4.18

Resource: www.Wikipedia.org

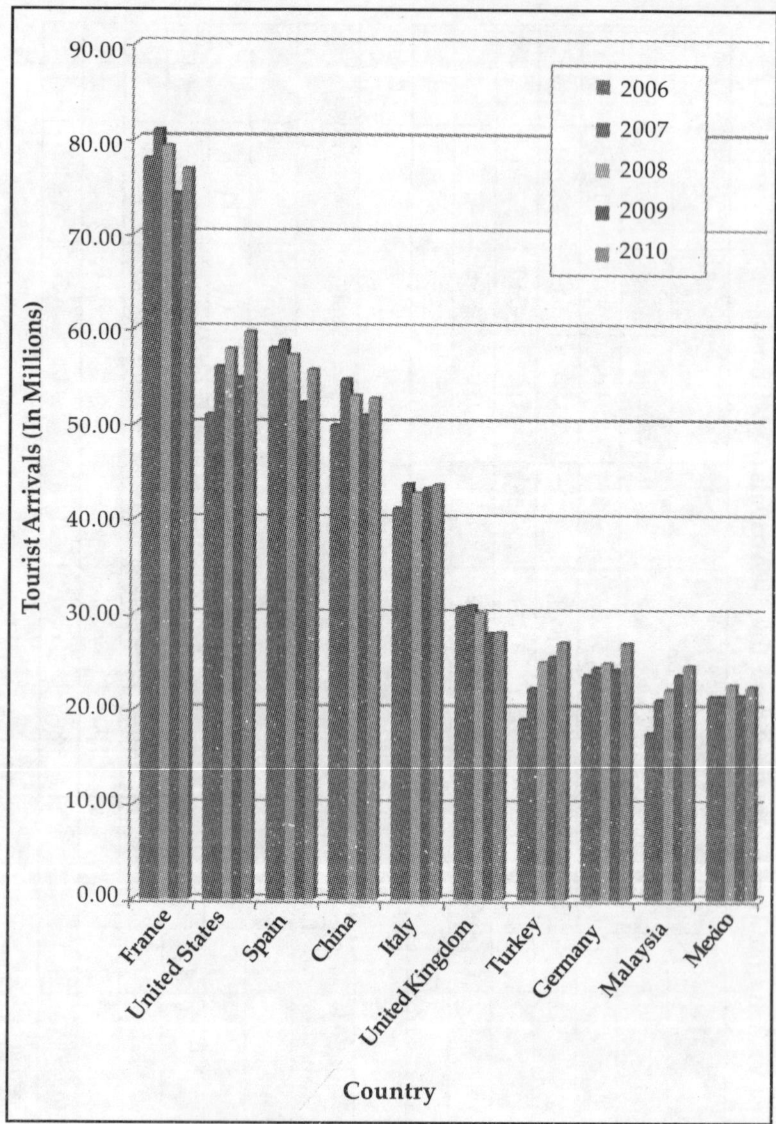

Fig. 1.1: Most Visited Countries by International Tourist Arrivals

Resource: www.wikipedia.org

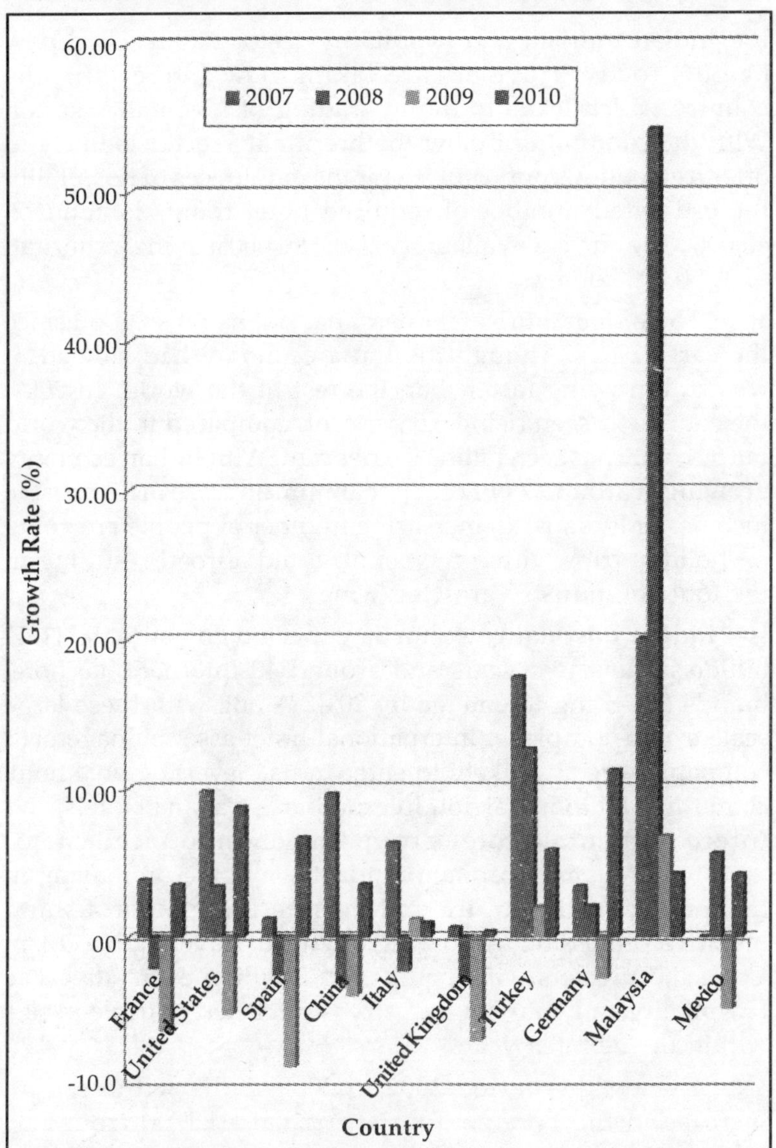

Fig. 1.2: Growth Rate of Most Visited Countries by International Tourist Arrivals

Resource: www.wikipedia.org

Indian tourism and hospitality sector has reached new heights today. Travelers are taking new interests in the country which leads to the upgrading of hospitality sector. With the continuing inflow the hospitality sector is likely to offer tremendous opportunity for the employees of hospitality the estimated number of required hotel rooms is about 2, 40,000 . The current availability is just 90,000 leaving a shortfall of 1, 50,000 rooms.

"The Indian tourism industry has not had it so good since the early 1990s. Though the India economy had slowed, it was still growing faster than the rest of the world. In 2009, the country is seen rising 6.5 per cent, compared to the world output, which is seen falling 0.4 per cent. With Indian economy growing at around 7 per cent per annum and rise in disposable incomes of Indians, an increasing number of people are going on holiday trips within the country and abroad resulting in the tourism industry growing wings." [20]

Indian hospitality sector is expected to estimate 11.41 billion in next two years and around 40 International hotel brands are going to emerge by 2010. Along with these large scale expansion plans, International hotel asset management companies are also likely to enter India. Several global hotel chains like Hilton, Marriott International, Cabana Hotels, and Intercontinental Hotel groups have announced major investment plans. Hospitality Industry will recruit maximum manpower in the future and also be the glamorous and lucrative profession. According to World Travel and Tourism Council, Travelers will spend US $ 5 billion every day. The Hospitality and Tourism Industry is predicted to triple in size within the next ten years.

"During the period 2002 to 2009, India witnessed an increase in the Foreign Tourist Arrivals (FTAs) from 2.38 million to 5.11 million. Due to global slowdown, terrorist activities, H_1N_1 influenza pandemic, etc., growth rate in FTAs during 2009 fell by 3.3 per cent. The year witnessed a contraction in global tourism by 4.3 per cent; the declaration in India was, therefore, less than that of the scale of global slowdown. Foreign Exchange Earnings (FEEs) from tourism increased from Rs. 15,064 crore in 2002 to Rs. 54,960 crore in 2009. The growth rate in earnings in 2009 vis-a-vis 2008 was 8.3 per cent." [21]

Tourism in India has come into its own as a brand – India Tourism has been several innovative approaches in the Ministry's policy in 2009-10. The creation of niche tourism products like heliport tourism, medical tourism, wellness tourism, adventure tourism, cruise tourism and caravan tourism has served to widen the net of this sector. The Ministry is contemplating a workshop to discuss the modalities to evolve Sustainable Tourism Criteria for India. The Ministry had also commissioned a pilot survey to assess the impact of growth of infrastructure in and around Corbett National Park. The year has seen some firsts too. The Grand Prix for publicity related activity of India Tourism world-wide is a vindication of the Ministry's creative abilities to project Indian tourism as the world brand as also the stand that publicity is an important tool for development. Hotel projects have been enabled to obtain credit at relaxed norms due to the efforts put in to have the Reserve Bank of India delink credit for hotel projects from Commercial Real Estate. External Commercial Borrowings have been relaxed by the Ministry of Finance to solve the problem of liquidity being faced by the hotel industry due to economic slowdown.

The Ministry, in its efforts to deliver responsive governance has initiated some measures. It is the first Ministry to have a Performance Agreement signed between the Secretary (Tourism) and the senior officers of the Ministry of the rank of Joint Secretary and above. This agreement lays down timelines for implementation of specific tasks by the officers. This has culminated in the Results Framework Document for the Ministry being hosted in the official website highlighting its objectives, actions and measurable performance indicators.

"The year 2009-10 witnessed heightened engagements of the Ministry of Tourism with the States/UTs to strengthen initiatives to promote tourism to a new height. Also, recognizing the need for monitoring of projects supported by Central Financial Assistance, new Project Monitoring Information System (PMIS) software has been designed. This software permits online submission of projects and utilisation certificates as also the reporting of the status of implementation of projects." [22]

Table 1.3: Year-wise Foreign Tourist Arrivals in India

Year	FTA in India (In Millions)	Growth Rate (%)
1996	2.29	0.00
1997	2.37	3.49
1998	2.36	-0.42
1999	2.48	5.08
2000	2.65	6.85
2001	2.54	-4.15
2002	2.38	-6.29
2003	2.73	14.70
2004	3.46	26.73
2005	3.92	13.29
2006	4.45	13.52
2007	5.08	14.15
2008	5.37	5.70
2009	5.16	-3.91
2010	5.58	8.13

Source: India Tourism Statistics accessed and compiled from http://www.tourism.gov.in

The above table 1.3 depicted the foreign tourist arrivals in India during 1996-2010. It clearly showed that FTA in India increased from 2.29 Mn to 5.58 Mn from 1996 to 2010. Growth rate of FTA was increasing during that period however the years 1998, 2001, 2002 and 2009 showed decline in FTA in India. The year 2003 showed significant jump in growth of FTA form -6.29 per cent to 14.70 per cent. In 2008 FTA in India was 5.37 Mn which declined to 5.16 Mn in 2009 however it again revived in 2010 with growth rate of 8.13 per cent.

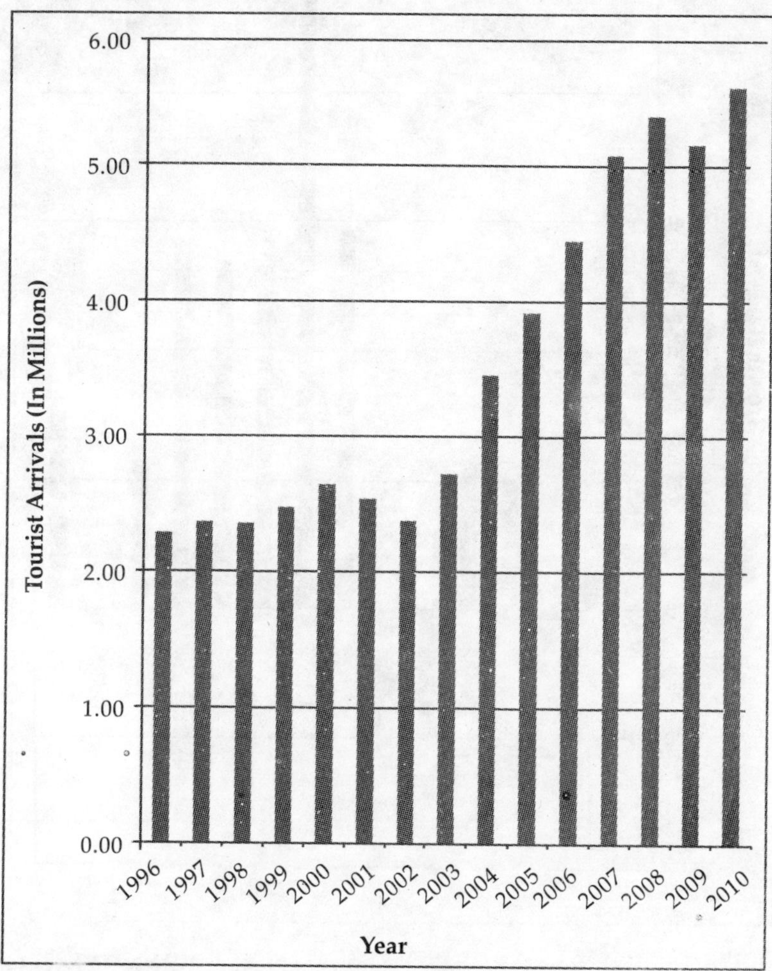

Fig. 1.3: Year-wise Foreign Tourist Arrivals in India

Source: India Tourism Statistics accessed and compiled from http://www.tourism.gov.in/

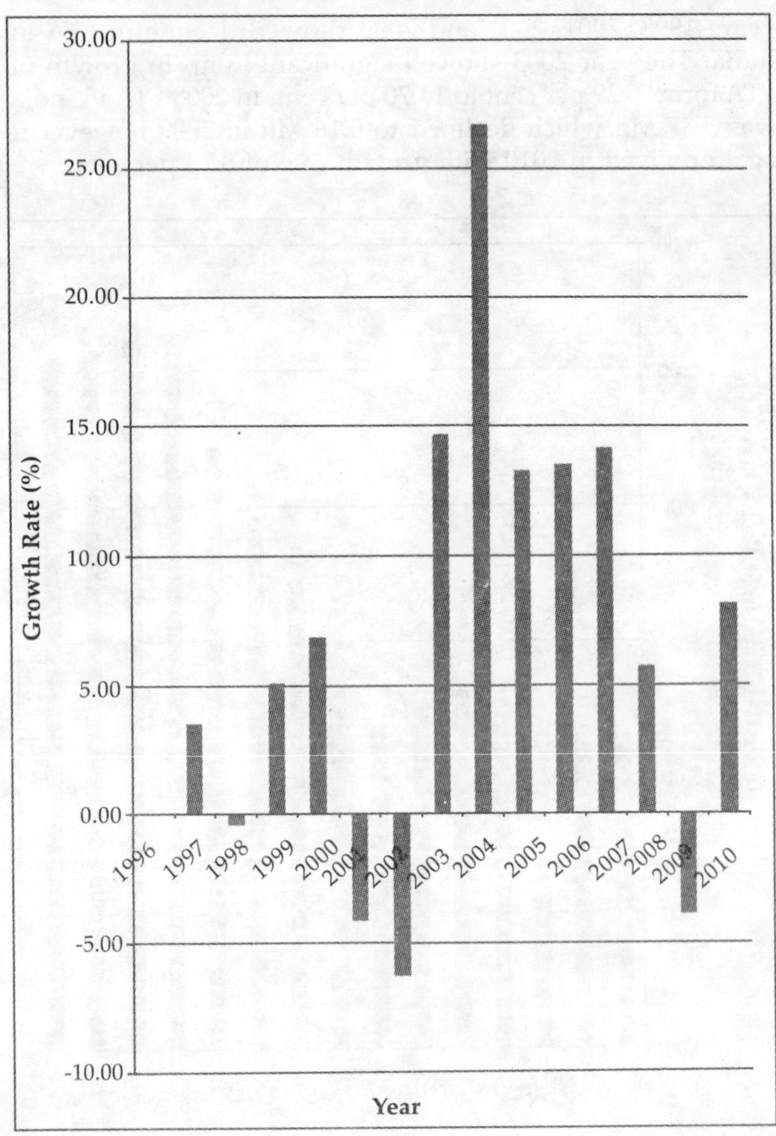

Fig. 1.4: Year-wise Growth Rate of Foreign Tourist Arrivals in India

Source: India Tourism Statistics accessed and compiled from http://www.tourism.gov.in

Growth rate of FTA was high in October (47.50%) whereas recorded least in the month of April (-25.84%) in the year 2007 as shown in Table 1.4. Growth rate of FTA in 2007 was positive in the month of May, June, July, October, November and December. The year 2008 showed that growth rate of FTA was 31.96 per cent in October whereas it was -24.63 per cent in the month of April. The year 2008 was also recorded with positive growth rate of FTA in the month of February, June, July, October, November and December. The month of October was recorded with highest growth rate of FTA during 2009 (38.78%) as well as 2010 (37.39%). Similarly both the year 2009-2010 (-21.49 % and -27.54 %) were holding least growth rate of FTA in the month of April.

In all it can be observed from the above table 1.4 that there was positive growth rate of FTA during 2007-2010 in June, July, October, November and December months as the said months are seasonal months of tourism in India. Therefore they show positive growth rate of FTA. (*See table on next page*)

Future Trends of Tourism and Hotel Industry in India

- "The real GDP growth for travel and tourism economy is expected to be 0.2 per cent in 2009 and is expected to grow at an average of 7.7 per cent per annum in the coming decade.
- Earning through exports from international visitors and tourism goods are expected to generate 6.0 per cent of total exports (nearly $16.9 billion) in 2009 and expected to increase to US$ 51.4 billion in 2019.
- According to the Ministry of Tourism, Foreign Tourist Arrivals (FTAs) for the period from January to March in 2009 was 1.461 million. For the month of March 2009 the FTAs was 4, 72,000. The reason for the decline is attributed to the ongoing economic crisis.
- In spite of the short term and medium term impediment due to the global meltdown the revenues from tourism is expected to increase by 42 per cent from 2007 to 2017." [23]

Table 1.4: Month-wise Foreign Tourist Arrivals in India

Month	2007		2008		2009		2010	
	Arrivals (In Lacs)	Growth Rate (%)	Arrivals (In Lacs)	Growth Rate (%)	Arrivals (In Lacs)	Growth Rate (%)	Arrivals (In Lacs)	Growth Rate (%)
January	5.35	0.00	5.11	0.00	4.81	0.00	5.68	0.00
February	5.01	-6.36	6.11	19.57	4.89	1.66	5.52	-2.82
March	4.72	-5.78	4.79	-21.60	4.42	-9.61	5.12	-7.24
April	3.50	-25.84	3.61	-24.63	3.47	-21.49	3.71	-27.54
May	2.77	20.85	3.04	-15.78	3.05	-12.10	3.32	-10.51
June	3.10	11.91	3.41	12.17	3.52	15.40	3.84	15.66
July	3.99	28.70	4.31	26.39	4.32	22.72	4.66	21.35
August	3.98	-0.25	3.83	-11.13	3.69	-14.58	4.22	-9.44
September	3.01	-24.37	3.41	-10.96	3.30	-10.57	3.69	-12.56
October	4.44	47.50	4.50	31.96	4.58	38.78	5.07	37.39
November	5.32	19.81	5.13	14.00	5.41	18.12	6.36	25.44
December	5.96	12.03	5.33	3.89	6.15	13.67	7.15	12.42

Source: India Tourism Statistics accessed and compiled from http://www.tourism.gov.in/

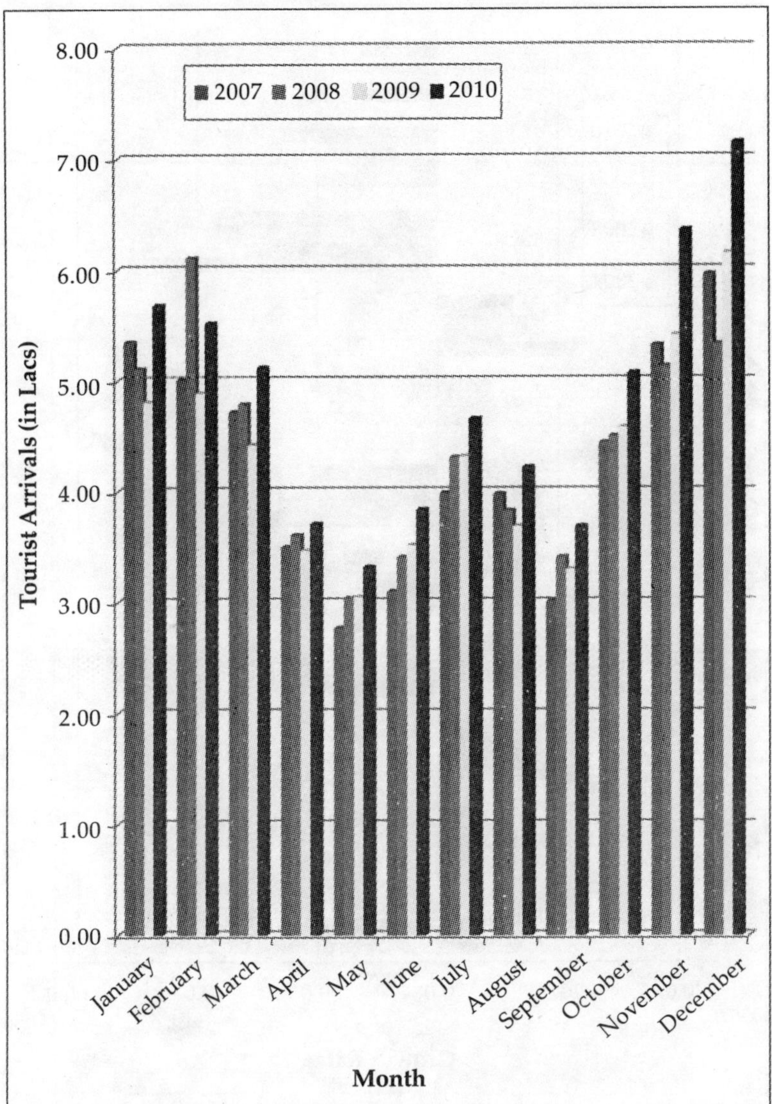

Fig. 1.5: Month-wise Foreign Tourist Arrivals in India

Source: India Tourism Statistics accessed and compiled from http://www.tourism.gov.in/

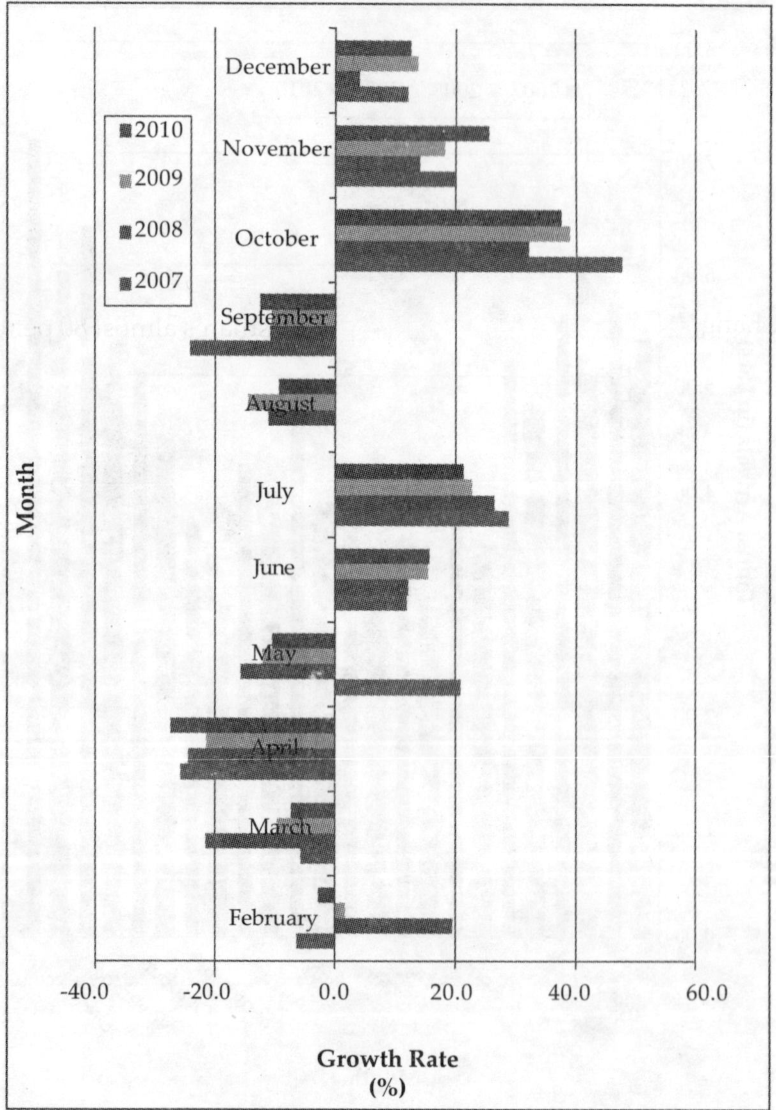

Fig. 1.6: Month-wise Growth Rate of Foreign Tourist Arrivals in India

Source: India Tourism Statistics accessed and compiled from http://www.tourism.gov.in/

Tourism in the Rajasthan State

Rajasthan, the 'Abode of Kings' is a favorite destination for all kinds of tourists. Its forts, places, temples, wild life, lakes, Aravlais and Thar, Colourful fair and festivals have been inviting tourists to visit Rajasthan. But it seems this 'Hot' destination has started losing its glory. "The share of state in tourist arrivals in India has come down to 25 per cent from 33 per cent in recent years." [24]

Rajasthan is culturally rich and has artistic and cultural traditions which reflect the ancient Indian way of life. There is rich and varied folk culture from villages which is often depicted and is symbolic of the state. Highly cultivated classical music and dance with its own distinct style is part of the cultural tradition of Rajasthan. The music is uncomplicated and songs depict day-to-day relationships and chores, more often focused around fetching water from wells or ponds.

It is known for its traditional, colourful art. The block prints, tie and dye prints, Bagaru prints, Sanganer prints, and Zari embroidery are major export products from Rajasthan. Handicraft items like wooden furniture and handicrafts, carpets, and blue pottery are some of the things commonly found here. Rajasthan is a shoppers' paradise, with beautiful goods found at low prices. Reflecting the colourful Rajasthani culture, Rajasthani clothes have a lot of mirror-work and embroidery. A Rajasthani traditional dress for females comprises an ankle length skirt and a short top, also known as a lehenga or a chaniya choli. A piece of cloth is used to cover the head, both for protection from heat and maintenance of modesty. Rajasthani dresses are usually designed in bright colours like blue, yellow and orange.

Rajasthan — The Land of Kings is a majestic tapestry of camels plodding over soft sand dunes of the Thar Desert. It is a kaleidoscope of brightly turbaned men with proud moustaches and women with twinkling anklets in colourful swirling ghagras. The landscape is dotted with island palaces shimmering on idyllic blue lakes; temples and fortresses situated on hilltops of the rugged and rocky Aravalli; exquisite palaces built during the reign of some of its many erstwhile

Rajput dynasties; and well laid out gardens with pavilions and kiosks, all of which add to the splendor and whimsical charm of this majestic land. But, it is the art of Rajasthan that makes it such a popular tourist destination of India.

Tourism Destination of Rajasthan State

Rajasthan is famous for the majestic forts, intricately carved temples and decorated havelis, which were built by Rajput kings in previous ages; they were the soul of pre-Muslim era Rajasthan. It is a classic blend of beauty and historicity. Rajasthan's almost 80 per cent of the places are regarded as the places of tourist interest. The old city of Jaipur, capital to the state of Rajasthan, painted pink that gives a magical glow to the city, is one of the must visit places of the state.

In the bleak desert that is Rajasthan, there is also a green oasis-Mount Abu, a cool hill station, a holy mountain retreat, the Aravalli range; the verdant forests alive with a variety of flora and fauna; the Nakki lake; the stunning Dilwara Jain temples; the city of Ajmer; the Dargah or tomb of the popular 13th century; the white marble Bara-dari on the Anasagar lake is exquisite; a number of monuments belonging to the Mughal era; the well-fed camels and citadels; the exotic camel safaris; the worship of thousands of holy rats at Mata Kali temple are some of the most interesting aspects of the state in general. The golden city of Jaisalmer, which lies courageously as the western sentinel of India, is a place worth visiting. Jaisalmer Fort and Havelis are part of the true architectural heritage of India. Major points of attraction are Manakchowk, Chittorgarh Fort, Lake Palace, City Palace, Ranakpur Temple dedicated to Lord Adinath near Udaipur, Jain temples in the fort complexes of Chittor, Kumbhalgarh, Lodarva Jain temples, Bhandasar Temple of Bikaner are some of the best examples.

Fairs and Festivals of Rajasthan State

Rajasthan has all the usual Hindu and Muslim festivals, some celebrated with special local fervor as well as a number of festivals of its own. The exact dates, determined by the lunar calendar have specific religious significance. Major festivals in the state are Camel Festival at Bikaner in January, Nagaur Fair in January - February; Desert Festival of Jaisalmer in February; Elephant Festival Jaipur; Gangaur Festival celebrated all over the state in March - April; Mewar Festival in Udaipur; Urs in Ajmer Sharif; Teej in the months of August; Marwar Festival at Jodhpur in October; and Camel and Cattle Fair of Pushkar in November.

The Ghoomar dance from Udaipur and Kalbeliya dance of Jaisalmer have gained international recognition. Folk music is a vital part of Rajasthani culture. Kathputali, Bhopa, Chang, Teratali, Ghindar, Kachchhighori, Tejaji etc., are the examples of the traditional Rajasthani culture. Folk songs are commonly ballads which relate heroic deeds and love stories; and religious or devotional songs known as bhajans and banis (often accompanied by musical instruments like dholak, sitar, sarangi etc.) are also sung.

The main religious festivals are Deepawali, Holi, Gangaur, Teej, Gogaji, Shri Devnarayan Jayanti, Makar Sankranti and Janmashtami, as the main religion is Hinduism. Rajasthan's desert festival is celebrated with great zest and zeal. This festival is held once a year during winter. Dressed in brilliantly hued costumes, the people of the desert dance and sing haunting ballads of valor, romance and tragedy. There are fairs with snake charmers, puppeteers, acrobats and folk performers. Camels, of course, play a stellar role in this festival.

Growth and Development of Tourism in the State of Rajasthan

The art of Rajasthan has attracted numerous visitors. At present, the State receives approximately one fourth of the foreign tourists who visit India annually. Additionally, over 6.50 million domestic tourists also visit Rajasthan annually. The rate of growth of tourism in Rajasthan has been sustained at around 5-7 per cent per annum in the last few years. Some of the tourism products of Rajasthan have become popular among the tourists such as Palace-on-Wheels, Heritage Hotels, Camel Safaris, Pushkar Fair, Desert festival, Palace Hotels and

Wild Life Sanctuaries/National Parks. The State with its rich historical, cultural and environmental heritage, coupled with colourful fairs and festivals and popular tourist products has become one of the important tourist destinations for both domestic and international tourists in India.

The Government and the Tourism Industry both have been striving to improve the quality of the product and services made available for visiting tourists. Efforts are being made for providing necessary information, facilities to connect visiting sites and suitable accommodation to the visitors: The Department of Tourism is undertaking the important activities for development and conservation of tourist sites and also to develop infrastructure facilities around the tourist places.

"Rajasthan attracted 14 per cent of total foreign visitors during 2009-10 which is fourth highest in all states of India. It positioned fourth place also in Domestic tourist visitors. Endowed with natural beauty and a great history, tourism is a flourishing industry in Rajasthan. The palaces of Jaipur, lakes of Udaipur, and desert forts of Jodhpur, Bikaner and Jaisalmer rank among the most preferred destinations in India for many tourists both Indian and foreign. Tourism accounts for eight per cent of the state's domestic product. Many old and neglected palaces and forts have been converted into heritage hotels. Tourism has increased employment in the hospitality sector." [25]

The number of tourist arrivals in the state has increased fourfold in the last thirty years and in 2001, the state received 0.6 Mn foreign tourist and over 7 Mn domestic tourists. The state is known for its diversity in terms of natural resources, cultural heritage, historical as well as archaeological wonders and rare wild life. The forts and palaces, heritage hotels, colourful fairs and festivals, local art and handicrafts, etc. has been a unique selling proposition for tourists coming to the state. The desert environment in the western parts of the state is also a major attraction for visitors, particularly the foreign tourist. Four decades ago tourism in Rajasthan was small industry that was largely confined to the elite foreign tourists and domestic pilgrim traffic. Tourist arrivals were restricted to a few thousand tourists annually and were primarily recorded in select places such as Jaipur, the state capital, Udaipur and Jodhpur (for foreign tourists) and the pilgrim centers of Ajmer, Pushkar and Nathdwara (for domestic tourists). The employment in the sector and the sector's contribution to the state economy, as well as employment potential were limited. However, over the last few decades, due to the focused efforts of Rajasthan Tourism, various State Government agencies, select entrepreneurs / individuals, tourism has grown from an elite and pilgrim phenomenon to a mass phenomenon putting Rajasthan firmly on the foreign and domestic tourist map. Also, as compared to the past, where the tourism in the state meant desert tourism, heritage tourism (forts, palaces, etc.) and pilgrim tourism, today the tourists have a wide canvas of places, attractions and activities to choose from in the state, which enhances the overall tourism experience. The industry today employs over one lac people directly and over three lacs people indirectly. Its contribution to the State economy is estimated to be over two thousand Crore presently. Given the increasingly important role that the sector plays in the overall socioeconomic development of the state, the State Government of Rajasthan has accorded an industry status to tourism from the year 1989. As the nodal agency to promote tourism in the state, the Department of Tourism (DoT), Rajasthan has played a key role in this growth along with the Department of Tourism. "Tourism Development Corporation (RTDC), which was established in November, 1978 primarily to act as catalyst by developing tourism infrastructure facilities (for domestic and foreign tourists), particularly by way of basic amenities like accommodation, catering and organized tours/sightseeing facilities." [26]

Table 1.5 revealed the year wise tourist arrivals in Rajasthan state during 2000 to 2010. Domestic tourists in Rajasthan increased from 73.70 Lac to 255 lacs during 2000-10. Foreign tourists increased from 6.23 lacs to 13 lacs in the

Table 1.5: Year-wise Tourist Arrivals in Rajasthan State

Year	Domestic Tourists (In Lacs)		Foreign Tourists (In Lacs)		Total Tourists (In Lacs)	
	Arrivals	Growth Rate (%)	Arrivals	Growth Rate (%)	Arrivals	Growth Rate (%)
2000	73.70	0.00	6.23	0.00	79.90	0.00
2001	77.50	5.16	6.08	-2.41	83.60	4.63
2002	83.00	7.09	4.28	-29.60	87.20	-4.30
2003	125.40	51.08	6.28	46.72	131.70	51.03
2004	160.30	27.83	9.71	54.61	170.00	29.08
2005	187.80	17.15	11.31	16.47	119.10	-29.94
2006	234.80	25.02	12.20	7.86	247.00	107.38
2007	259.20	10.39	14.01	14.83	273.20	10.60
2008	283.50	9.37	14.77	5.42	298.30	9.18
2009	255.50	-9.87	10.73	-27.35	266.30	-10.72
2010	255.00	-0.19	13.00	21.15	268.00	0.63

Source: Department of Tourism – Ministry of Tourism, Government of India (1st April, 2010).

same period. The year 2008 was recorded with highest tourists (domestic as well as foreign) arrivals in Rajasthan. After 2008, the year 2007 recorded with 273 lacs tourist arrivals in Rajasthan. It is noticeable that growth rate of foreign tourists in Rajasthan became negative in 2002, 2005, and 2009 however in the year 2006 (107.38%) it showed highest growth rate as compared to 2005 (-29.94).

Table 1.6 shows the city wise spread of accommodation (as on 2009). The total no. of hotels, rooms and bed were 1689, 29202 and 58763 respectively, in Rajasthan. Jaipur owns highest no. of hotels in Rajasthan followed by Jodhpur, Udaipur, Ajmer and Mt. Abu which is having 386, 211, 181, 139 and 120 no. of hotels respectively. (*See table on page 27*)

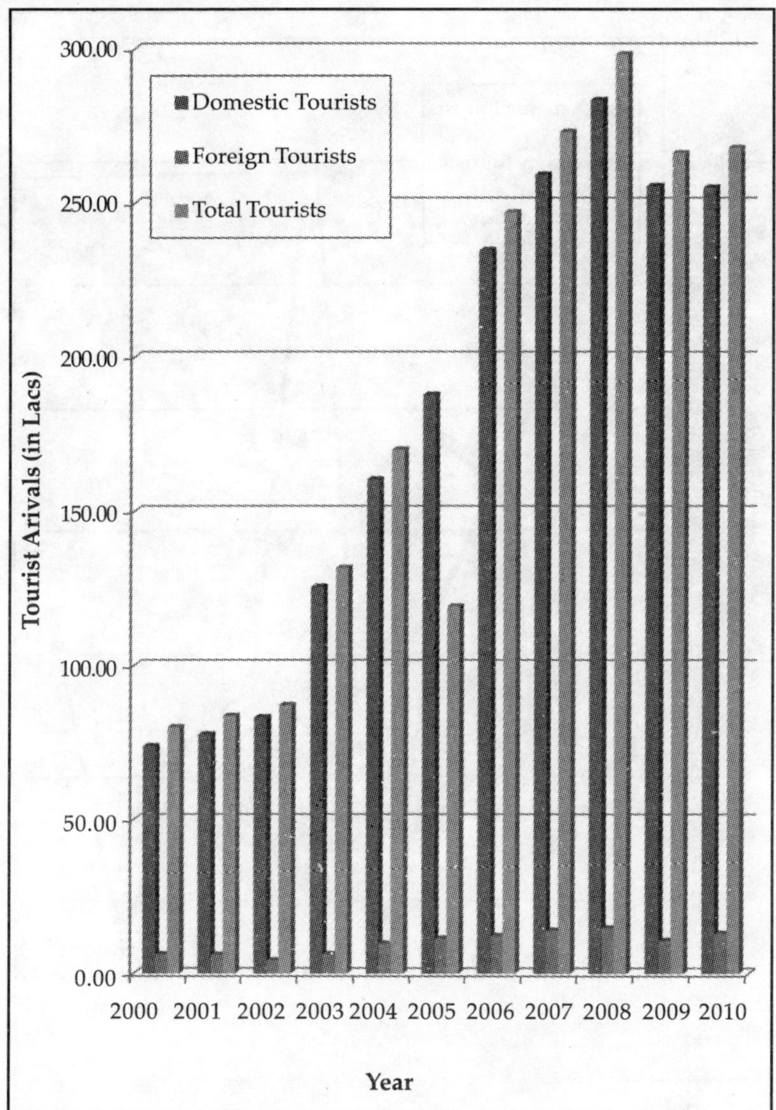

Fig. 1.7: Year-wise Tourist Arrivals in Rajasthan State

Source: Department of tourism – Ministry of Tourism, Government of India (1st April, 2010)

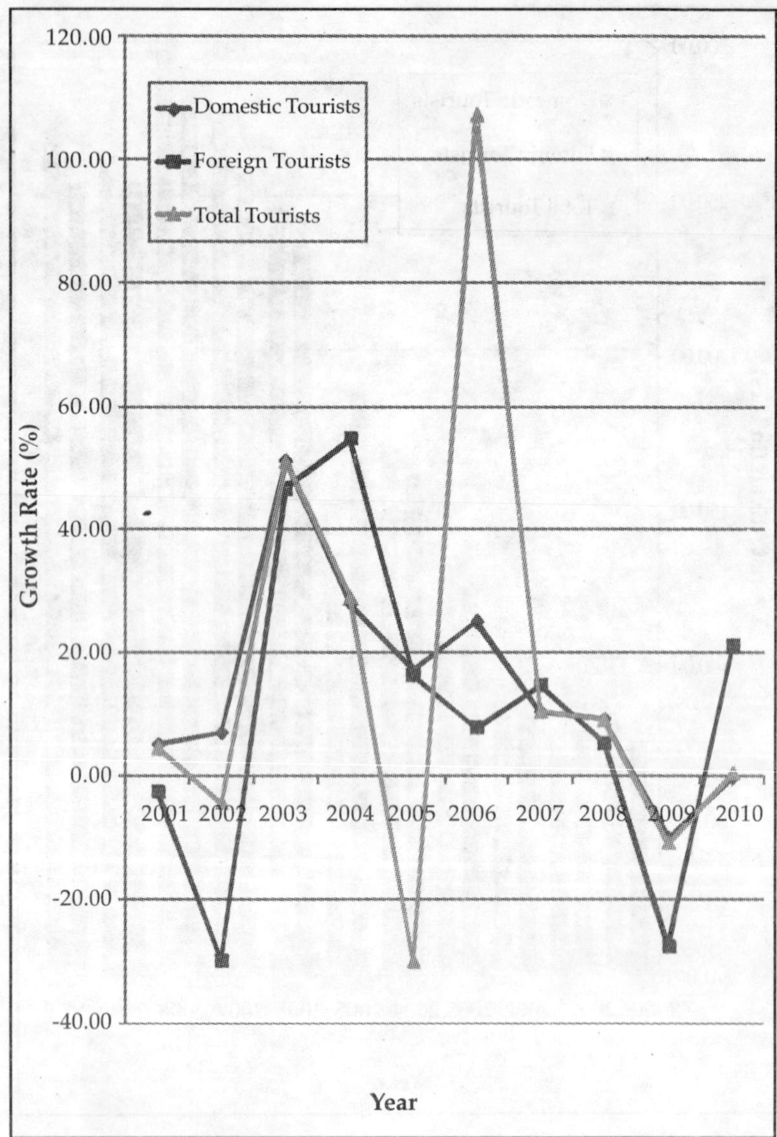

Fig. 1.8: Year-wise Growth of Tourist in Rajasthan State

Source: Department of tourism – Ministry of Tourism, Government of India (1st April, 2010)

Table 1.6: Location-wise Hotel Facilities in the State of Rajasthan

Sr. No.	Location	No. of Hotels	No. of Rooms	No. of Bed
1.	Bikaner	49	1163	2280
2.	Ajmer	139	2016	3889
3.	Pushker	92	1172	2235
4.	Bundi	31	279	617
5.	Kota	67	1422	2678
6.	Jhalawar	07	238	376
7.	Bharatpur	55	638	1276
8.	Jaipur	386	7032	14318
9.	Savimadhopur	45	698	1360
10.	Jaisalmer	110	1609	3232
11.	Jodhpur	211	3516	6922
12.	Mount Abu	120	2171	4550
13.	Udaipur	181	3762	7456
14.	Nathdawara	33	615	1245
15.	Rajsamand	21	318	678
16.	Chittorgarh	68	1241	2914
17.	Alwar	31	568	1124
18.	Shekhawati Town	29	524	1187
19.	Mandawa	07	208	402
	Total	**1686**	**29202**	**58763**

Source: Tourist Department Government of Rajasthan Jaipur, 1 April, 2010.

Tourism in the Gujarat State

Aavo Padharo, words of welcome in the language of Gujarat because it is here that these words ring truly and the guest is 'God' and the people of Gujarat are gregariously friendly, inviting and enticing to come again and again. Gujarat will discover centuries of history as spanning the geological core of the earth onto a fascinatingly vibrant future. Gujarat is unique in its geological and topographical landscape. From volcanic outpourings through bedrock to fossil fields of indigenous dinosaurs; from the art of the Neolithic cave painter to the stone masterpieces of a series of civilized architecture. Ancient cave paintings to historic murals, natural and manmade caves. Art, history, music, culture, all dovetails within each other to form a wondrous matrix that is the cultural exuberance of the people of the state.

The Gujarat growth has now expanded to include tourism — a sector that despite much potential has always lagged behind in making it to the mainstream. "The state government's focus on the sector in countdown to the Vibrant Gujarat Global Investors' Summit 2011 certainly seems to be helping matters. The Maverick Vithal Kamat, executive chairman and managing director of Kamat Hotels India Ltd. He is bullish on Gujarat and it was evident as he announced his interests in taking over old heritage buildings, opening roadside hotels and more." [27]

Tourism Destination of Gujarat State

"Tourism Corporation Of Gujarat Ltd. (TCGL) has selected 37 destinations for integrated tourism development. In last 2 years more than 600 projects in 300 tourist destination have been taken up with a cost more than USD 24 million 35 Pravasi Path of international standards has been taken up in Gujarat, involving an investment of USD 19 million Tourism year budget have been increased from USD 7 million to USD 24 million. This provision is continued in the new 5 year plan. The increase of budget has been provided for Tourism Infrastructure projects." [28] The famous destinations in Gujarat are as follows: Saputara Lake, Somnath – The Shrine Eternal, Dwarka Temple, Gir Wildlife Sanctuary, Gandhi Ashram, Hutheesing Jain Temple, Sidi Sayeed Masjid, Walled city and gates, Mercado Ravivar (domingo), Swaminarayan Temple, Jama Masjid, Dada Harir Vav, Heritage Walk, Rani no Hajiro, Badshah no Hajiro, Manek Chowk, Pols of Old City, Vishala, Vechaar Utensils Museum, Calico Museum and

Sarabhai Foundation, Sanskar Kendra, N C Mehta Gallery, Shreyas Folk Museum, Hussain Doshi's Gufa , Kanoria Centre for Arts, Hutheesing Visual Arts Centre, Community Science Center, Sardar Patel Museum, Jhulta Minara, Sundarvan, Sarkhej Roza, Kankaria Lake, Kochrab Ashram, The Adalaj Stepwell, Science City , Indroda Nature Park, Mahudi Jain Temple, Akshardham, Teen Darwaja, Nal Sarovar Bird Sanctuary, Thol Lake Bird Sanctuary.

Fairs and Festivals of Gujarat State

Around more than 1000 festivals are celebrated in Gujarat—the state is known as the land of fairs and festivals. Some of these fairs and festivals are as follows:

> Bhavnath Mahadev Mela (February) situated at the foot of Mount Girnar in the city of Junagadh, is the site of the Bhavnath Mahadev fair held for five days in February. Dangs Darbar is the name of the annual fair held every year in Ahwa, the most important town in the Dangs a few days before Holi, Chitra — Vichitra Mela (March) fairs, is attended by around 60,000 to 70,000 tribal people. It takes place every year in the village of Gunbhakhari in Sabarkantha district, very near the borders of Rajasthan. It is held a fortnight after Holi, the festival of colours, The Sanskruti kunj Festival shows the different cultures of the states of India. It is organized in the winter session in the capital city, Gandhinagar. All the competitors of India come during this fair and show their state's culture and dance.

Other than those festivals observed throughout India, there are festivities specific to Gujarat. Navaratri celebrations in Ahmedabad, Makar Sankranti and Kite Flying Festival (14 January), The Kite Flying Festival takes place in mid January and marks the time when the Sun's direct rays reach the Tropic of Capricorn after the winter solstice. It is celebrated with lots of folk music and dance as well as kite flying, Dance Festival — Modhera (January) Resting on a knoll in the village of Modhera are the ruins of the 11th century Sun Temple. The outer walls of the temple are covered with sculptures in which the figures of Surya, the sun god, are prominent, The Kutch

Mahotsav (February–March) is celebrated at the time of the Shiv Ratri in February/March. The centre of the festival is Bhuj in Kutch. It has crafts, fairs and folk dances and music and cultural shows, all organized by the Gujarat Tourism, Bhadra Purnima (September) is one of the four most important festival days of the year when farmers and agriculturists come to Ambaji, a place that derives its name from Goddess Ambaji, whose shrine is located there.

Growth and Development of Tourism in the State of Gujarat

The Gujarat government has identified 39 tourism places for hospitality development. If Gujarat has to grow, its hospitality industry has to grow simultaneously. Gujarat has realized that the path of migratory bird is one that of a great potential. Orissa has already started bird tourism. There the locals treat animals like human beings. They call it 'Bhoot Daya' — loving animals and birds as creations of God. That is the base for tourism.

"The State Government decided the year 2006 as 'Tourism year', keeping in view the importance of tourism industry as an important factor of the development process and generator of large scale employment. The Government formulated "Gujarat Ni Chetanyatra" – Gujarat tourism policy for the year 2003-2006. Total of 38 Memorandum of Understanding (MOUs) for 69 projects in the tourism sector amounting to INR 20,821 crore was signed at the recent Vibrant Gujarat Global Investor's Summit. The efforts of the Gujarat Government worked in some measure as the State registered an increase of 32 per cent in tourist arrivals in 2006, compared to the figures of 2005.The State witnessed 2.5 million domestic tourists and 50,000 foreign tourists. The average contribution of tourism industry to the State's GDP is close to 2.5 per cent, while the comparable figure for India is 5.3 per cent. The average foreign tourist spend per person per day is close to USD 700 to 1050. With world class health facilities, zero waiting time and most importantly, one tenth of the medical cost in US or UK, Gujarat is becoming a preferred medical tourist destination. About 1,200 to 1,500 NRI's, Non-resident

Gujaratis (NRG's) and a small percentage of foreigners come every year for different medical treatments. Gujarat contributes close to 25-31 per cent of the total medical tourism business in India." [29]

There can be a Khadi and related industries tour. Handicrafts tour or even an industrial tour of Gujarat. Success in tourism means sending back a happy and satisfied tourist; it is the best marketing. Gujarat can strive for an 80:20 tourist ratio - domestic: international.

Tourists come to see old buildings, not new. Circuits should be planned with a minimum stay of 7-15 days. Typically one trip should cover 70 per cent of Gujarat. The product should be a basket for tourist, packaged into a neat tablet. One hotel room gives 35 people direct job and 75 people indirect jobs. Gujarat has to encourage talent.

Table 1.7: Year-wise Tourists Arrivals in Gujarat State

Year	Domestic Tourists (In Lacs)		Foreign Tourists (In Lacs)		Total Tourists (In Lacs)	
	Arrivals	Growth Rate (%)	Arrivals	Growth Rate (%)	Arrivals	Growth Rate (%)
2002-03	62.46	0.00	4.23	0.00	66.69	0.00
2003-04	79.76	27.70	6.08	43.74	85.84	28.71
2004-05	64.28	-19.40	2.04	-66.44	66.32	-22.74
2005-06	112.40	74.86	9.08	345.09	121.48	83.17
2006-07	121.60	8.18	20.04	120.70	141.46	16.44
2007-08	137.70	13.24	24.28	21.15	161.98	14.50
2008-09	151.20	9.80	32.03	27.80	183.23	13.11
2009-10	164.30	8.66	42.07	31.34	206.37	12.63

Source: www.gujaratcmfellowship.org

As shown in Table 1.7, the number of tourists (Domestic and Foreign) who visited Gujarat in 2002-03 was only 66.69 lacs. In 2003-04, it was increased up to 85.84 lacs. Tourist's arrival has been decreasing in the year 2004-05 and this year

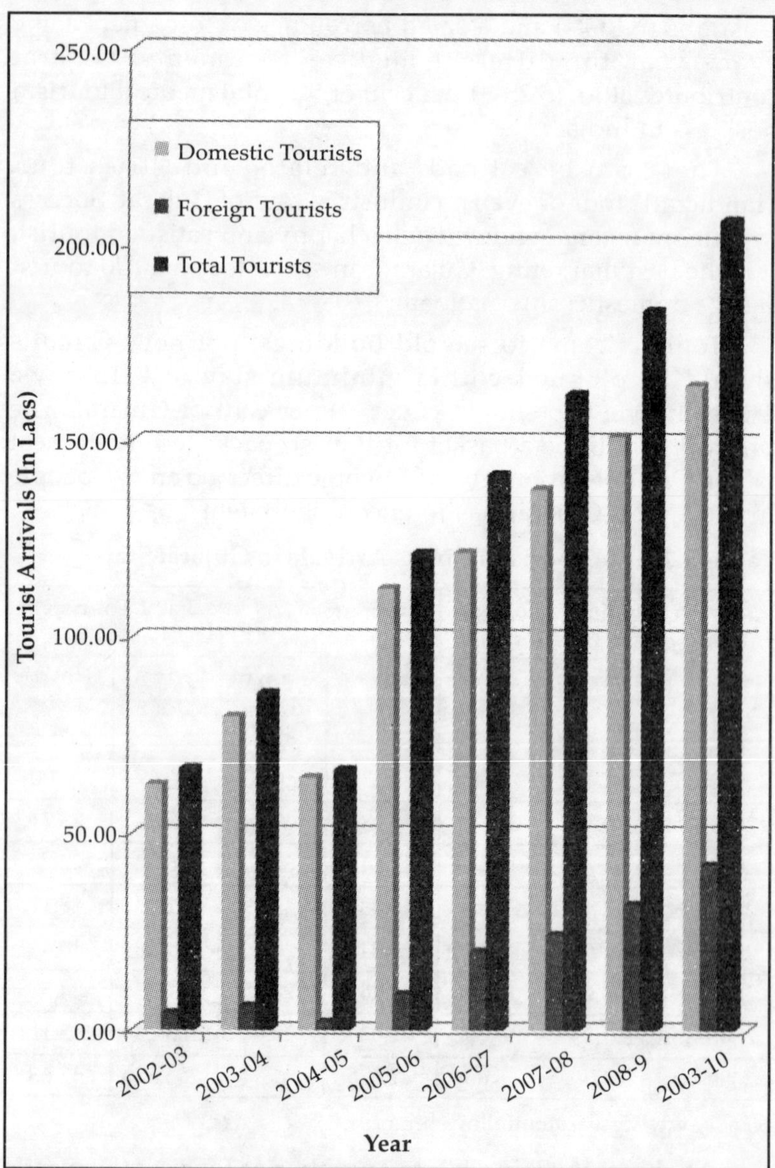

Fig. 1.9: Year-wise Tourists Arrivals in Gujarat State

Source: www.gujaratcmfellowship.org

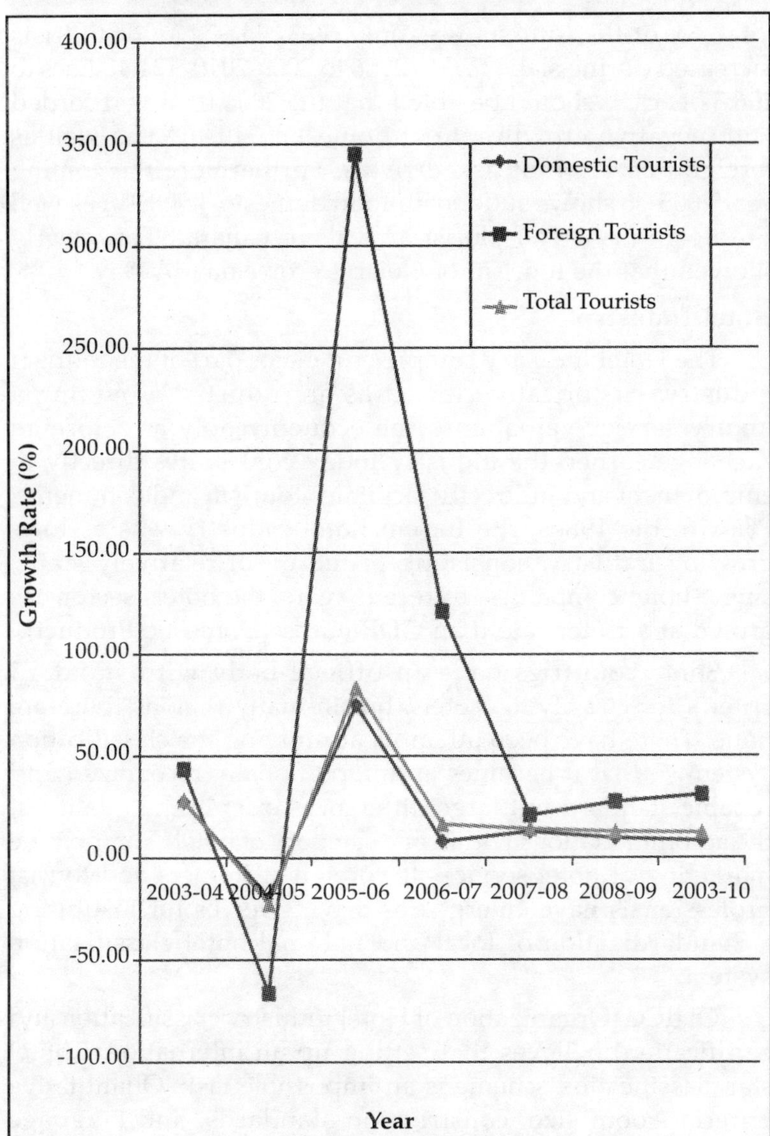

Fig. 1.10: Year-wise Growth of Tourist in Gujarat State

Source: www.gujaratcmfellowship.org

total no. of the tourists was only 66.32 lacs. No. of tourists increased during slab of 2005-2006 to 2009-2010. 121.48 Lacs to 206.37 Lacs. It should be noted that the 2004-05 was recorded with negative growth rate of domestic (-19.40%) as well as foreign (-66.44%) tourists arrivals. Furthermore the coming year 2005-06 shows sudden jump in domestic (74.86%) as well as foreign (345.09%) tourist arrivals in Gujarat. This clearly showed that the tourism of Gujarat grows day-by-day.

Hotel Industry

The Hotel Industry comprises a major part of the tourism industry. Historically viewed as an industry providing a luxury service valuable to the economy only as a foreign exchange earner, the industry today contributes directly to employment and indirectly facilitates tourism and commerce. Prior to the 1980s, the Indian hotel industry was a slow-growing industry, consisting primarily of relatively static, single-hotel companies. In recent years, the hotels sector has grown at a faster rate than GDP (Gross Domestic Product).

Some countries have an official body with standard criteria for classifying hotels, but in many regions there are none. There have been attempts at unifying the classification system so that it becomes an internationally recognized and reliable standard but large differences exist in the quality of the accommodations within one category of hotel. Competitive marketing of hotel services to foreign customers and tourist professionals have emerged as driving forces for instituting a Standardization of local and national hotel classification system.

OHICC (Organization of Hotel Industry classification and certification) believes that setting up an international hotel star classification scheme is an impossible task. Quantitative criteria (room size, construction standards, and language proficiency) vary too much from country to country. Qualitative criteria remain highly subjective. Many online travel agencies have established their own rating systems, providing enhanced, current evaluations.

Structure of Hotel Industry

"The Department of Tourism had constituted committee, Hotel and Restaurant approval and classification committee (HRACC) which inspects the Hotel (the applicant hotel) to assess its suitability and for awarding the star category. There are 5 such committees in the country – one central committee and four Regional Committees. The classification or reclassification of 4 star, 5 star and 5 star deluxe hotels is handled by the central committee. The classification and reclassification of 1, 2, 3 star and heritage hotels and approval of restaurants is done by the regional committee." [30] The ratings are reviewed every five years.

Category of Star Hotels

Hotels in India are broadly classified into 7 categories (five star deluxe, five star, four stars, three stars, two star, one-star and heritage hotels) by the Ministry of Tourism, Government of India, based on the general features and facilities offered.

Five Star Deluxe Hotel

The five star deluxe hotels having reception opened 24 hours, multilingual staff, doorman-service or valet parking, concierge, page boy, spacious reception hall with several seats and beverage service, personalized greeting for each guest with fresh flowers or a present in the room, minibar and food and beverage offer via room service during 24 hours, personal care products in flacons, internet-PC in the room, safe in the room, ironing service (return within 1 hour), shoe polish service, turndown service in the evening. The deluxe hotels need to attain high expectations of an international guest service. The Superior luxury star is only awarded with a system of intensive guest care.

Five Star Hotel

The finest hotels in the world. A five star hotel is characterized by luxury appointments, superlative service, and the highest standards of comfort. Five star hotels offer originality in architecture and interior design, high-grade materials in construction and décor, and such special touches as fresh flowers and plants in abundance. These properties also maintain a high staff-to-guest ratio, gourmet dining, and 24-hour room service. Guestrooms offer ample space, the finest furnishings and decor, premium bedding, and luxury bath products. Room amenities generally include high-speed Internet access and CD and/or DVD players. Five star hotels may offer additional recreation facilities such as tennis courts and golf-course access. On-site spa services, a top-notch fitness centre, and a pool are generally available, as well.

Four Star Hotel

These upscale establishments usually offer a fine-dining restaurant, lounge, and room service with extended hours. Service features usually include baggage assistance, concierge service, and valet parking. A conference centre with up-to-date technology and full business services are usually offered. Public spaces and guestrooms are thoughtfully designed and constructed with high-quality materials. Guestrooms generally offer stylish furnishings, high-quality bedding and bath products, and a wide array of amenities.

Three Star Hotel

Three-star establishments place a greater emphasis on style, comfort, and personalized service. They generally feature on-site dining room service, a pool and/or fitness centre, a gift shop, and may provide baggage assistance. Conference rooms for meetings and extended services for business travelers are usually offered. Guestrooms offer more extensive amenities and more careful attention to decor and comfort. Usually located near a major expressway, business center and/or shopping area, these hotels offer nice, spacious rooms and decorative lobbies.

Two Star Hotel

These limited-service establishments are expected to offer clean, basic accommodation. These properties may offer some business services but generally lack meeting rooms, baggage assistance, and full fitness and recreation facilities. On-site dining is usually limited to coffee or Continental breakfast service. Guestrooms generally offer private bathroom, telephone, TV, and limited amenities. These hotels are generally part of a chain that offers consistent quality and limited amenities. While not have the convenience of room service, there should be a small restaurant on site.

One Star Hotel

A one-star establishment is expected to offer clean, no-frills accommodation with minimal on-site facilities for the budget traveler for whom cost is the primary concern. Guestrooms generally are small, functionally decorated, and may not have a private bathroom, in-room telephone, or amenities. On-site dining is usually not available. Public access and guest reception may not be available at all hours. Expect a small hotel managed and operated by the owner. Restaurant service should be within walking distance, as well as nearby public transportation, major intersections and entertainment that is reasonable in price.

Heritage Hotel

The Maharajas in India have left a royal legacy with their palaces and residences still holding on to the glory. Vacation in one of the heritage hotels in India would be like steering by vacation ship to the port of royalty and comfort to live king size while being awake to the hospitality and facilities. The erstwhile residences of the royal families in various states of India serve as luxury and boutique hotels presently. Guests at such palace turned hotels enjoy great ambience, royal food, huge rooms, old furniture, yet modern facilities. The rooms have been renovated to satisfy a modern guest who is looking to make his vacation and business trip worthwhile. The concept of heritage hotels took off mainly from the Rajputana state of Rajasthan, land of the Marwar rulers too. There were several havelis and palaces owned by the Maharajas that stood abandoned and were simply tourist attractions. Today, it remains to be an attraction, but tourists are offered the chance of reliving history. In this hotel a guest is graciously welcomed, offered room that have their own history, serve traditional cuisine and are entertained by folk artist. These hotels put their best efforts to give the glimpse of their region. Example: Jai Mahal palace in Jaipur.

Star Hotels in Rajasthan State

Rajasthan is the Suitable Location for putting up world class hotels and also the safest state in India in terms of Law and Order. It offers to its tourists a safe and secure environment. It is also very easily accessible by air, train and road. It is also the leading tourist destination state of India will start getting International Chartered Flights in view of extended Airport run way of Jaipur Airport. Rajasthan is going to make headway in the area of spiritual tourism, eco tourism, health tourism and rural tourism. Heritage tourism, which is one of the strengths of Rajasthan Tourism, is going to be strengthened further. Therefore Rajasthan is one of the most favoured tourism destinations in India.

Many tourists travel and enjoy this beautiful place. With such reasons accommodation facilities are improving in Rajasthan moreover high class tourist prefer five star only. Therefore five star hotels have been selected for our study. Some of the Five Star Hotels in Rajasthan are —

Hotel Inder Residency (Udaipur)

It is located at Ellisbridge Goverdhan Vilas, Shikharbadi Road Udaipur, lose to the business areas enables the esteemed business class barons and visitors to easily access the hotel. The hold offers world class luxury and comfort and best accommodation facilities to their guests with modern amenities that any star hotels offer.

Taj Lake Palace (Udaipur)

The Taj Lake Palace, located in the middle of Lake Pichola is a dream of white marble and mosaic glistening in the moonlight, very reminiscent of the most beautiful tourist cliché in the world, the palace was built in 1746 by Maharana Jagat Singh II, 62nd successor to the royal dynasty of Mewar – believed to be descendants of the Sun God. Set against the backdrop of the majestic Aravalli Mountains on one side of the lake, and lofty palaces on the other, the Taj Lake Palace spreads across a four-acre island – an almost surreal vision in marble.

Hotel Udaivilas (Udaipur)

Udaivilas at Udaipur (Rajasthan, India) is an Oberoi Group Hotel, located on the banks of Lake Pichola and is a 40 minute-drive from Udaipur's Dabok airport. The Oberoi Group's new Luxury hotel encompasses 30 acres of manicured gardens and courtyards. Designed as a Mewari palace, the hotel recreates the luxurious ambience of a royal residence, complete with decorative water bodies and carved stone pillars.

Country Inn (Jaipur)

Country Inn and Suites by Carlson Jaipur proudly stands tall and stands out as a smart and unique a structure in a city that prides itself upon its lavish and historical monuments. Breaking away from the tradition; it's simple yet stylish and contemporary design creates a calm environment.

Rambagh Palace (Jaipur)

The Rambagh Palace is a magnificent building spread over 47 acres of gardens. This former residence of the Maharaja of Jaipur is centrally located, near the main shopping area and historical monuments. The Rambagh offers 106 rooms, including 4 special suites. All rooms are elegantly appointed and air conditioned, with Superior rooms tastefully decorated in traditional Rajasthani style. The hotel offers guests an indoor swimming pool and fitness centre among its facilities and has two banquet halls with a capacity of 30 to 200, depending on arrangement.

Taj Jai Mahal Palace (Jaipur)

Jai Mahal Palace, the former residence of the Prime Minister of the princely state of Jaipur, recreates the aura of the city's royal past. The majestic palace, a vast complex of regal rooms, pretty pavilions and charming colonnades set amidst 18 acres of landscaped gardens in the heart of the city, traces its origins to 1747. The stately Moghul gardens of the Jai Mahal palace are the finest Moghul gardens in existence.

Le Meridien (Jaipur)

Le Meridien Jaipur is a mere 20 miles from the international airport, eight miles from the City Palace/Jantar Mantar, and 10 miles from the Nahargarh Fort - Historic Fort. This property is an extravagantly regal hotel, a hotel that pays homage to the grandeur of Indian architecture with peacock arches and gleaming white stone. Built upon 25 acres of lush gardens, Le Meridien Jaipur offers a sanctuary of serene tranquility. The hotel features a world-class spa with massage and meditation rooms, two innovative restaurants, a sleek bar, a cinema seating 42 guests, and a Penguin Club for children. The hotel also includes a state-of-the-art conference centre and magnificent banquet halls.

Taj Hari Mahal (Jodhpur)

Taj Hari Mahal Hotel is just an ideal place to stay in Jodhpur. Belonging to the prestigious Taj Group of Hotel, Taj Hari Mahal Hotel has it all from perfect accommodation, dining and recreation. It is located at a distance of 5 kms from the airport, 3 kms from the railway station and 2 kms from the bus stand.

Star Hotels in Gujarat State

Gujarat also known as the Manchester of the East was famous for textile industries from the medieval times is visited by numerous big and small business travelers to make trade; they form the bulk of the patrons in these hotels. Some of the five star Hotels in Gujarat are:

Hotel Taj Residency (Gujarat)

It is Located at International Airport Circle, Hansol, Ahmedabad 382 475, the Hotel Taj Residency consists of 91 centrally air-conditioned rooms and suites. The rooms are centrally air conditioned with world class modern amenities of international standard like the ISD direct dial facility, 24 hours room service, mini bar, restaurants, television and more. Other facilities available for their guests include airline desk, beauty salon, drug store, porters, conference facilities, boutiques, business center, indoor parking, car rental desk, currency exchange, 24 hour room service and front desk, baby sitting, fax, health club, restaurant, safe deposit box, refrigerator, free newspaper, smoke detectors and more.

Cambay Grand (Gujarat)

A five star luxury hotel is centrally situated in the heart of business hub. Major corporate houses, entertainment, recreation and shopping centers are in the vicinity of the hotel. Cambay Grand, Ahmedabad offers beautifully appointed rooms, excellent conference and banquet facilities with impeccable service.

Hotel Le Meridien (Gujarat)

It is located near Nehru Bridge, the Hotel Le Meridien has sixty three well equipped rooms with decorated lobby having granite pillars and marble floors enhance the external view of the hotel. Basically planned for business and leisure travelers, the hotels offer guests with the best luxury and true value for money. The hotel also provides best of opportunities. Esteemed business class barons get the opportunity to conduct successful conferences, mock tails, meeting, wedding receptions, seminars, dinners etc.

Holiday Inn Hotel (Gujarat)

The rooms of the hotel are centrally air conditioned with world class modern amenities of international standard and all sorts of facilities enjoyed in a star hotel. The waterfall, the restaurant inside the hotel offer multi cuisine according to individual taste. Antigravity is the 24-hr coffee shop inside the hotel. The hotel has conference and banquet facilities as well.

Hotel Fortune Landmark (Gujarat)

Fortune Landmark in Ahmedabad is one of the most prestigious Five Star Hotel in Ahmedabad. This hotel is known for providing personalized service, devoted and well trained staffs and the beautiful ambience. This hotel provides all the needed facilities to the tourists at an affordable price. Fortune Hotel Landmark is a luxurious hotel beautifully located in the heart of commercial hub of Ahmedabad. The hotel provides most comfortable and well-equipped accommodation facilities keeping in mind the need of the modern business traveler. It offers state-of-the-art business facilities along with well-trained staff services. Fortune Hotel Landmark is a great place to stay and experience the finest hospitable services.

Hotel The Pride (Gujarat)

The Pride Hotel is one of the best luxury hotel of Ahmedabad which possesses unparallel elegance and grace. As it is a world-class five star hotel, it provides finest amenities and accommodation along with warm hospitality services. The hotel offers state-of-the-art conference hall and banquet hall to host any occasion. With classy metropolitan richness, The Pride Hotel is ideal place for an enthused business trip, social events, or pleasure-seeking escape from the anarchy of the city.

Sample Hotels

The usefulness of such in-depth studies is widely accepted because human resource development is backbone of every hotel. As although upper class family prefer to go five or seven star hotel, that's why this category of hotel give much emphasis on training and development of their employees as compare to other category of hotels.

So we selected the five star category hotels. That is – Hotel Inder Residency (Udaipur) and Hotel Cambay Grand (Ahemdabad).

Hotel Inder Residency (Udaipur)

Hotel Inder Residency, Udaipur is a modern and luxurious hotel. The hotel was established in October 2008. The hotel overcome to its popularity with its most luxurious and perfectly located space, it is surrounded by lovely gardens, misty hills and breath taking lakes and ponds. This hotel is the unit of 'Seasons Hotel Pvt Ltd'. The Inder Residency Hotel is located at Goverdhan Vilas, Shikharbadi Road, Udaipur. Hotel Inder Residency is frequented by both the business as well as leisure travelers for its unparalleled services and facilities. Stylish settings, the ultimate in modern comfort, gracious hospitality, state of the art facilities and intuitive service seamlessly come together to create an inspired regal experience, that is quintessentially.

Hotel Inder Residency, Udaipur – Rajasthan

Ideally poised to offer breathtaking sunset and stunning morning views of Aravalies is the essence of Mewar charm. This charming hotel on 3.75 lacs square feet of well landscaped gardens is strategically located at Udaipur - the jewel of Rajasthan – the city of lakes, palaces, forts located on hilltop and tails of valor. A historical step well "BAWARI" within the gardens dates back in history allowing a glimpse of ancient irrigation methods.

Outdoor adult's swimming pools and toddlers pool at the bottom of "MAGRI" a landscaped hillock within the courtyard. Gym, steam, sauna, play scape, beauty salon, spa and business centre, etc. are the few of the facilities available at the hotel.

Hotel Inder Residency features 144 aesthetically appointed rooms and suites. The rooms and suites are segregated into different categories such as deluxe room, super deluxe room, Hawa Mahal balcony room, grand suite, Maharaja Suite and presidential suite. These cocoons of comfort are well furnished with scores of modern amenities that cater to daily needs. Some of the most sought -after in-room facilities are cable television, direct dial telephone, tea or coffee maker, attached baths and washroom amenities. The refreshing spa facilities remain fit and energetic even after a day of long traveling.

Inder Residency hotel in Udaipur offers plenty of modern facilities and services to make stay comfortable. The hotel has a multi cuisine restaurant bask in the fine dining experiences. Bar, poolside barbeque restaurant and coffee shops are the other ideal places to enjoy refreshing drinks and tasty preparations.

Room Type

(a) Deluxe Garden View (88 Nos.)

Description – large and spacious room with lush green garden view.

(b) Super Deluxe Pool View (35 Nos.)

Description – Room with very nice view of pool and pool side.

(c) Hawa Mahal with Balcony (14 Nos.)

Description – Spacious room with private balcony.

(d) Grand Suite (05 Nos.)

Description – A suite with one beautifully made living and bed room with balcony overlooking garden and mountain.

(e) Maharaja Suite (1 Nos.)

Description – A suite with one living room overlooking all the nice views of pool and garden. It has a large bathroom with jacuzzi inside and a cubical shower.

(*f*) Presidential Suite (1 Nos.)

Description – One of the best suite amongst all the rooms. It has a private bar in room, spacious bed room and living room, bathroom with jacuzzi.

Dinning

Laziz – The Fine-Dining Restaurant

Savour unrivalled range of delectable multi-cuisine in contemporary and cozy ambience. Laziz is a fine-dining restaurant situated at lobby level, open for dinners from 7.00 pm to 11 pm. It has an exotic bar card and serves International gourmet cuisines with Indian touch.

Tashkeen – The Coffee Shop

This swanky café has reflection of subtle International trends. Enjoy coffees and conversations. Relish scrumptious quick bites. Savor buffets for breakfast, luncheons and dinner.

Harbour – The Bar

Exhaustive collection of International and Indian wines, aperitifs/liquours, beers, spirits, etc. Located at the lobby level and designed to represent ship harbour, this one-of-a-kind bar also features a menu of heady cocktails and mocktails and a synchronized menu of short-eats – Barbeque and International too. Open 11 am to 11 pm.

Pool Side Bar-be-que Restaurant

The poolside outlet near the Bawri on the Foothills of beautifully landscaped Magri is a perfect place to cool-off with a drink and snack. Bar-be-Que operational every evening from 7 pm serving tandoor specialities along with the best of beers, wines and spirits.

Kohinoor Hall and Pre-function

Kohinoor, our banquet hall is the largest in Udaipur with capacity of 1000 persons. And it's not just about space we provide services and facilities of highest level to make sure your occasion becomes memorable.

Front Office

In the hotel, the front office welcomes guests to the accommodation section: meeting and greeting them, taking and organizing reservations, allocating check in and out of rooms, organizing porter service, issuing keys and other security arrangements, passing on messages to customers and settling the accounts. This particular department is responsible for the sale of the hotel rooms, reservations followed by registrations.

Following are the different sections in the Front Office

Front Desk

This section handles the guest complaints, verifies different files and formats and follows the formalities of check-In and Check-Out guests, Flash reports, etc. It is also called as Reception.

GRE Desk

The GRE is also called as Guest Relation Executive. The section is responsible for handling different guest's relation and keeps the average detailed information about the guest for future relation.

Back Office

A back office is a part of most corporations where tasks dedicated to running the company itself take place. The term comes from the building layout of early companies where the front office would contain the sales and other customer-facing staff and the back office would be those manufacturing or developing the products or involved in administration but without being seen by customers. Although the operations of a back office are usually not given a lot of consideration, they are a major contributor to a business. The internal operations of an organization that is not accessible or visible to the general public.

Board Room

It has an 831 sq.ft area and meant for different meeting. It has 24 covers.

Lobby

It has 4982 sq.ft area where the guest can relax and spend their sufficient time before the check-In or Check-Out procedures take starts.

Shopping Arcade

This is a boutique shop which has traditional, cultural and luxurious sufficient boutiques from all over India and especially from the local state Rajasthan itself it has 1102 sq.ft area.

Business Centre

It has 119 sq.ft. area and meant for the guests who can use the modern browsing technology for different purposes and premises.

Gymnasium, Steam and Sauna

It has 454 area sq.ft. This particular section provides the modern, world class facility for body fitness and exercises and provides the facilities to experience the efficient best services for 24 hours.

Other Facilities

The hotel provided other facilities like adult and toddlers swimming pool, in-house laundry, doctor on call, money exchange facility, extensive parking for buses, cars and two wheelers, one room for physically challenged and also facilities for public cloak rooms and in all public areas including non-skid ramps to access these areas.

Table 1.8: Income of Hotel Inder Residency

Year	Income (Rs. In Crore)	Growth Rate (%)
2008-2009	2.56	—
2009-2010	8.38	227.34
2010-2011	10.14	21.00
2011-2012	10.46	3.15

Table1.8 showed income of hotel Inder Residency during 2009-12. In 2009, the hotel made the total business of 2.56 Crore which increased to 8.38 Crore in 2010. During 20010-11 and 2011-12, the business was 10.14 crores and 10.46 crores respectively. Growth rate in 2010-11 and 2011-12 was decline.

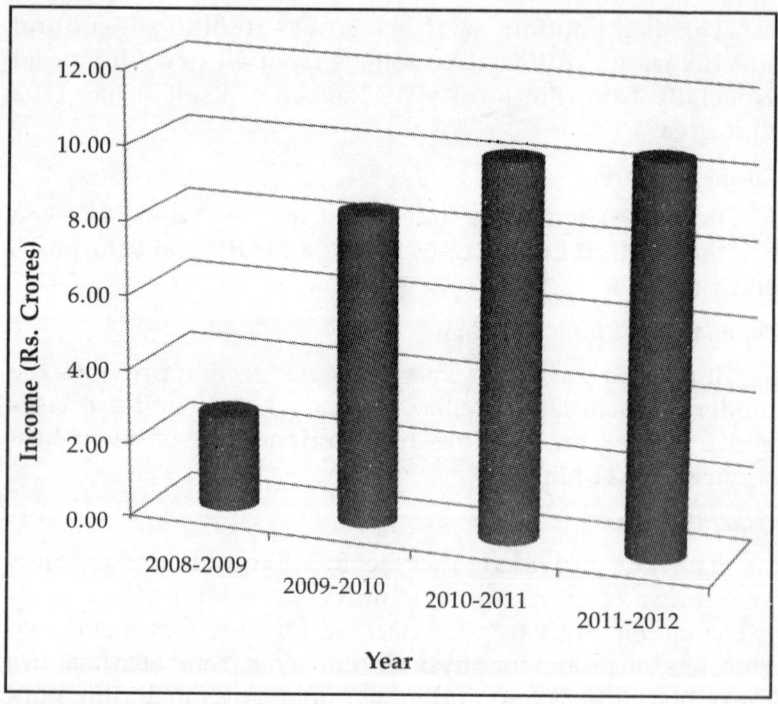

Fig. 1.11: Income of Hotel Inder Residency

Hotel Cambay Grand (Ahmedabad)

The Hotel Cambay Grand is an upscale five (5) Star category hotel spread with a built up area of 28485 Sq. Mtrs. This hotel is located near the Thaltej, Ahmebabad with close proximity to city's business areas. This hotel has been operational since November 2009 with 168 rooms including suites. It provides a range of facilities to its guest including business centre, spa, swimming pool, fitness centre,

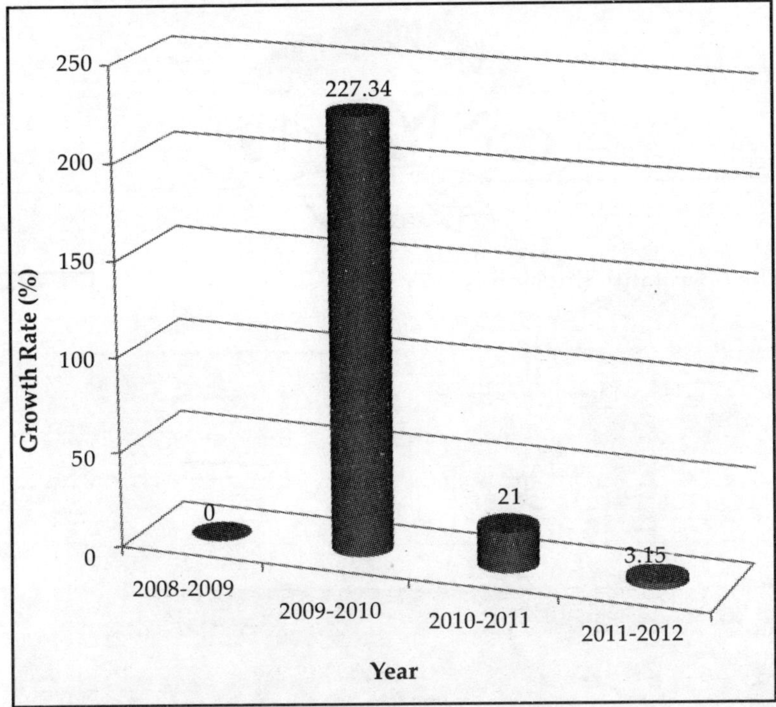

Fig. 1.12: Growth Rate of Hotel Inder Residency

discotheque and a beauty salon. The hotel has multi-cuisine restaurants and food and beverage outlets. The hotel also has meeting rooms and banquet halls with capacity for up to 1,500 persons. This hotel is RCI affiliated.

The premium luxury hotel has been pushing the envelope of business hospitality. Best - known for hosting high-end business meets, leadership summits, musical extravaganza, etc. Cambay Grand is setting a precedent of sorts in hospitality business. Located at a driving distance of 20 minutes from the airport and 10 minutes from the new commercial and business hub of Ahmedabad, Cambay Grand offers tastefully appointed rooms and suites equipped with high speed internet access, restaurants, conference halls, in-house entertainment facilities and much more.

Hotel Cambay Grand, Ahmedabad — Gujarat

All its properties are located in lush green pastures with pristine surroundings to achieve that much elusive joy. With 10 properties across Ahmedabad, Gandhinagar, Gurgaon, Jaipur, Udaipur, Kerala and Goa, Cambay offers undiluted opulence through their superior ambience, hospitality and service. In the year 2011, the Group is poised to become a 1500+ room, 13 property companies. Cambay also has upcoming properties at Jodhpur, Neemrana and Dahej. Cambay properties are all embellished with state-of-the-art features like golf and spas, giving them a competitive edge. While golf distinctly attracts the corporate world, spas are a natural extension of modern lifestyle. The latest of all ventures is the hospitality education institute that will certainly meet the requirement of hospitality maestros, for the group and also the entire hospitality industry. Cambay offers innovative and integrated hospitality solutions. From corporate hospitality to holiday management, it ensures the best services in absolute luxury. The hospitality division is segmented into hotels, resorts, spas, clubs, golf, family holidays and education. Cambay is a part of Neesa Leisure Ltd.

Room Type

(*a*) Deluxe Rooms (95 Nos.)

(*b*) Premium Rooms (65 Nos.)

(*c*) Cambay Club Suites (08 Nos.)

Room Amenities at Cambay Grand reflect the ethos of modern living. Wooden flooring, king-size beds, motorized blinds and thermostat air conditioning exude the sensation of sheer luxury. Additional amenities like tea-coffee maker, Wi-Fi connectivity, LCD TV, electronic safe, hairdryer, mini bar, direct dialing telephone and other faultless services add ease to stay.

Dining

Our gourmet chefs whip up delicious recipes to pander your gastronomical indulgences.

Indus Multi-cuisine Restaurant

Authentic world class flavors combine to create culinary magic at Indus. Savour cuisines from the northern and coastal regions, exotic Oriental dishes like Thai, Chinese, Malaysian, Lebanese and various Continental delicacies.

Golden Cilantro - Multi Cuisine Restaurant

Explore the wonders of great food by renowned chefs at Golden Cilantro. Every dish of global cuisine is a piece of art. Done up in a blend of lively and earthy tone, the restaurant offers a wide range of cuisine from Indian, Continental to

Oriental. Serving a la carte and buffet, each dish at Golden Cilantro is distinct and created with perfection to cater individual taste buds. The cheerful ambience, delicious food and efficient service are sure to surprise the bon vivant of Ahmedabad.

Pool Side Grill Restaurant

At Pool Side Grill, experience the grilled sensations created by swaggering chefs. The newly launched restaurant will have a Live Tandoor, Live Mock tail bar, in addition to plethora of luxurious trappings which includes a green canopy and a swimming pool attached with one-of-its-kind Jacuzzi of the city. Chefs can also take breath away while serving soups, mock tails, salads and many other surprises. Guests can soak in the summer sun reposing by the pool side, before gorging on varied grilled delicacies. So, experience the thrill at Poolside Grill.

Cambay Cafe

Sit back, chat up friends and family or catch up on some leisurely reading. A hangout for all ages, Cambay Café lets you unwind and reinvigorate with an assortment of beverages, hot and cold, freshly baked cookies and divine desserts.

Orient Spa

Opulence and grandeur loom in every corner of the place. It offers the ultimate exuberance in spa therapy and reflects the expression - 'wellness, fitness and makeover,' as its core element. Providing an alternative to conquer the curse of daily stress through its aromatic massages, luxurious settings and expert techniques, the Orient Spa in Ahmedabad instils the essence of spa therapy in the heart of Indian culture.

Meetings and Banquets

Refined to the modern businessman's taste, business centre settle in with ease. Superior conferencing facilities and state-of-the-art amenities take care of all business requirements flawlessly. Cambay will create an atmosphere where elegance, warmth, ambience, impeccable service, and superb food offered to the guests. Well appointed rooms with all the luxurious facilities like Golf, Spa, Beauty Salon, Gym, Swimming pool, Mini Theater, Discotheque, Gaming centres and unmatched services that would make stay very comfortable. It tie-ups with event management companies and have a very good team to arrange entertainment acts and decor like Magician, Musicians, Dance Troops, DJ, Gaming Jockey, Florist etc.

Board Room

Elegant and spacious boardroom is designed to offer premium luxury to its occupants. Executive seats are cushioned to provide extra comfort for those day-long businesses meets and are supported by state-of-the-art audio-visual facilities.

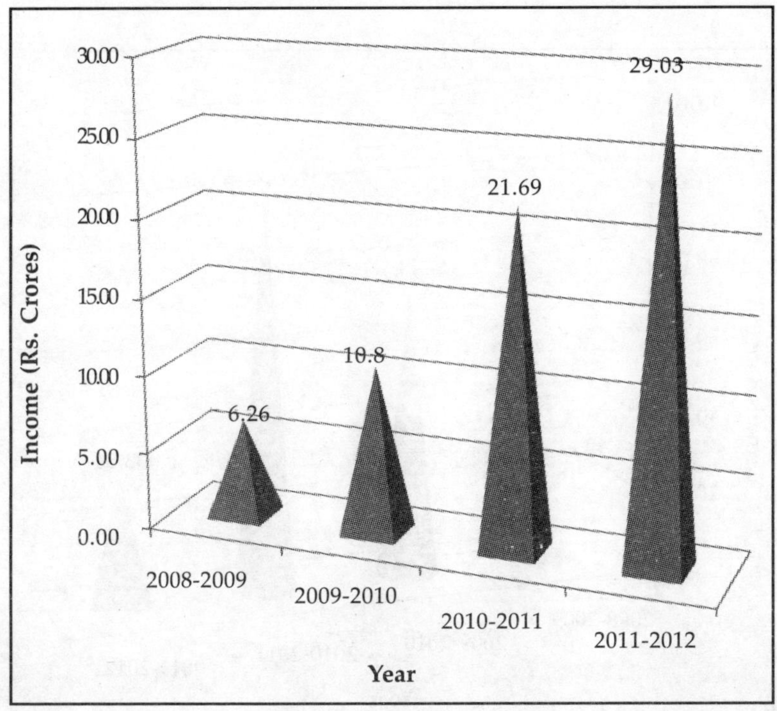

Fig. 1.13: Income of Hotel Cambay Grand

Other Facilities

The hotel provided other facilities like wi-fi, swimming pool, travel desk, restaurant, car rental, health club, valet parking, baby sitting on request, currency exchange, business centre, special handicap facility, audio visual equipment, florist - on request, discotheque, computer games, library etc.

Table 1.9: Income of Hotel Cambay Grand

Year	Income (Rs. In Crore)	Growth Rate (%)
2008-2009	6.26	—
2009-2010	10.8	72.52
2010-2011	21.69	100.83
2011-2012	29.03	33.84

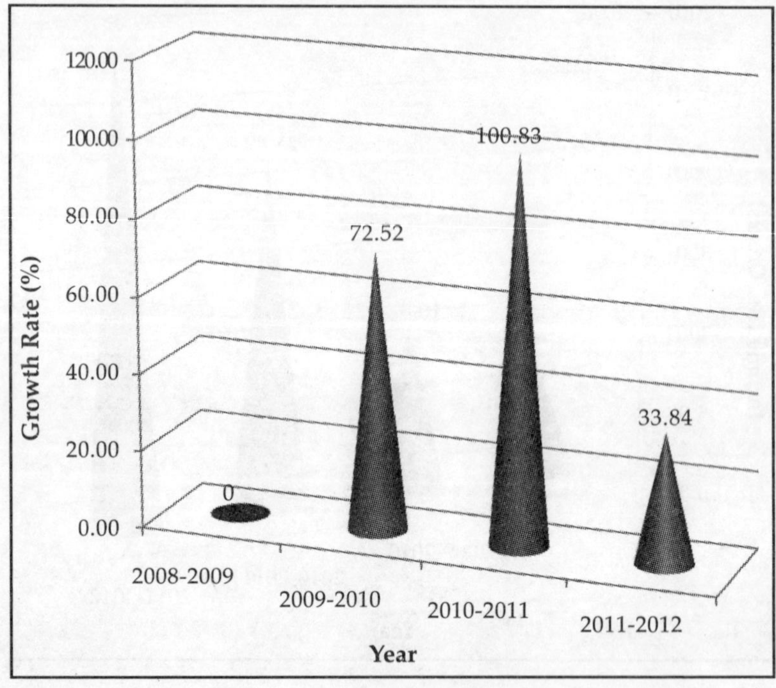

Fig. 1.14: Growth Rate of Hotel Cambay Grand

Table 1.9 indicated that hotel Cambay Grand business was 6.26 Crore Rs. This increased to 29.03 Crore Rs. in the year 2011-12. The growth rate was high in 2010-11.

REFERENCE

1. Floyd Miller, Statler – America's Extra Ordinary Hotelman, Statler Foundation, New York, 1968, p. 36.
2. Kasavana, M.L., and Brooks, R.M., Front Office Procedures 4th E.D., Educational Institute of AHMA, Michigan, 1996, p. 3.
3. Joseph D. Fridgen Dimensions of Tourism, Educational Institute of AHMA, Michigan, 1996, p. 193.
4. Indian Management, A Blueprint: Welcoming more Tourists, May 1997, p. 54.
5. Travel and Tourism: The World's Largest Industry, World Travel and Tourism Council Report, 1992.
6 Yojna, Paryatan Vikas Ki Sambhavana, June 1998, pp. 2-3.
7. Indian Management, A Blueprint: Welcoming more Tourists, May 1997, p. 55.
8. Negi J.M.S., Hotels for Tourism Development, Metropolitan Book Co., New Delhi, 1997, p. 17.
9. *Ibid* pp. 3.
10. *1bid* pp. 8.
11. Indian Management, A: Blueprint: Welcoming more Tourists, May 1997, p. 58.
12 Report of Bhagwati Committee on Unemployment, 1973.
13. Negi .J.M.S , Hotels for Tourism Development, Metropolitan Book Co., New Delhi, 1997., p. 9.
14. *Ibid.*
15. UNWTO Technical Manual: Collection of Tourism Expenditure Statistics". World Tourism Organization. 1995. p. 14.
16. UNWTO World Tourism Barometer (World Tourism Organization) 2007/2 June 2009.
17 UNWTO World Tourism Barometer June 2008, 6 World Tourism Organization, June 2008.
18. http://www.tourismroi.com/Content_Attachments/27670/File_633513750035785076.pdf.
19. UNWTO World Tourism Barometer January 2010.8.World Tourism Organization.January2010. http://unwto.org/facts/eng/pdf/barometer/UNWTO_Barom10_1_en_excerpt.

20. http://www.indiacore.com/tourism.html
21. Annual Report 2009-10, Ministry of Tourism, Government of India, Available at www.incredibleindia.org
22. *Ibid*
23. http://www.tradechakra.com/indian-economy/service-sector/tourism-industry.html
24. http://en.wikipedia.org/wiki/Tourism_in_India
25. Sharma, Bimla, Foreign Tourist Arrivals Falling, Times of India, July 2nd, 1997.
26. http://en.wikipedia.org/wiki/Rajasthan
27. http://tourism.gov.in/pplan/rajasthan.pdf
28. www.resortsinindia.ca/5-star-hotels-in-gujarat.htm
29 http://www.vibrantgujarat.jp/detailed-sector-profiles/tourism.pdf
30. http://www.dtpt.com/pdfs/Gujarat_KPMGReport.pdf
31. Hotel and Food Service Review, Hotel Classification, Aug. 1997, p. 25

CHAPTER

2 Human Resource Development in Hotel Industry

HUMAN RESOURCE DEVELOPMENT

INTRODUCTION

"THE ACHIEVEMENT of sustained and equitable development remains the greatest challenge facing the human race. Despite good progress over the past generation, more than one billion people still live in acute poverty and suffer grossly inadequate access to resource — education, health services, infrastructure, land and credit – required to give them a chance for a better life. The essential task of development is to provide opportunities so that these people and the hundreds of millions not much better off, can reach their potential." [1] People make things happen. If people have to make things happen, they need a set of circumstances to make things happen. However, it is the people who create circumstances that can help them to others in making things happen. HRD is the process of enabling people to make things happen. It deals both the process of competency development in people and creation of conditions to help people apply these competencies for their own benefit and for that of others. Man is the creator of all the organizations. It is the human beings who make things happen. It is the people who make the difference between success and failure. On several occasions, in spite outdated plant, equipment and technology, a committed group of people have produced 'the best' on the contrary, in many cases organizations with latest technologies and equipments could not yield satisfactorily because of people. It is possible to buy best equipment, quality material, sophisticated machines, robots technology, super computers, design and fully automatic unit, but it is not possible to buy people, their commitment and dedication.

As *Prof. T.V Rao* observed "It is not enough to engage on employee as individuals but it is more important to develop boss-subordinate relationships, team spirit, organizational climate and culture with the help of workers." [2]

According to *Leon. C. Magginson* the term Human Resources can be thought of as "The total knowledge, skills, creative abilities, talents and aptitudes of an organization's work force, as well as the value, attitudes and belief of the individual involved." [3]

The term 'Human Resources' can also be explained in the sense that it is resource like any other natural resource. The term human resources from the organizational point of view can be defined is the total success of any organization depends on the quality of its human resources studies in the growth pattern of advanced countries have shown that improvements in the quality and utilisation of personnel have been a major factor in accelerating face of economic growth. It is the effectiveness of human system.

Therefore, that differentiates successful dynamics and progressive organizations from others as noted by *Thomas J. Peter and Robers H. Waterman* in their management classic in search of excellence. "Treat people as an adult, treat them as partners, treat them with dignity, treat them with respect, and treat them not as a capital spending automation or the primary source of productivity gains. These are fundamental lessons from the excellent company research. In other words, if you want productivity and the financial reward that goes with it, you must treat your employees as your most important asset."

This is more especially true in hotels as it is essential a people's business and improvement in service and quality of work as also the commitment towards social and development policies of government will largely depend on the attitudes and caliber of its employees at different levels. It is for this reason that all hotels have started laying much greater emphasis on the development of the most important resource *i.e.* 'Human Resource' and the important philosophy over the past few years. HRD has emerged as a profession in itself with tremendous relevance to the service sector. The emphasis of HRD is not only on production and productivity but also an overall quality of work life. Knowledge, skills, creative effective and efficient decision making abilities talents values, beliefs, aptitudes, attitudes and commitment of individual and groups involved in and concerned with the hotels. Human Resource plays a critical role in the development process of modern economy.

"It is often felt that, though the exploitation of natural resources availability of physical and financial resources and international aid play prominent roles in the growth of modern economics none of these factors is more significant than efficient and committed manpower. A nation with an abundance of physical resources will not benefit itself unless human resources will not benefit it unless human resources make use of them." [4]

In fact, one of the fundamental activity areas of management is the management of human resources. Thus, "In management of four M's – Money, Machine, Material and Men. It is need less to be labour the obvious point that considering the nature of man, the management of men...." [5] "Successful management depends significantly upon the ability to predict and control human bahaviour. Among other things, if a company is economically successful, it means, the management has been able to manage human resources effectively." [6] "The human Resources are the active force in industrialization, and strategies for development should concentrate particularly on their enhancement." [7]

It is observed that Human Resource being the most significant and active factor of production, becomes the key to optimize the utilisation of all the other material resources, developing the Human Resources, upgrading their skills and knowledge would lead to economic development. The concept of Human Development was originally introduced as an alternative to conceptions of development that focused on economic growth with or without equity consideration. "Today H.R.D is fast developing into a fad and fashionable tool, because its suits the culture and managerial styles of organizations, power play, obedience through fear and coercion, ensuing implementation of policies more through punished and less through rewards." [8]

In the period of rapidly changing technology and increasing competition, the organizations are become highly conscious about the development of its human resources. No organizations can effort to ignore the development of its Human Resources, if it desires to achieve the standards of excellence. Almost all the major industrialist organization has now established H.R.D departments separately to effectively deal with the Human Resources. Realizing the importance of utilising this vital resource, even our Government has setup a separate H.R.D ministry at the national level.

Human Resource System is an organization is not only a unique sub-system but a principal and central sub system as it operates upon and controls all other sub-systems. Thus in the words of *Wendell L. French* "Personnel management is a major pervasive sub system of all organizations." [9]

Whatever is in the environment affects the organization as a whole hence also affects the Human Resources system. The human resources receive inputs from the organization in the form of a objective and it results in that may viewed as individual and organizational output. Both the human resources system and the entire organization operate under the same culture economic, social, legal, and political and under constraints. Hence, greater the effectiveness and productivity of human resources, the more will be the effective functioning of an organization.

"According to *Peter F. Drucker* the significance of human resources as manager are fond of saying 'our greatest asset is people.' They are fond of repeating the truism that only real difference between one organization and another is the performance of people." [10] In essence the survival, development and performance of an organization, although not solely but heavily, depends on the quality of human resources.

Need of Human Resource Development

The need of H.R.D was aptly expresses by an environment philosopher of *China, Kuang Chungturm* during 7th century in the following words:

"If you wish to plan for a year, sow seeds,
If you wish to plan for 10 years, plant trees,
If you wish to plan a life time, develop men."

According to *T.V Rao and D.F Pereira* "HRD is needed by any organization that wants to be dynamic and fast growth oriented or to succeed in a fast changing environment. Organizations can become dynamic and grow only through the efforts and competencies for their human resources." Personal policies can keep the morale and motivation of employees high, but these efforts are not enough to make the organization dynamic and take it in new directions. Employee capabilities must continuously be acquired sharpened and used. For this purpose on 'enabling' organizational culture is essential. "When employee use their initiative, take risks, experiment, innovate and make things happen, the organization may be said to have an enabling culture." [11] Even an organization that has reached its peak, has to adopt to the changing environment. All the organizations do require and increase its capabilities for stability and renewal. H.R.D is not an activity carried out in an isolated environment. It basically aims at developing the individual for his own growth. In turn it also contributes to the fulfilled of the company objectives. Therefore the H.R.D does not keep the individual from his normal area of activities it goes towards him placed in the very context of life at his work place, home and society. Among other things H.R.D gives attention towards a creating a home environment in the work place where the workers gains an assurance of being cared for in the most personalized manner. The worker should not carry the worries of the work place to his home. As normally a worker spend a major portion of his day time in the shop floor, the management should concentrate on the work place and improvements in the quality of work life. The concept of quality of work life is 'A process of work organization which enables its members at all levels to participate activity and efficiently in shaping the organization environment methods out comes.' "It is value based process which is aimed towards meetings the twin goals of enhances effectiveness of organization and improvement quality of life at work for employees." [12]

Concept of Human Resource Development

In the field of management human resource development concept is of recent origin. The term 'HRD' was tested by *Len Neudler*. In America Society for Training and Development conference, did a planned study they inferred that promotion of it in last two decades and specially from the late eighties only, the management thinkers, behavioural scientists and practicing managers have started looking for other systematic and planned ways of developing human resources other than 'Training' which is often misunderstood as HRD The vigorous exercise carried out by these thinkers to develop human resource has resulted into emergence and exploration of a field *i.e.*, Human Resource Development. Where the knowledge is getting generated experience and multiplies and molding of man to human resource is being taken care of today, the term HRD enjoys a high profile and increasing attention being paid by policy makers, human resource specialist's chief executive, line managers, training and development specialties management consultant etc.

In so far as HRD is concerned it is multi faceted process involving areas like selection, placement and induction, training objective, performance appraisal, career planning and potential development. It also includes area like motivation and development of entire work force within an organization. It not only aims to provide knowledge and skills to employees but also brings about changes in the attitudes of people with a view to developing them. HRD policies and exercises with an organization help the individual employees in sharpening those existing capabilities and acquiring new capabilities. "Infact an effective HRD policy enables an individual to improve his overall personality and career prospects and helps him to perform existing and future roles effectively. It also develops a sense of belonging of the employees towards the organization and society and a commitment to work." [13]

According to *Venkateshwara Rao* there are various methods available for developing human resources, HRD is not a piecemeal or a onetime exercise but "It is a continuous process requiring to keep pace with the changes and developments taking place by which employees an organization are helped in a continuous and planned way to —

- Acquire and sharpen capabilities required to perform various functions associated with their present or expected future roles.
- Develop their general capabilities as individual and discover and exploit their own inner potentials for their own or organizational development purposes.
- Develop an organizational culture in which supervisor, subordinate relationships, team work and collaboration among sub-units are strong and contribute to the professional well being motivation and pride of employees." [14]

Thus a careful observation of the above definitions clearly states that HRD is a continuous process through which mere human being is developed to 'Human Resource' which enables individual development of skills, competencies, capabilities, attitudes, commitment towards the job as well as organizational development in the form of creative development, effective and healthy work culture which not only motivates employees but also ensures a great amount of success, overall effectiveness, devotional dynamism and positive direction. The important influential factor that affects the organizational climate is the philosophy of the top management. Management's philosophy can help an organization to link its activities to the needs of society and legitimize its existence." [15]

Apart from a corporate unit building on its products or services having consistent distribution channels, cohesive marketing strategies and cost leadership, it cannot choose to ignore it's human resources and neither can it employees of a company from the basic and real assets and therefore must also be relates as such. "It is these employees that facilitate the organization to grow hence the importance of imparting knowledge, skills and facilitating an adequate organization climate to them so as "to enable the corporate unit by dynamic and growth oriented." [16]. "Indeed organization cannot service beyond a point unless they are continuously alert to the fast changing business environment and continuously prepare their employee to meet the challenges of the future. After all, unlike other resources human resources have rather unlimited potential capabilities." [17]

According to *A.K.Singh* HRD is "the development of abilities and attitudes of the individual leading to personal growth and self-actualization which enables the individual to contribute to societal well being and development in achieving personal satisfaction and happiness." [18]

The definition by Singh A.K. seems to point out that HRD in the broad sense extends beyond the organization premises to include individual growth and the contribution he/she makes towards the society and national at large. This view is further added weight on by *T.V., Verma K.K.,* who define H.R.D in the national context as "a process by which the people in various groups (*viz* age groups, regional groups, socio-economic groups, community groups etc.). All helped (by the government or otherwise) to acquire new competencies continuously so as to make them more self reliant and simultaneously develop a sense of pride in their country. Such self reliance and sense of pride could be developed through a variety of intervention at national, regional and organizational level." [19]

On the other hand according to *Leonard Nadler* the definition of HRD means "those learning experiences which are organized for a specified time and assigned to bring about the possibility of behavioural change." [20]

From the above definition it can be realized that HRD is basically viewed from two aspects:

1. HRD in the national context (Macro – HRD)
2. HRD in the organizational context (Micro – HRD)

"As discussed above while the former view of HRD extends beyond the organization for the matter with specific reference to personnel there in the term Micro – HRD" [21]

Objective of Human Resource Development

Man is not merely pair of hands but he goes to work with intelligence, imagination, feelings and inspiration. The working condition should, therefore, be such that these are enough scope for his various abilities.

The development of human resource at macro level needs carrying out —

- Man power resource and planning to anticipate long run labour market needs.
- Man power development through training and retraining programmes.
- Man power distribution through an effective placement services.
- Man power for full utilisation of national resources.

At the micro organization level, it is a comprehensive system to help the employees in a systematic way to acquire, sharpen or mould capabilities which need to achieve the objectives mentioned as:

(a) To increase the productivity;

(b) To improve the employee's morale;

(c) To create right organizational environment;

(d) To identify talents and develop them;

(e) To reduce absenteeism and

(f) To reduce the expenditure.

Dimension of Human Resource Development

Now-a-days HRD is considered as the key to the higher productivity, better relations and greater profitability for any organization. According to different manager these are the main dimensions of HRD

According to *T.V. Rao* "HRD sub systems comprise performance appraisal, potential appraisal, career planning, training programme, performance coaching, organization development, employee welfare rewards, quality of work life and human resource information system."

According to *Udai Pareek* "Performance appraisal, feedback, counseling, potential appraisal, career achievement, career planning and training as dimensions of HRD"

According to *M.S.S. Varandran* "HRD mechanism into performance appraisal, role analysis, organization development and quality circles."

A well structured HRD programme is expected to have the following component.

Manpower Planning

Manpower planning is a process for determining and assessing that the organization will have an adequate number of qualified persons, available at proper time, performing jobs which would meet the needs of the organization and which would provide satisfaction for the individuals involve.

1. Estimation of present and future requirements and supply of human resources based on the objectives and long-term plans of the organization.
2. Calculation of net human resource requirements based on present level of human resource.
3. Initiating steps to change mould and develop the existing human resources to meet the future human resource requirements.

4. Planning the necessary programme to get the rest of human resources from outside the organization and to develop the human resources of existing employees.

Recruitment, Selection and Placement

Recruitment is the generation of application for specific positions for actual or anticipated vacancies. The ideal recruitment efforts will be to generate adequate number of suitable applications.

Selection is the process of ascertaining the qualifications, experience, skill, knowledge etc., of an application with a view to appraising his/her suitability to a job.

Placement is the process of assigning the selected candidate with the most suitable job. Scientific placement underlies the need for placing right men at the right job so that the best results could be obtained.

Training and Development

Training is a learning process that seeks to bring about a permanent improvement in the ability and behaviour of the employees by enabling them to acquire new skills, knowledge and attitude for more efficient performance.

Training includes:

1. Identification of training needs;
2. Developing suitable training programme;
3. Imparting requisite job skills and knowledge to employees; and
4. Evaluating the effectiveness of training programme.

Developing is basically an educational process which is directed to increase the ability of employees to perceive and apply knowledge in terms of cause and effect relationship.

Development includes:

1. Identification of areas;
2. Conducting development programmes;
3. Motivating the executives;

4. Taking the services of specialists; and
5. Evaluating the effectiveness of development programmes.

Performance Appraisal

Performance Appraisal is a process of determining how well a worker is performing his job. It provides a mechanism for identification of merit and deficiencies observed in an employee in relation to his job performance. The object of appraisal is to determine the present state of efficiency of a worker in order to establish the actual need for training. The process of Performance Appraisal consists of:

(a) Setting standards for performance.

(b) Communicating the performance; and

(c) Comprising the actual performance with the standard set.

Job Rotation

It is said that distribution of responsibilities will result in specialization but to be able to utilise their specialization in the best possible way, the work tasks should be rotated among the employees. So as to broaden their field of specialization as well as their knowledge about the organizations operation as a whole. The work tasks, therefore be rotated once a year among the various employees depending upon their qualifications and suitability to perform a new work task.

Wage and Salary Administration

This is also a fairly complex aspect requiring professional handling, determining and fairing salary scales. Giving weightage to differential work process, job responsibilities hazards encountered and stress borne would call for continuous study of different factors *viz.*, compensation, increments, incentives etc.

Career Planning and Development

Career Management is aimed at generating among employees an awareness of their strength and weakness and a helping them to match their skills and abilities to the needs and demand of the organization. This idea denotes that the careers of employees should be planned in such a manner that each one in the department has a chance to improve his portion.

Feedback and Counseling

In the Indian context counseling requires stress. It is yet at its infancy in most Indian organization in regard to HRD Counseling may resolve many frustrations, misunderstandings and misgivings which an employee may harbor effecting his work and performance. Counseling can serve several purposes; it can help strength the superior – subordinate relationships help the executive understand. The limitations of his seniors and problems of his juniors, improve communications. There by facilitating quality decisions help employees, recognize their strength and weakness, gain role clarity, evaluate the impact of their decisions and so on.

Organization Development

This component implies a process of graduation from experience. Behavioural scientists have underlined organizational development as a key process of HRD as such in which team work is emphasized; The O.D. exercises includes team building programme, role clarity, interpersonal sensitivity, personal growth and stress.

Industrial Relations

The manifestation of the attitudes of workers and other employees to work hopes and aspirations natured and realization or frustration ultimately faced. It covers a fairly wide ground. Strains may develop on different counts and HRD takes account of these promises.

Quality Circles

It is an approach which allows employees to become more involved by solving their own job related problems in an organized way.

Human Resource Information System

"The personal inventory has to be maintaining which contains information on the personal bio-data of officers, including their academic and professional qualification, their assignments, aptitudes and training. This inventory is used for selection of suitable officers for different specialized assignments and for taking decisions regarding transfer, placement and training. The feedback and reference can be further facilitated if computerization is introduced to maintain this inventory." [22]

"These subs-system when well implemented, reduce over – supply of labour, increase morale and motivation reduces accidents. Improve quality (both of the product and employee in value terms), reduce inefficiency enable prevalence of a self renovation thrust, improve communications and personal relations within and outside of the firm, increase both quality of life and quality of work life. Create avenues for promotion, increase organization effectiveness efficiency and consequently profits and goodwill, increase the effective use of the data bank among a host of others." [23]

Importance of Human Resource or Human Capital

- *Country Develop If the Human Resource is Developed*: To enhance economic development the state constructs road, building dredges, dams, power houses, hospital, etc. to run these units doctors, engineers, scientist, teachers, are required. So if the state invests in a human resource it pays dividend in response.
- *Increase in Productivity:* The batter education, improved skills and provision of healthy atmosphere will result in proper and most efficient use of resources (non-natural and natural) which will result in increase in economic production.
- *Eradication of Social and Economic Backwardness:* Human Resource development has an ample effect on the backwardness economy and society. The provision of education will increase literacy which will produce skilled Human Resource. Similarly provision of health facilities will result in healthy Human Resource which will contribute to the national economic development.

- *Entrepreneurship Increase:* Education, clean environment, good health, investment on the human resource, will all have its positive effect. Job opportunities would be created in the country. And even business environment will flourish in which creates many job opportunities.
- *Social Revolution:* Because of human Resource development the socio economic life of the peoples a country changes drastically. Over all look changes thinking phenomena change, progressive thoughts are endorsed in to the mind of peoples.

Importance of HRD for Effective Management Control

"Control is a function of management which extends to all other functions of management *viz.*, planning, organization, staffing, directing, coordinating and budgeting." [24] Many a times umbrage arises when managers introduce a control system which is then misconstrued by the employees to be a punitive measure." [25] It is thus the responsibility of the management to bring to rest such misconception lest should it have a devastating negative effect on the firm.

Most of the economies are dependent upon the level of management of human resources. In fact it is said that all development comes from human mind. Human Resources are responsible for the transformation of fundamental tasks of management is to manage human resources in the service of the economic objectives of the enterprise. Among other things, if a company is economically successful it means that management has been able to manage human resources effectively.

"HRD plays an important role in management control for the reason that it develops more competent people, brings about better developed roles. Higher work commitment and job involvement. Higher job satisfaction, better generation of internal resources and reduces conflicts." [26]

"However while dysfunctional/destructive conflicts misrouted out, functional constructive conflicts is allowed to prevail for the betterment of the organization as a derived

from HRD reduce significantly supervision and control from the top hierarchy besides employees prefer self control than control which is effected from above." [27]

HUMAN RESOURCE DEVELOPMENT IN HOTEL INDUSTRY

Human Resource Development (HRD) is the frameworks for helping employees develop their personal and organizational skills, knowledge, and abilities. Human Resource Development includes such opportunities as employee training, employee career development, performance management and development, coaching, succession planning, key employee identification, tuition assistance, and organization development. The focus of all aspects of Human Resource Development is on developing the most superior workforce so that the organization and individual employees can accomplish their work goals in service to customers.

Human Resource Development can be formal such as in classroom training, a college course, or an organizational planned change effort. Or, Human Resource Development can be informal as in employee coaching by a manager. Healthy organizations believe in Human Resource Development and cover all of these bases.

The most important function in a hotel is that of Management. The entire hotel system works or does not work on the basis of Management and its efficiency. The term 'Management' may refer either to those individuals who have authority and control over a system or to function carried out by those individuals. Management may also be considered as a process that is designed to accomplish certain goal, organizing, directing, motivating and controlling processes to achieve these goals. From the functional point of view, management involves the utilisation of six available resources, commonly as the 6 M's of Management. These are –

1. Manpower,
2. Money,

3. Materials,
4. Minutes,
5. Machines,
6. Market.

According to the American Management Association, "Management is the process by which human and physical resource are guided into dynamic and viable organizational units that attain objectives to the satisfaction of those served, and with a high degree of morale and sense of attainment on the part of those providing the service." [28]

The main resources available to the management in the hotel business are —

1. Human Resources,
2. Physical Resources such as equipment and ingredients, and
3. Monetary Resources.

Many Hotels spend considerable effort and skill in planning the purchase, installation and maintenance of machinery and often pay little attention to the need for planning their manpower requirements. New Hotels and restaurants are built and almost as an afterthought, management applies itself to the recruitment and training of staff. There are some Hotels where future needs to various categories of staff are considered and plans are set in hand for their training and development. But such arrangements, even in management level, are apt to be frustrated by what seems to be an endemic proclivity of employees in this industry to seek constant changes in employment perhaps in the hope of findings something better elsewhere or perhaps merely from a general sense of dissatisfaction and a feeling that the alternative cannot be worse.

In utilising resources to meet organizational objectives, the following important functions are carried out – Decision-making, Planning, Organizing, Communicating, Directing, Controlling.

Training within a Hotel provides the best opportunity to influence the attitude and performance of employees. The training programmes include fire, food hygiene, and control of substances hazardous to health, manual handling first-aid, technical skills, and product knowledge and customer service. In many other areas, there is a statutory requirement to carry out training.

In small hotels the various aspect of personnel functions are the responsibility of the hotel manager. Medium-sized hotels delegate these responsibilities to the assistant manager. Whereas in large hotels due to increase in the size of operation, the personnel function is the responsibility of a separate personnel department headed by a Personnel Manager.

Some of the positions in this department are:

1. Personnel Director;
2. Personnel Research and Development Officer;
3. Recruitment Officer;
4. Training Officer and
5. Welfare Officer.

Figure 2.1 shows the various Human Resource Department in the five star hotels. This is the hierarchy of five star hotels. In the order of hierarchy, General Manager is headed by Director HRD. General Manager is authorized to control the overall system and decision making. Director HRD is followed by Personnel Manager and Personnel Officer. Personnel Officer is responsible for Personnel and Training Department Recruitment and selection, Training and Development, Security and Welfare Department are controlled by Personnel Department. And the separate Training cell controls the overall training programmes only.

Figure 2.2 indicated the break – up of the employee's working in the various sections of the department. This shows the administration and functions of five star hotels. Administration Department is supervised by General

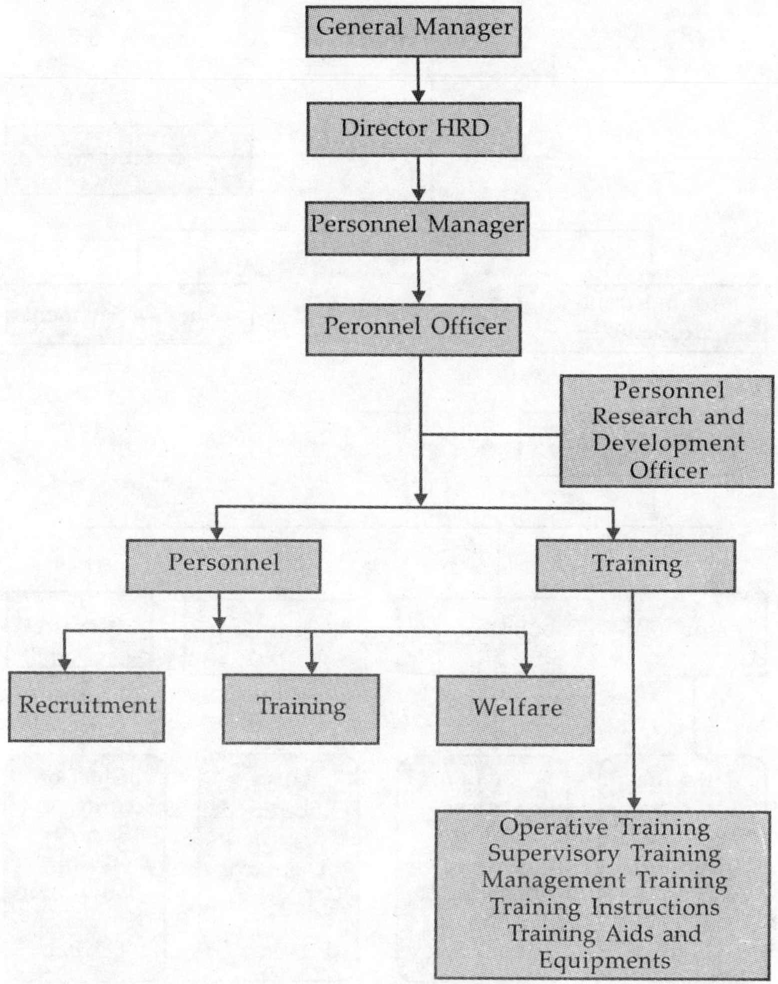

Fig. 2.1: Human Resource Department

Source: Dr. Jagmohan Negi "Human Resource Development and Management in the Hotel Industry." [2000] Frank Bros. and Co. (Publishers) Ltd., New Delhi. ISBN 81-7170-453-0

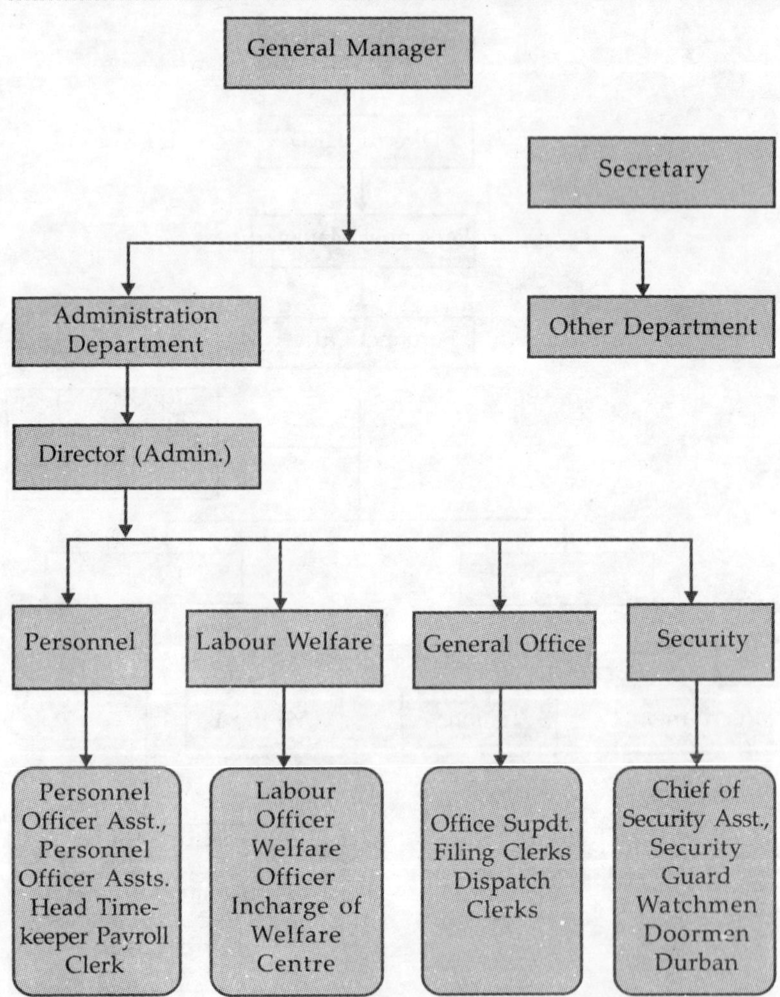

Fig. 2.2: Organization and Administration – Personnel and Security

Source Dr. Jagmohan Negi "Human Resource Development and Management in the Hotel Industry." [2000] Frank Bros. and Co. (Publishers) Ltd., New Delhi. ISBN 81-7170-453-0

Manager. Director Administration control following departments such as – Personnel, Labour Welfare, General Office and Security. Personnel Department deals with all payroll functions and time office. Labour Welfare Department deals with all welfare and Recreational facilities provided to the employees. And general office taking care of all clerical works. And security department handle Watchmen, Doormen, Durban.

REFERENCE

1. Rao T.V Human Resource Development, Concept and Background, Oxford and IBM Publishing Co. Pvt. Ltd., New Delhi, p. 25.
2. World Bank, Human Resource, Concept and Background, 1992, p.1.
3. Leon C. Megginson, Personnel and Human Resources Administration, Richard d. Irwin Inc. Home wood, Illionis, 1977, p. 4.
4. Leon C. Megginson, *Op Cit*, p. 14.
5. Rudrabasavaraj M.N., Dynamic Personnel Administration, Himalaya Publishing House, Bombay, 1979, p. 39.
6. Douglas McGregor, The Human Side of Enterprise, Tata Mc Graw Hill Publishing Co. Ltd., Bombay, 1971, pp. 3-4.
7. Dunlop, John T., Industrialism and Industrial Man Reconsidered: Some Perspective on a Study Over Two Decades of the Problems of Labour and Management in Economics Growth, The Inter – University Study of Human Resources in National Development, New Jersey, 1975, p. 41.
8. Garg M. C., Emerging Dimension of HRD, Deep and Deep Publications, New Delhi, 1993, p. 3.
9. Wendell L. French, The Personnel Management Houghton Mifflin Company, Boston, 1978, p. 3.
10. Peter F. Drucker, Management, Tasks, Responsibilities, Practices, William Heinemann Ltd., London, 1973, p. 308.
11. Ahuja K.K, Personnel Management, Kalyani Publishers, New Delhi.
12. Balu. V, Human Resource Development.
13. Nadler Len, "Defining the Field – It is HRD or O.D.?" *Training and Development Journal*, Vol. 34, No. 2, pp. 66-68.
14. Venkateshwara T. Rao, "Integrated Human Resource Development System" in T.V. Rao and D.F. Pereira, Recent Experiences in Human Resource Development, Oxford and IBM Publishing Co. Pvt. Ltd., New Delhi, 1986, pp. 3-4.

15. Kazmi Azhar, Business Policy, Tata Mc-Graw Hill Publishing Company Ltd., New Delhi, 1992, p. 19.
16. Tripathi P. C. and Reddy R.N., Principles of Management, New Delhi, Tata Mc-Grow Hill Publishing Company Ltd., New Delhi, 1999, pp. 155-156.
17. Mathur B.L., 'Human Resource Development' Arihant Publications, Jaipur, 1989, p. 23.
18. Singh A.K., HRD in India – Barries and Prospects, Gurgeon, The Academic Press, 1986, p. 128.
19. Rao T.V. and Verma K.K., "Alternatives Approaches and Strategies of HRD", Rawat Publications, Jaipur, 1988, p. (vii) F
20. Leonard Nadler, *Op cit.*, No. 12, Dec. 1980, p. 66.
21. Rao T.V. and Verma K.K., *Op cit.*, p. (vii) F.
22. M.C. Garg, *Op.cit.*, pp. 5-8.
23. Galphin, T. The Human Side of Change, Sanfrancisco Jossey, Bass Publication, Allahabad, 1988, pp. 28-29 and 87-92.
24. Chhabra Singh, 'Business Organization and Management' Kitab Mahal Publications, Allahabad, 1988, p. 184.
25. Rao, V.S.P. and Narayan, P. S., p. 676.
26 Rao T.V. and Verma K.K., *Op cit.*, pp. 12-37.
27. Drucker Peter, The Practice of Management, Harper and Brother Publication, New York, 1974, p. 63, 101.
28. Negi Jagmohan "Human Resource Development and Management in the Hotel Industry." [2000] Frank Bros. and Co. (Publishers) Ltd., New Delhi. ISBN 81-7170-453-0.

CHAPTER

3

Review of Literature and Research Methodology

INTRODUCTION

HUMAN RESOURCE DEVELOPMENT (HRD) can be described as a continuous process or virtuous cycle which uses investment in human capital in order to improve productive output, enhance the quality of that output, provide increased benefits for those employed and contribute to an improved quality of life for those involved and their dependants. At the same time, HRD is a process which is at the core of an organization's investment in its human capital and, as such, can make a significant contribution to improved performance, productivity and profitability.

HRD is a key functional aspect of human resource management (HRM) and, in its broadest sense, encompasses the complementary process of ecotourists, training and developing personnel for or in an organization.

An important part of all the organizations is Human Resource Development. Human resources can be counted in one of the most valuable assets for a company. It is very necessary that human resource development runs smoothly for the benefit of the organization. Employing the right person for the right job with right personality is what human resource management is. Hospitality management and human resource management when combined together bring about a new opportunity that helps one to understand the critical issues in managing people in an organization. The combination also highlights work's social context and expertise with reference to operating and managing hospitality business. In order to gain competitive power for the hotel, human resource development is an elementary issue. Human resource development can be regarded as the foundation for the hotel to acquire competitive advantage. Innovative activities and ideas of the hotel get highlighted by the talents of the hotel thereby affecting the overall development of the hotel. It's all about service in the hotel industry. Human resources play an important role in developing the greatest asset, the people and helping them to outstand others. Recruiting qualified, energetic and motivated people and developing their skills so that they remain in the field for a long time. As it is said there is no business without customers and hospitality industry is all about getting customers. It's true that hospitality management and human resource development go hand in hand. Honoring the employees through effective communication, training programmes for the employees and benefit programmes is what effective hospitality management is all about. Human resource development and effective hospitality management is the corner stone of successful business in hospitality industry. Hospitality management along with apt human resource development provides:

- Training the employees,
- Involvement of management in achieving key goals,
- Conducting surveys,
- Encouraging the feeling of team spirit in employees,
- Retaining the talented professionals,
- Focusing on core business.

Human resource development deals not only with recruitment but includes: staffing, training, working in a team and much more! Effective human resource development is all about creating better relationships between employees and employers. Quality of staff is another important issue involved in human resource development. Human resource professionals in hospitality industry ought to manage the staff differently. Thus, the human resource professionals in this industry ought to manage the pool of staff in their companies differently from other industries. Effective human resources management for hotels helps to provide a basis to increase the productivity of the hotel.

Human Resource Development and Hospitality cannot be separated. Managing human resources effectively along with hotel industry takes a look at HRM policies and practices followed in the tourism industry.

Human Resource is considered to be a newly emerging concept. Development of human is a specialized function and is one of the fundamental operative functions of personnel administration. In the development and growth of human lies the nation's growth and progress.

It is said 'Knowledge is key to success.' If he has sound knowledge of part he can take lessons from it and perform infallibly in present making his future rich. Similarly, in research the past studies and investigation can contribute to show the path where the work has been done, how much that work has contributed, what are the limitations. To develop and prosper the knowledge base perusal of literature directly or indirectly related to the proposed study has made.

Review of Literature

The first step in any research study is the Review of Literature. A literature survey usually turns up a number of ideas for further investigation that will advance the research. Keeping this in view, the empirical studies available in India and abroad and allied areas, having direct and indirect bearing on the objective of present study, have been scanned. Only those studies have been selected for the survey which provides some insight directly or indirectly into the Human Resource Development in Hotel Industry. The survey covers reference books, research papers, reports and articles published and unpublished documents in this area, the prominent among them include:

Mervyn D.J. Wilson (1977), In recent times the importance of training and education have been recognized as important tools to foster economic growth within companies and industries in the global marketplace. Unfortunately the UK hospitality industry in general has been unwilling to train and develop its managers. This paper examines the contract catering sector of the hospitality industry in Northern Ireland. It commences by investigating the educational qualifications and training of managers within the contract catering sector and then proceeds to discuss the transference of hospitality skills and practices. [1]

Egon Smeral (1998), The pressure of globalization is having a major impact on the small and medium enterprises (SMEs) of the European tourism industry. Globally acting suppliers, decreasing transportation costs and emerging new destinations have put pressure on the European SMEs in traditional destinations. As many European countries are economically very dependent on tourism, a need for effective policy support arises. The paper focuses on the questions: What could be done to restore the European tourism industry as a growth engine for income and employment? as well as: What roles should the government sector and the private sector respectively play? The implementation of flexible operating network alliances and holistic destination management techniques geared to meet 'post-modern' tourism demand are suggested to alleviate the impacts of globalization on SMEs. [2]

K. J. Jithendran, Tom Baum (2000), The goal of sustainability oriented tourism development requires a number of human resources development (HRD) strategies aimed at the tourism industry personnel, host community and the tourists, and underpinned by concepts and practices of sustainability. Sustainability based 'work culture', 'professional ethics' and operational practices are basic to sustainability in tourism. Indian tourism, despite its immense potential, has seen tardy development, and shortcomings in the HRD domain have been one of the reasons for this below par performance. This paper suggests a comprehensive and strategic approach to HRD, catering to the training and education needs of Indian tourism at various levels for the major target groups. The paper also identifies the pressing issues confronting HRD in Indian tourism and potential strategies to address them within the context of sustainability. [3]

Olsen, Michael D; Chathoth, Prakash; Sharma, Amit (2001), Competing in today's global market place is daunting. The global flow of capital is forcing countries to open their doors to free trade if they expect to maintain economic growth within their borders. This imposes many new challenges for executives who now must rely upon their ability to understand what changes will result from this and how they will impact their organizations if they hope to compete successfully in this environment. This translates into the need to think strategically by developing foresight into those forces that will drive this change. This is not a competency that has been achieved by many management professionals who have competed in the free markets of the world. [4]

Kuthiala, S K (2001), India is known worldwide as ancient and mysterious civilization and the second most populated country of the world after China, with a population of one billion. With increasing worldwide tourism and travel for leisure, business and cultural purposes are on the rise, India attracts only 2.4 million visitors annually of the 600 million who travel. India can develop a sound policy to attract tourism and travel to generate jobs at the lowest cost of investment per job in this industry as well as promote sustainable development and cultural heritage, which has been so precious to India. India needs to shed its reluctance of encouraging tourism by affluent Westerners. [5]

Ciara Nolan (2002), Human resource development in the Irish hotel industry: the case of the small firm: Presents an examination of human resource development (HRD) in the Irish hotel industry and focuses primarily on the case of the small firm as part of a larger study examining best practice HRD within the Irish hotel sector. HR utilisation has clearly become a critical feature for those firms where HRs is potential assets in the search for competitive advantage; this is particularly pertinent for the hotel industry. Almost every hotel firm claims to be people-oriented and to believe in HRD. In practice, however, a much smaller number follow through on these claims. All in all, it is clear that many employers in the hotel industry still have to be convinced of the benefits to be derived from HRD. Current research suggests that small hotel firms tend to favour informal training methods and usually value training which is specific to the job in question. In addition, HRD activity is almost exclusively directed at the solution of immediate work problems rather than the long-term development of people. Where a more strategic HRD approach is adopted, the most significant driving force is the importance placed on training and learning by owner-managers. Their positive attitude and belief in staff development is a key feature. Concludes that until the connection between sound HR practices and organizational success is firmly rooted in the mindset of the hotel industry, HRD will not gain the status it deserves. [6]

Paul Hyland; Terry Sloan; Ron Beckett (2002), Learning to compete: post-graduate training in an aerospace company: Over a period of nearly five years a large number of technology oriented employees in an Australian aerospace company were exposed to a wide variety of post-graduate coursework modules intended to add a business management perspective to the technology background of those employees. Not all of the students had prior experience with university education, but some of these people completed Masters Degrees. Their experience is also discussed. Over the duration of the programme the company was in a constant state of significant change. The number of employees initially increased, adding a further training load, but later on the number of employees decreased and the programme was wound back. This paper looks at how the programme was integrated with work, the perceived upsides and downsides several years down the track, and the influence of organizational culture on the learning styles of the participants. [7]

Sharon Kemp (2002), The hidden workforce: volunteers' learning in the Olympics: Examines the demographic make-up of volunteers and their motives for participating in a mega-event. Compares the Olympic Winter Games held in Lillehammer, Norway in 1994 and the Olympic Summer Games held in Sydney, Australia in 2000. Finds that volunteers in these events had similar demographic characteristics to more conventional volunteers and similar conventional motives. Also finds that volunteers in these events are strongly motivated by pride in their country and its culture, social contact and friendship. Concludes that there are important implications for organizations to glean from these findings in the area of human resource development. [8]

John S. Akama (2002), This study uses the case study of Kenya to analyze the role of government in the development of tourism in the Third World. Usually, government involvement in the development of tourism reflects on the uniqueness and peculiarity of the tourism industry. By its nature, the development and provision of tourism product involves diverse stakeholders and activities. In the diverse socio-economic situation, it is usually the government that has the required social and political capacity and legitimacy to bring together and co-ordinate the activities of diverse and different interest groups which are involved in the development of tourism and, also, establish the required level playing field. In this regard, as probably is the case in most less developed countries where tourism is a major socio-economic activity, the Kenya Government has, over the years, played a crucial role in the development of the country's tourism industry. Particularly, during the exploratory stage of tourism development in Kenya, it was government involvement that helped lay the required groundwork and, as a consequence, jump-started the rapid development of the country's tourism industry. However, in recent years, particularly in the 1990s, Kenya's tourism industry is confronted with serious problems including declining international visitor arrivals and decreasing tourism revenues.

Ironically, the same government that played a crucial role, especially in the initial development of the country's tourism industry, is currently being blamed as being responsible for the industry's current poor performance. Thus, this study will also examine the underlying factors responsible for the current downturns in Kenya's tourism industry and how they relate to the role of government in the development of tourism. [9]

Vinnie Jauhari (2006), Competencies for a career in the hospitality industry: an Indian perspective: The purpose of this paper is to examine the link between industry competency requirements and the current provisions for hospitality management education in India. [10]

Ravinder Rena (2006), Education is a lifelong process. Twentieth century has witnessed the miracles of Human Resource Development (HRD) activities reflected through increase in GNP and overall productive activities. The Government of Eritrea offering both formal and informal training programmes at different levels in order to develop the human resources. This prosperity in education is obviously a great thing for Eritrea, and the dream to make Eritrea a technological-oriented and advanced nation would become real, because the cumulative effort done so far in the human development is noteworthy. As Human Resource Development Programmes concentrate much on the category of major raw human resource to be processed into the work force and its role in reconstructing the economy. An attempt is made in this article to analyze the educational and human resource development after independence. This article also provides detailed account of technical and vocation education with special reference to skill development programme. [11]

Yu Wang (2006), Training and development is increasingly important to the international hotel industry, especially in China. This paper examines some Chinese four-and five-star hotels' training and development (T and D) practices from a Western human resource development (HRD) perspective and compares the results between the Chinese state ownership and Sino-foreign joint ventures using multiple case studies.

Results seem to show that the western way of training and development may not necessarily lead to superior training effects in the Chinese context than those used by state-owned hotels. It suggests that a better T and D model for Chinese hotels may emerge by learning the lessons from both kinds of hotels' good practices. [12]

Tom Bauma, and Edith Szivas (2007), Government's engagement with tourism and in the development of the sector is widely accepted but academic debate about the form and level of such involvement is limited. This is particularly the case when specific facets of state engagement, relating for example to support for human resource development (HRD) in tourism, are concerned. The purpose of this paper is to explore the substantially neglected role of the state and its agencies in creating an enabling environment for effective HRD within tourism, through policy and planning as well as the delivery of actual HRD initiatives. In this paper, we briefly address the contested role of government in economic development and, in particular, in HRD. We address the nature of tourism as a sector within the economy and identify its salient features in terms of the key themes in this paper. The role of human resources in enabling tourism businesses, destinations and countries to operate effectively and competitively in the contemporary global economy is addressed and the paper considers the impact that tourism's defining structural and operational characteristics have on the role of people. Finally, building on the experience of the Irish Republic over the past 40 years, we will consider whether government and its agencies can play a useful role in guiding policy and delivering programmes that act to enhance the quality and productivity of people in the delivery of products and services to guests within tourism and, if they can, how this role can best be defined and operationalised. [13]

Philip Lye (2007), Human Resource Issues in the Hospitality Industry: Many businesses in the hospitality industry-both small and large have difficulty in understanding their human resource and employment relations obligations whichever country or countries they operate in. This is understandable given the raft of legislation and regulations governing (drowning) the employment environment in which governments seem to revel in. The hospitality industry is certainly no exception and in many cases is more complex than the average business. In this publication Biz Momentum will outline important employment matters that will assist in reducing the 'stress' factors you may be experiencing directly related to the hospitality industry which Biz Momentum is actively involved in a hands on capacity. [14]

Sjoerd A. Gehrels (2007), Is of the view that work in progress describes the value systems and other driving powers of hotel upper segment restaurant managers (HUSRM's) and the way that these can influence hospitality management Curriculum design. The outcomes of the research provided an overview of the diver's value systems and driving powers of the respondents. Recommendations were made to have these values Systems, driving powers and other characteristics to be taken into account by hospitality management schools in the curricula content and proximity to the industry. [15]

Richard A. Swanson (2007), This article was based on a study of Business Leaders. The popular perception that HRD costs organizations more than it returns in benefits has haunted the HRD profession since its inception. And not being able to change this perception is its Achilles heel, although organizations are more than economic entities, they are nonetheless economic entities. Any organization that remains alive will ultimately judge each of its components from a return-on-investment framework and it will do so with or without valid data. To face this challenge, four views of HRD have been presented: *(i)* A major business process, *(ii)* A value added activity, *(iii)* An optional activity and *(iv)*. A waste of Business Resources, something that has costs exceeding the benefits. [16]

Ian D. Clark, David A. Cahir (2008), The purpose of this article is to describe and understand the nascent state of hospitality on the Victorian goldfields in the 1850s. The primary sources for such an account are the journals of miners, public officials, and other travelers spanning this decade. The gold rushes transformed hospitality in numerous ways; the number of travelers requiring hospitality increased exponentially, and significant commercialization occurred to meet this increased demand. Despite mining representing a new wave of occupation of their lands (pestoralism being the first) Aboriginal people were often renowned for their hospitality on Victorian goldfields. [17]

Fujun Shen, Kenneth F.D. Hughey, David G. Simmons (2008), Tourism has been increasingly used for, and directly linked with, rural poverty reduction in developing countries. However, the application, and to an extent the principles, of the widely used organizing framework for considering poverty reduction, the Sustainable Livelihoods Approach (SLA), may not fit fully the tourism situation, and vice versa. Based on a review of the literature we first suggest that sustainable livelihoods for tourism should be viewed in a broader tourism context, rather than merely taking tourism as a development tool. Second, the SLA seeks household livelihood sustainability at the individual or household level, while tourism sustainability is often applied to the industry and destinations at wider, more macro level scales. Thus, a reconciliation of the tensions and opportunities between the SLA and tourism needs to be found. Third, tourism research has demonstrated local residents" increasing concern about participation in political governance associated with tourism development, with less participation jeopardizing local people's assets from a livelihood perspective. Therefore, an additional concept of institutional asset (mainly community participation) needs to be incorporated within the SLA. Given the above understandings, a sustainable tourism livelihood was defined and a Sustainable Tourism Livelihoods Approach (STLA) is proposed. The potential applications of the STLA are discussed and future research is recommended. [18]

Abel D Alonso and Alfred Ogle (2008), Despite numerous efforts by researchers to examine the importance of design among hospitality and tourism operations, little if any attention has been paid to small operations of these industries, for example, to the level of importance operators place on facility design. Semi-structured face-to-face and phone interviews among 30 businesses located in Western Australia were used in the data collection process. Overall, respondents not only indicated being actively involved in the design of their small businesses, but also emphasized the importance of maintaining a balance between the physical aspect and their operations' natural surroundings. Simplicity and efficiency are also identified and used as operations' appealing factors. Because of the important role that small enterprises play in the hospitality and tourism industries, the findings of this study have important implications for ways in which design is being utilised among these operations to promote efficiency, comfort and value to guests' experience. These areas, in turn, could positively contribute to businesses' well-being. [19]

Dominique Keeffe, Rebekah Russell-Bennett and Alastair Tombs (2008), The service encounter is the point where employees and customers interact both positively and negatively. When things go wrong (service failure), initially it is the employee who is required to remedy the situation (recover the service). While positive service recovery outcomes are well investigated, there is little research that investigates whether specific service recovery strategies can be used to reduce customer anger and retaliation. Further, there is little research regarding whether an organization's acceptance of blame has an effect on customer anger and retaliation. These gaps are addressed using a quasi-experimental study of 120 respondents that examines customers' emotional and behavioural responses to specific service recovery strategies following a service failure. The results show that high-level service recovery strategies directly reduce the occurrence of retaliation, as well as indirectly reduce retaliation through the mediating effects of customer anger. [20]

Greg G. Wang, Richard A. Swanson (2008), Economics and Human Resource Development: A Rejoinder: This article focuses on the areas agreement between two recent and seemingly disparate Human Resource Development Review articles by Wang and Swanson (2008) and McLean, Lynham, Azevedo, Lawrence, and Nafukho (2008). The foundational roles of economics in human resource development theory and practice are highlighted as well as the need for comparative studies. A framework for conducting comparative human resource development policy studies is proposed. [21]

Lynn Perry Wooten, Erika Hayes James (2008), Linking Crisis Management and Leadership Competencies: The Role of Human Resource Development: Most executives are aware of the negative consequences associated with an organizational crisis and focus on communications and public relations as a reactive strategy. However, much neglect the other leadership responsibilities associated with organizational crises. This may result from lack of formal training and on-the-job experiences that prepare executives to lead crises. Executives who enable their organizations to recover from a crisis exhibit a complex set of competencies in each of the five phases of a crisis — signal detection, preparation and prevention, damage control and containment, business recovery, and reflection and learning. In this article, through the use of qualitative research design and the analysis of firms in crises, we examine leadership competencies during each phase of a crisis. In addition, this article links the important role of human resource development to building organizational capabilities through crisis management activities. [22]

Mary J. Fambrough (2008), Emotions in Leadership Development: A Critique of Emotional Intelligence: In this conceptual article, emotional intelligence (EI) is critiqued, particularly as a resource for leadership development. Ultimately, this article seeks to answer the question: "What should human resource development (HRD) professionals know and reflect on as they consider the use of EI instruments and interventions in leadership development? The transmutation of emotions in organizations from negative and irrational to a positive attribute of successful leaders is traced, demonstrating how emotions have traditionally been mobilized in organizations to achieve instrumental goals. The following questions are explored: Is there one accepted model of EI? What are the instruments and measures for EI? Is there a definitive association between EI and leadership effectiveness? What issues are raised by generalizing EI abilities and competencies across cultures or in multicultural contexts? How might EI training enable leaders to abuse power more skillfully to achieve personal or organizational ends?" In conclusion, suggested areas of concern for HRD practitioners are raised, and alternative ways to include increased awareness of emotions in leadership development are discussed. [23]

Heisler, William J (2008), The relationship between human resource systems and organizational performance is a timely topic. Because the authors use a framework of their own devising, comparison of this study with others is challenging. Also needed is a way of establishing causality between an HR system and a hotel's performance. The connection between a hotel's human resources system and its strategy and performance is well worth studying, although the accompanying case did not make firm causal connections. Perhaps the key issue is how to measure the connection, as existing studies in the hospitality industry and other industries offer various metrics. As an example, one hotel is cited in the case as having the greatest employee satisfaction, but there is no indication of whether that satisfaction led to higher financial performance. Indeed, the constructs used to assess human resources systems are particular to this case, while other researchers have applied different constructs. In the accompanying case study of the role of human resource systems in the hospitality industry in Kenya, the authors address a significant issue under discussion within the human resource community, namely, the relationship between human resource management systems and organizational performance. [24]

Grant Cairncross Stephen Kelly (2008), This paper provides an analysis of human resource development and knowledge capital management relations practices used by hotels and resorts in 2007. The study examined the employment instruments used, methods of employee recruitment, selection, staff turnover trends, remuneration policies, attitudes to knowledge capital and the application of service quality measurement. The findings indicate that larger foreign-owned organizations have adopted more innovative approaches than smaller Australian-owned hotels and resorts, while skill shortages and generational attitude changes have driven more inventive retention strategies in both groups. It was also found that in spite of the adoption of more enlightened human resource strategies, staff turnover, particularly casual staff turnover, remains problematic and could negatively impact upon customer satisfaction. [25]

Abel D. Alonso and Alfred Ogle (2008), This study examines the impacts of daylight savings among small businesses represented by a group of 41 operators consisting of small wineries, bed and breakfast, food factories and other facilities open to the public located in and around Perth, the capital of Western Australia. While the largest group of respondents in this study did not perceive any major impacts of daylight savings to their businesses, just over one-third of operators viewed daylight savings as detrimental to their businesses. The overall findings clearly reflect the ongoing heated political debate in Western Australia and have a number of implications for businesses, including the fact that daylight savings is affecting operators' lifestyle and working patterns. Further, as some respondents indicated, daylight savings also appears to be affecting their customers' behaviour, with resulting potential negative consequences for their operations. [26]

Oh, Juliana Kheng Mei Ms (2008), The Tourism industry in Asia is booming with casinos, attractions and integrated resorts opening up in the next decade. Being a labour-intensive industry, the issue of human resource development is significant as there is not a shortage of manpower but an acute shortage of trained manpower. This paper addresses the human resource strategies that can be adapted to alleviate the shortage of trained manpower. These strategies form part of the integrated plan covering tourism development overall in three countries mainly Singapore, Macau, China and Thailand. [27]

Ahmed Naama, Claire Haven-Tang, Eleri Jones (2008), The Libyan government emphasizes the importance of tourism in economic diversification through its Libyan Tourism Master Plan identifying various initiatives to develop the Libyan tourism industry, including human resource development (HRD). Hotels are key to an internationally competitive industry and human resources critical to perceptions of service quality. This paper analyses issues relating to the Libyan hotel sector, including the need to strengthen the private sector; to match education/training programmes to industrial needs, and to address cultural and religious dimensions which exacerbate poor industry image. [28]

Daniel Edward Craig (2009), Hotels have always taken the high road when dealing with guest complaints. 'The guest is always right' is a cornerstone of hospitality, and social media hasn't changed that. In the case of a false or exaggerated review, hotels are sometimes better off not to dignify the comments with a response. Travelers are smart enough to read between the lines, and there's a good chance the hotel's fans will spring to its defense. This doesn't mean that all negative reviews should be left uncontested. Social media provides unprecedented opportunities for hotels to engage travelers and is only gaining in influence. Sticking our heads in the sand has never been a prudent survival strategy. However, there's a big difference between sites like Face book and Twitter, where consumers opt in to receive communications, and traveler review sites, where consumers are seeking traveler testimonials, not hotel propaganda. If a hotel weighs in on the conversation, it better have some value to add. [29]

Dylan Tanner (2009), While eco-tourism emerged in the 1970s and 1980s, it remains a fairly fringe industry, attracting only a few per cent of the total number of tourists. The hotel industry, responding to criticism that it was not taking its environmental impacts seriously, enacted a series of voluntary industry initiatives in the 1990s. Further, standards to define "eco tourism", and to prevent fraudulent use of the term, began to emerge. However these have proved not to be hugely effective neither in marketing nor reputation protection. NGOs such as Greenpeace have criticized many such standards/schemes as being superficial and not addressing the key environmental impacts of resorts and hotels, namely energy and water use and land conversion. In the niche of eco-tourism, standards and schemes remain important as a means of informing their customers (who are by nature environmentally aware and curious) of their credibility. Perhaps the key issue at present for the hospitality and events sector is carbon emissions and this is the focus of standardization at present. [30]

Mahima Kini (2009), The global tourism industry is booming presently. Number of domestic as well as international arrivals has more than tripled. The tourism industry accounts for more than $1000 billion and is expected to grow by 200 per cent in next five years. Tourism also in a major way contributes to the economy indirectly through its association with other sectors such as horticulture, agriculture, poultry, handicrafts and construction. Travel and tourism is United States' 2nd largest service export industry, 3rd largest trade industry and one of the largest employment providers. There are various courses available that can help you become a part of this sector. [31]

Debpath (2010), Indian Airlines Ltd., and Air India Ltd. The two nationalized air transport industries in India have been merged since 2007 officially. But in practice both the organizations have been maintaining their separate identities both in respect of operations and on financial matters as well. While one company is engaged on domestic operation, the other one in international operation. The purpose of the merger was to bring forth-maximum leverage in utilisation of aircraft, engineering/maintenance infrastructures, and trained manpower. Despite synergy in both the companies for realizing the leverage by utilising the resources at optimum level, the merged entity is now in mess incurring huge accumulated loss of about $3000 million. What are the main reasons of such huge loss? It is the seer lack of integration of Human Resources of both the companies that are responsible for the failure of merger. The merged entity inherited huge number of over staff. The emoluments mainly consist of hefty amount of 'Productivity Linked Incentive' which was not based on the tangible performance of the companies. The employees are divided craft-wise and 'Productivity Linked Incentives' are distributed according to craft. Hefty PLI fails to motivate the employees towards performance. Employees are more interested for next month's PLI or the next promotions rather than their performance. The case in point is an example of failure in Human Resource Management, which actually pampered the lot instead of motivating them towards better performance for a quality product in highly competitive environment. Since airline is hospitality based service industry, HRD plays a very important role. It has also shown that hefty emoluments cannot be the only incentive for better performance. [32]

Esther Hertzfeld (2010), The latest PTACs are all about efficiency, thanks to this year's R-22 phase out and next year's planned energy-management guidelines. The goal for 2010 was to make PTACs work with new refrigerants, namely R-410A, said Ben Broido, national sales manager—PTAC for LG Electronics. "Many manufacturers were having the same problems with new refrigerants," he said. Along with the refrigerant change, manufacturers have stepped up energy-efficiency efforts, both to appeal to guests and to comply with 2012's energy-management guidelines. "There are several things the customer is looking for: Ease of service, ease of maintenance, controlling capital expenditures and lowering operating costs," said Jim Benz, marketing manager, air conditioning products for GE. [33]

Dawn M R Martin (2010), Phillip Vincent was a determined man who had firm ideas on how a motorcycle should perform, and more importantly, how a motorcycle should be built. In the 1920s, he built his first motorcycle. Like all others, it had rear suspension with a triangulated pivoted fork and the springs were mounted beneath the saddle to work against the upper frame. It had a Swiss Mag engine, a Moss gearbox, Webb forks and Enfield hubs. In 1927, at the age of 19, he decided to go into business making motorcycles. After taking advice from Arthur Bourne, he purchased the established HRD name from the OK Supreme Company. The HRD name may have only been three years old, but the name Howard R Davies was well known, as he had tied for second in the 1914 Senior TT, been reported as killed in Action in 1917, and had won the 1921 Senior with his 350 AJS. After forming his company, he was second in the junior and won the senior in 1925. [34]

Simon Waker Haughtone (2010), A wide variety of activities are included in human resource management. Key factors among them are to decide the staffing that is required for smoothly running the enterprise. Entrepreneurs can use independent contractors to hire the employees or recruit such employees directly on their own efforts. Besides recruitment and finding the best talents, another aspect of the HRM is appropriate training. Quality training can render even the insipid people skillful and they can turn out to be assets for the enterprise. At the same time training the best employees will ensure very high performance level. Entrepreneurs and employers have to deal with the performance issues. Ensuring such personnel and management practices would conform to various regulations. Management of approach to employee's benefits as well compensation paid to them is a vital aspect of human resource management process. [35]

Balu Rankonda (2010), Human Resources Department in an organization will take the responsibility of selection and recruitment of eligible candidates for the organization. The entire process of recruitment which includes assessment of required posts, getting approval for additional posts from the management, notification, collection of applications from the candidates, scrutinizing the applications, compiling the data of applicants, invitation for interviews, conducting interviews, selecting proper candidates, recruiting successful candidates from the interviewed panel will be handled by HRD. Performance of each and every employee in the organization is monitored and evaluated HR sections for assessing them for appraisal benefits. During this process HR sections will know the weakness of the employees and plan for training them to impart knowledge and prepare them to stand at par with their colleagues who are in the race of intensive schemes. These efforts will boost the employee performance and in turn result in better returns to the organization on human investment. [36]

Kaye (Kye-Sung) Chon (2010), Welcome to Hospitality: An Introduction, International Edition provides a detailed description of the many facets of the Hospitality and Tourism sector, including Tour and Travel, Hotels, Restaurants, Culinary, Casino Operations, Cruises, and the Recreation and Leisure industries. Personal profiles of industry leaders highlight the wide range of career opportunities available in the field. The authors discuss the Hospitality and Tourism industry's evolution toward increased internationalization and integration. Industry Insight vignettes offer a behind-the-scenes view of real-life job tasks and career success stories. Each chapter features practical case study scenarios, including business and social attitude comparatives, advertising and marketing messaging, financial modeling, and competitive analysis formulation. New To This Edition: Expanded coverage of industry career opportunities, a comprehensive new chapter on the Gaming Industry, and expanded coverage of Events Management. [37]

Kathleenchester (2011), Business owners demand instant and low-cost solutions that are easy to upkeep and maximize return on their investment. Enterprise Resource Planning - ERP systems fit the bill perfectly and hence have become popular with many businesses, especially in implementing the resource efficiency lessons learned during recent recessionary periods. In fact, now not only multi-million dollar businesses that deploy such systems, but also small-sized units and even start-ups. Reduction in Operational Costs: Deploying an ERP software system holds benefits for all three process streams of an organization-strategic planning, production control, and management control. Such a system integrates varied business processes across the myriad of departments in an organization into a single and comprehensive information repository. This integration makes communication smooth in-between departments and this improved communication, in turn, imparts a degree of efficiency in the production, planning, and decision making processes. This efficiency is manifested in various ways-lower production costs, less marketing expenses incurred, and less need for securing help desk support. [38]

Fred Fish (2011), Industry experts have designed restaurant POS software that assists food service organizations in eliminating waste and increasing profit. Your business management can benefit in many ways from the uniquely designed computer software that performs time-consuming business transactions efficiently and quickly. Your business can go to a whole new level with the computer expertise available for smoothly managing restaurants including delivery and sit down.

Restaurant POS software is available for your restaurant, bar, quick service or delivery service. This unique software is designed by computer experts to service your restaurant so that it runs smoothly and efficiently saving money and eliminating waste. Your restaurant management can be computerized which will allow your business to run efficiently without the costly waste of employee power or products that can easily hide in the management of restaurants. One of the biggest profit pickpockets in food service is waste and there is a specific and uniquely designed computer software system that will work to eliminate waste and protect profit in the food service industry and businesses of all kinds benefit from delivery only pizza parlors and sub shops to beautiful sit down establishments. [39]

Emelia Ennin (2011), A recent inspection conducted by the Ghana Tourist Board, the main regulator of the hospitality industry, led to stunning revelations. The team that toured hotel facilities in the country discovered poor kitchen hygiene, housekeeping and supervision, inadequate provision of mandatory furnishing and unskilled staff who are not professional. These developments, among other things, have hampered the growth of the hospitality industry. Over the years, tourists have not been impressed with facilities in the country, which has prompted calls to address their concerns to make Ghana the preferred destination for international tourists. The Ministry Of Tourism has announced plans to strengthen its Inspectorate Directorate in order check hoteliers. According to the Deputy Minister of Tourism, Kobby Acheampong, government is committed to adopting policies to streamline the operations of hoteliers. Currently, there is no Operational Service Standards which would serve as a guideline to service providers to deliver excellently in the hospitality industry. [40]

Location

This is the study of Human Resource Development in five star hotel Industries in the state of Rajasthan and Gujarat. The hotel Industries of Rajasthan and Gujarat has been selected on the following bases —

In India due to cultural as well as due to physical diversity there are significant numbers of tourist centres. But out of them Rajasthan and Gujarat has a considerable share of number of attractions and also number of tourists coming here. Rajasthan and Gujarat is culturally rich and has artistic and cultural traditions which reflect the ancient Indian way of life. There is rich and varied folk culture from villages which is often depicted and is symbolic of the state. Highly cultivated classical music and dance with its own distinct style is part of the cultural tradition of both the state .Due to development of tourism, hotel Industry has full-fledged day by day.

Rajasthan and Gujarat are attracting visitors from other countries and is emerging as a favorite holiday destination and due to this reason; hospitality industry is working overtime towards improving itself. The incoming national and international tourists are being taken care of by hotels specially five star hotels offering comfort, warmth and amusement amenities to their guests.

Hospitality sector plays a key role in the total economic growth of the country. Along with the speedy industrial growth and advancement of tourism, the five star hotel sectors are flourishing at a speedy pace. The Indian middle class is becoming prosperous day by day and domestic Indian tourist travel is springing up speedily, allowing this class to avail five star hotel facilities.

Thus due to all these characteristics Rajasthan and Gujarat state has been selected to carry out the study of Human Resource Development in Hotel Inder Residency and Hotel Cambay Grand in the state of Rajasthan and Gujarat.

Objectives of the Research

It is desirable here to spell out the broad objective of the study in the light of the work done or already in progress in this field in the country. The study mainly focuses on Human Resource Development of employees of five star hotels in Rajasthan and Gujarat state. The main objectives of the study were:

1. To assess the development and growth of stars hotel in the state of Rajasthan and Gujarat.
2. To study the Human Resource Development philosophy, policies and practices in Hotel Industries.
3. To study Recruitment and Selection process of hotel industry.
4. To study how Training and Development programmes are organized for employees of hotel industry.
5. To analyze the Employee's Satisfaction regarding the salary, incentives and other fringe benefits.

6. To analyze and compare the Promotion and Demotion practices in hotel industry.
7. To examine Social Security facilities (Pension, Provident Fund and Gratuity etc.) provide by hotel management to their employees.
8. To suggest suitable suggestions in the light of findings of this investigation for improvement in Humar Resource Development in hotel industry.

Research Hypothesis

The hypotheses formulated for testing under this study were as follows:

1. "Advertisement is the best method of recruitment than any other method of recruitment."
2. "Motivation method adopted by hotel management increases productivity in hotels."
3. "In Hotel Industry employees have less grievances and dispute with management."
4. "In Hotel Industries proper social security facilities have been provided by management to their employees."

Research Methodology

Sources of the Data Eollection

To conduct the investigation, data were collected from both primary and secondary sources:

- *Primary data:* A structured questionnaire was designed to collect the primary data. Along with the questionnaire personal interviews was conducted for managers and employees to know the opinion and suggestion about the hotel.
- *Secondary data:* Secondary data were collected from journals, research papers, articles, newspapers, books, annual reports of Cambay and Inder Residency hotel, website, past studies, periodicals and persons who may have any information on the subject.

Tools for Data Collection

For collection of primary data we designed two types of questionnaire and used.

(i) Questionnaire for management of hotel industries.

(ii) Questionnaire for employees of hotel industries.

Two structured questionnaire separately for managers and employees were designed to collect the primary data.

The first questionnaire for management was related to motivation, reward system, encouragement about grievance and discipline procedure in the hotel industry.

The second questionnaire was designed to analyze the responses of employees. The first segment of questionnaire was carrying general information about the respondents. Next segment was commenced with simple questions related to HRD functions in hotel industry thereby moving to the questions important for our study like proper recruitment and selection procedures followed by hotel or not, whether training has been imparted to the employees or not, about the working hours, salary and incentives benefits, accommodation, medical and welfare and other recreational facilities. They were also asked questions related to promotion and demotion policy, P.F, gratuity and pension scheme if applicable after leaving the hotel or not.

Sample Design

Table 3.1 showed the two category of management which we selected to this study. We prepared a list of 50 top management, 100 middle management and 100 junior management, than we selected randomly 20, 50 and 50 employees respectively from top management, middle management and junior management from Hotel Cambay Grand and Inder Residency hotels for this study. In all we selected 240 employees from both the hotels. (*See table on next page*)

Table 3.1: Sample of Employees

Sr. No.	Category	Sample Size (Hotel Cambay Grand)	Sample Size (Hotel Inder Residency)
1.	Top Management	20	20
2.	Middle/Junior Management	100	100

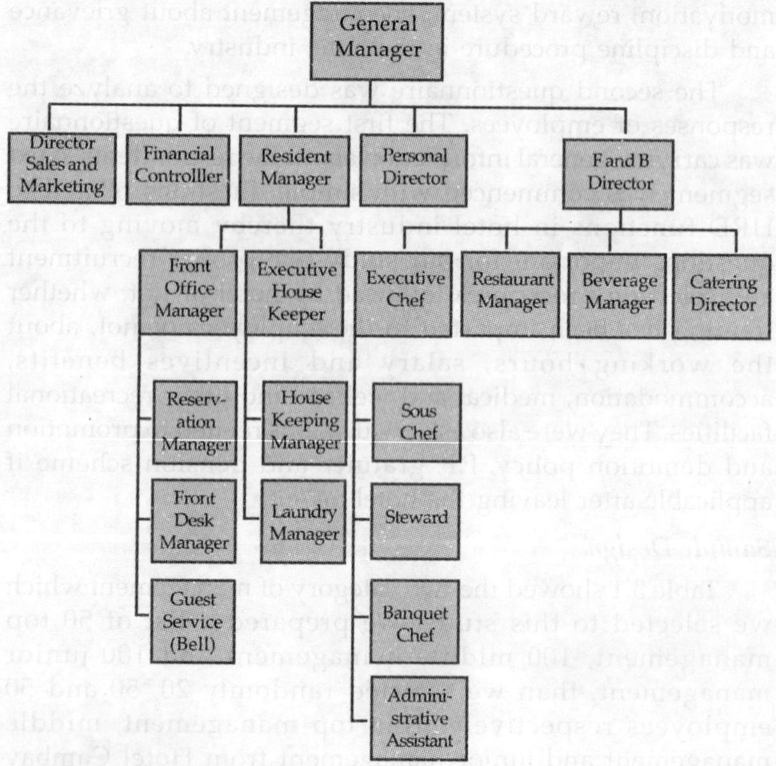

Fig. 3.1: Hierarchy of Hotel Industry

Source: Dr. Jagmohan Negi "Human Resource Development and Management in the Hotel Industry." [2000] Frank Bros. and Co. (Publishers) Ltd., New Delhi. ISBN 81-7170-453-0

Field Work

Field work of the present study was carried out during January, 2011 to June, 2011.

Tools for Analysis of Data

Various statistical tools such as percentage method, chi-square test and bar diagrams used to analyze the primary and secondary data.

Importance of the Study

Human Resource Development plays a vital role in a hotel industry. It has gained importance in every hotel whether big or small. It is regarded as a 'must' for the successful running of any hotel. It may be worthwhile to mention here that enormous changes have taken place in the field of HRD in the last three decades. Many new HRD techniques, programmes have been launched in hotel industry. It is therefore high time that a proper assessment and evaluation were made of HRD in hotel industry.

The success of any hotel depends on the people employed in it as manpower is the most valuable asset of hotels. Successful management depends upon the management of human development. Human Resource Development of the hotels is invaluable asset and the success of the hotels in long run depends very much on the quality of its human resources. Most of the problems in hotels functioning are human and social rather than physical, technical or economic. The recognition of human aspect in the hotel and its continued development has assumed highest priority. If human resources are properly managed it may prove as dynamic motive force for running the hotels at this optimum level.

The present investigation is an attempt to study Human Resource Development in hotel industry in the state of Rajasthan and Gujarat. The research mainly concentrates on to study, how people are procured, motivated, trained, developed and maintained in hotels. It also tries to compare the HRD function between two hotels. This type of study would be helpful to the Government, Tourism Department, Economic Planners and management of hotel group's in preparing the future programme for the development and growth of the Hotel Industry. The usefulness of such in depth studies are widely accepted because hotel industry is backbone of tourism.

REFERENCES

1. Wilson Mervyn D.J. (1977), "Training and Education in Contract Catering Management," *Journal of European Industrial Training Publisher*: MCB UP Ltd., ISSN: 0309-0590.
2. Smeral Egon (1998), "The Impact of Globalization on Small and Medium Enterprises: New Challenges for Tourism Policies in European Countries." Volume 19, Issue 4, pp. 371-380.
3. Jithendran K. J., Baum Tom (2000) "Human Resources Development and Sustainability — The Case of Indian Tourism", *International Journal of Tourism Research,* Volume 2, Issue 6, pp. 403-421.
4. Olsen, Michael D; Chathoth, Prakash; Sharma, Amit (2001), "Forces Driving Change in the Hospitality Industry in India", *Journal of Services Research.*
5 Kuthiala, S K (2001), "Tourism and Hospitality Industry in India", *Journal of Services Research.*
6. Ciara Nolan (2002) "Human Resource Development in the Irish Hotel Industry: *The Case of the Small Firm Journal of European Industrial Training*", Volume 26, Numbers 2-4, 2002, pp. 88-99.
7 Paul Hyland; Terry Sloan; Ron Beckett (2002) "Learning to Compete: *Post-graduate Training in an Aerospace Company Journal of European Industrial Training*", Volume 26, Numbers 2-4, 2002, pp. 100-108(9).
8. Sharon Kemp (2002) "The Hidden Workforce: Volunteers' *Learning in the Olympics Journal of European Industrial Training*", Volume 26, Numbers 2-4, 2002, pp. 109-116(8).
9. Akama John S. (2002) "The Role of Government in the Development of Tourism in Kenya" *International Journal of Tourism Research,* Volume 4, Issue 1, pp. 1-14.
10. Jauhari Vinnie (2006) "Competencies for a Career in the Hospitality Industry: An Indian Perspective" www.emeraldinsight.com
11. Rena Ravinder (2006), "Education and Human Resource Development in Post-independent Eritrea: An Explanatory Note." International *Journal of Education and Development Using* Vol. 2, No. 4.
12 Wang Yu (2006), "Strategic Employee Training And Development In Chinese Luxury Hotels." Article from: *Tourismos: an International Multidisciplinary Journal of Tourism,* ISSN: 17908418 Volume: 1 Issue: 1 pp. 109-116.

13. Bauma Tom, and Szivas Edith (2008), "HRD in Tourism: A Role for Government?" Volume 29, Issue 4, pp. 783-794.

14. Lye Philip (2007) "Human Resource Issues in the Hospitality Industry", www.biz-momentum.com

15. Gehrels, Sjoerd A. (2007) "How Hospitality Industry Managers' Characteristics Could Influence Hospitality Management Curricula" *The Electronic Journal of Business Research Methods* Volume 5 Issue pp. 37-48, www.ejbrm.com

16. Richard A. Swanson (2007), "Demonstrating the Financial Benefit of Human Resource Development: Status and Update on the Theory and Practice." *Journal of Human Resource Development Quarterly*, 9:285-295. Doi: 10.1002/hrdq.3920090307

17. Ian D. Clark, David A. Cahir (2008), 'The Comfort of Strangers': Hospitality on the Victorian Goldfields, 1850-1860, *Journal of Hospitality and Tourism Management*.

18. Fujun Shen, Kenneth F.D. Hughey, David G. Simmons (2008), "Connecting the Sustainable Livelihoods Approach and Tourism: A Review of the Literature," *Journal of Hospitality and Tourism Management*.

19. Abel D Alonso and Alfred Ogle (2008), "Exploring Design among Small Hospitality and Tourism Operations." *Journal of Retail and Leisure Property* (2008) 7, 325-337; doi:10.1057/rlp.2008.23;

20. Dominique Keeffe, Rebekah Russell-Bennett and Alastair Tombs (2008), "Customer Retaliation at the Employee-customer Interface." ISSN: 1833-3672 Volume: 14 Issue: 4, pp. 438-450.

21. Greg G. Wang, Richard A. Swanson (2008) "Economics and Human Resource Development: *A Rejoinder Human Resource Development Review*", Vol. 7, No. 3, pp. 358-36.

22. Lynn Perry Wooten, Erika Hayes James (2008) "Linking Crisis Management and Leadership Competencies: The Role of Human Resource Development" Advances in Developing Human Resources, Vol. 10, No. 3, pp. 352-379.

23. Mary J. Fambrough (2008) "Emotions in Leadership Development: A Critique of Emotional Intelligence Advances in Developing Human Resources", Vol. 10, No. 5, pp. 740-758.

24. Heisler, William J. (2008) "The Challenge of Causality: A Commentary on "Human Resource Systems in Kenya", *Cornell Hospitality Quarterly Journal*.

25. Grant Cairncross Stephen Kelly (2008), Human Resource Development and 'Casualisation' in Hotels and Resorts in Eastern Australia. ISSN: 1833-3672 Volume: 14 Issue: pp. 367-385.

26. Abel D. Alonso and Alfred Ogle (2008), "Impact of Daylight Savings on Small Hospitality and Tourism Businesses: A Western Australian Case Study" 314-324; doi:10.1057/thr.2009.16.

27 Oh, Juliana Kheng Mei Ms (2008), "Human Resource Development in the Tourism Sector in Asia," Perspectives in Asian Leisure and Tourism: Vol. 1: Iss. 1, Article 7. http://scholarworks.umass.edu/palat/vol1/iss1/7

28. Ahmed Naama, Claire Haven-Tang, Eleri Jones (2008), "Human Resource Development Issues for the Hotel Sector in Libya: A Government Perspective", *International Journal of Tourism Research* DOI: 10.1002/jtr.683Volume 10, Issue 5, pp. 481-492.

29. Daniel Edward Craig (2009) "Online Reviews: The Bane of Hotels' Existence or an Unprecedented Opportunity?" www.danieledwardcraig.com

30. Dylan Tanner (2009) "A New Standard for Sustainable Events and Tourism." http://ezinearticles.com. A--New--Standard--For--Sustainable--Events--and--Tourismandid=3355383

31. Kini Mahima (2009) "A Rewarding Career in Travel and Tourism Industry." http://ezinearticles.com. A--Rewarding--Career--in--Travel--and- Tourism--Industryandid=2408032.

32. Debpath (2010) "New Horizon in Change Management – HRD Aspect" www.expertscolumn.com

33. Esther Hertzfeld (2010), "PTACs are all about efficiency for hoteliers." Articles.com. 04 Feb, 2011.http://findarticles.com/p/articles/mi_m3072/is_14_225/ai_n56737231.

34. Dawn M R Martin (2010), "History of Vincent HRD." http://EzineArticles.com/?expert=Dawn_M_R_Martin.

35. Simon Waker Haughtone (2010), "Human Resource Management — An Integral Part of Human Resource Development." http://EzineArticles.com/?expert=Simon_Waker_Haughtone.

36. Balu Rankonda (2010), "Human Resource Development — How it Affects an Organization." http://EzineArticles.com/?expert=Dawn_M_R_Martin.

37. Kaye (Kye-Sung) Chon (2010), "Welcome to Hospitality 3e." ISBN-13: 9781439057377/ISBN-10:1439057370. www. http://edu.cengage.co.uk/catalogue/product.aspx?isbn=1439057370

38. Kathleenchester (2011), "Benefits of Enterprise Resource planning (erp) Systems." www.articlesnatch.com

39. Fred Fish (2011), "Restaurant Pos Software Is Provided by Expert." www.articlesnatch.com

40. Emelia Ennin (2011), "Boosting the Hospitality Industry." Ghana Business Guide.

CHAPTER

4

A Case Study of Five Star Hotels

In this study we selected two five star hotels that is Hotel Cambay Grand from Ahmedabad and Inder Residency Hotel from Udaipur.

In order to examine the opinion of managers and employees about HRD functions in hotels, the two structured questionnaire separately for managements and employees were designed to collect the primary data.

Questionnaire for management of hotel industries.

Questionnaire for employees of hotel industries.

Questionnaire for Management of Hotel Industries

Success of human resource development depends upon facilities provided by management to employees. Here comes an eminent role of management to development of human resources in the hotel. With this point in consideration it was decided to meet and interview the managers of hotel industries. For this purpose 20 managers were selected at random from these categories (General Manager, Director Sales and Marketing, Financial Controller, Resident Manager, Personnel Director, F and B Controller, GM HR, Executive Chief, Front office Manager etc.) from Cambay hotel and 20 from Inder Residency, so in all 40 managers were selected for this study.

The managers were met in person to get acquainted with their view – point related to recruitment, selection, training, motivation, reward system, promotion and demotion, employee encouragement, grievance and discipline procedure in the hotel industry and also know managers view with basic facilities like accommodation, educational, welfare, medical and recreational facilities, safety measures, reward, incentive plans, industrial relations and social security facilities.

Questionnaire for Employees of Hotel Industries

To study the human resource development in hotel industries. It was decided to collect information and views of employees of hotel industries. For this purpose, 100 employees were selected at random from these categories (*i.e.*, Personnel Officer, Executive HR, Front Office Executive, House Keeping Executive, Asst. Time Keeper, Security Guard, Bell Boy, Doormen, Durban, and Dispatch Clerks etc.) from each hotel. Hence 200 employees were selected from both the hotels for this study.

They were personally interviewed. They were asked to fill up the questionnaire containing questions relating to general information about the respondents. Next segment was commenced with questions related to HRD functions in hotel industry thereby moving to the questions important for our study like proper recruitment and development procedures followed by hotel or not, whether training has been imparted to the employees or not, about the working hours, salary and incentives benefits, accommodation, medical and welfare and other recreational facilities. They were also asked questions related to promotion and demotion, transfer policy, P.F, gratuity and pension scheme.

Analysis of Manager's Questionnaire

Profile of Sample Respondents

Distribution of Respondents

The sampling pattern has been shown in Table 4.1. In this study we selected 40 managers, 20 managers each from Cambay hotel and Inder Residency hotel.

Table 4.1: Distribution of Respondents

Cambay		Inder Residency		Total	
N	%	N	%	N	%
20	50.00	20	50.00	40	100.00

Age-wise Distribution

Table 4.2 revealed the age wise distribution of respondents. 10 (50%) respondents and 8 (40%) respondents from Cambay and Inder residency respectively belonged to the age group of 31-40. Only 10 per cent of Inder Residency respondents were above 50 years of age where as no respondents from Cambay belonged to this same age group. It is notable that most of the respondents of Inder Residency were old and more experienced; on the contrary Cambay is a new concern and in the selected units 8 (40%) respondents belonged to age of 30, young new generation given preference to increase productivity and profitability.

Table 4.2: Distribution of Respondents According to Age Group

Age Group	Cambay		Inder Residency	
	N	%	N	%
Up to 30	8	40.00	3	15.00
31 – 40	10	50.00	8	40.00
41 – 50	2	10.00	7	35.00
> 50	0	0.00	2	10.00
Total	**20**	**100.00**	**20**	**100.00**

Caste-wise Distribution

The caste-wise profile of the sample respondents is shown in Table 4.3. 18 (90%) respondents in Cambay and 11 (55%) respondents from Inder Residency belonged to Hindu caste. Only 10 per cent and 20 per cent respondents from Cambay and Inder Residency respectively were Christians. On the other hand percentage of Muslim and other S.C., S.T. and O.B.C., category were very low in both the Hotels. *(Table on next page)*

Educational Qualification-wise Distribution

Distribution of respondents according to education qualification depicts that 75 per cent managers in Cambay and 45 per cent managers in Inder Residency were Graduates in hotel management courses while 25 per cent managers in

Table 4.3: Distribution of Respondents According to Caste

Caste	Cambay		Inder Residency	
	N	%	N	%
Hindu	18	90.00	11	55.00
Muslim	0	0.00	3	15.00
Christian	2	10.00	4	20.00
Others	0	0.00	2	10.00
Total	**20**	**100.00**	**20**	**100.00**

Cambay and 40 per cent managers in Inder Residency were post graduate in Tourism Management and MBA in Hotel Management. This clearly indicated that most of respondents from both the hotels were graduates or post graduates in Hotel Management courses. (Table 4.4)

Table 4.4: Distribution of Respondents According to Educational Qualification

Educational Qualification	Cambay		Inder Residency	
	N	%	N	%
Graduate in Hotel Management	15	75.00	9	45.00
Post Graduate in Hotel Management	5	25.00	8	40.00
Others	0	0.00	3	15.00
Total	**20**	**100.00**	**20**	**100.00**

On the Basis of Length of Service

To study the samples on the basis of length of service above categories were formed as shown in table 4.5. Table 4.5 showed that 75 per cent *i.e.,* 15 respondents from Cambay and 40 per cent *i.e.,* 8 respondents from Inder Residency were in the service since last one year.

It showed that majority of people have less sustainability in the Cambay hotel when they are fresher wherein as the tenure of service increases they are more stable while in Inder Residency, 40 per cent respondents rendering their services in this field for more than 10 years.

Table 4.5: Distribution of Respondents According to Length of Service

Length of Service	Cambay		Inder Residency	
	N	%	N	%
Up to 1 year	15	75.00	8	40.00
2-5 years	3	15.00	3	15.00
6-10 years	2	10.00	1	5.00
> 10 years	0	0.00	8	40.00
Total	**20**	**100.00**	**20**	**100.00**

Chi Square Test

Chi square test is used to test for independence of two attributes or in other words to test whether the two attributes related to anything have any association. Assumption of independence of each other or no association between the two attributes is made. To calculate Chi Square value following formula is used —

$$\chi^2 = \Sigma \frac{(O - E)^2}{E}$$

Where O = observed frequency, E = Expected frequency

Degree of freedom (d.f) is calculated by (c – 1) x (r -1)

Where c = number of vertical columns or classes and r = number of horizontal rows or classes.

Significant value of Chi Square shows significant association between two attributes.

(*, ** & *** shows significant difference where * indicates $P < 0.05$, ** indicates $P < 0.01$, *** indicates $P < 0.001$, and NS indicates Not Significant difference.)

Chi Square	D.f	Result
10.464	3	*

(* $p < 0.05$)

Application of Chi Square Test

Test of association chi sqr was applied to see whether distribution of respondents according to length of service was associated with sampled hotels or not. The test result showed the significant association between sampled hotels and length of service ($\chi^2 = 10.464$, d.f = 3, $p < 0.05$). The observation table was observed that length of service in Inder Residency hotel was high than Cambay hotel.

Human Resource Development in Hotels

Essentiality of Separate Human Resource Department

The opinion of the managers about the human resource department was essential in hotels or not is shown in table 4.6. In both the hotels 100 per cent managers agreed that separate human resource department was essential in hotels.

Table 4.6: Essentiality of Separate Human Resource Department in Hotels

Essentiality of Separate Human Resource Department	Cambay		Inder Residency	
	N	%	N	%
Yes	20	100.00	20	100.00
No	0	0.00	0	0.00
Total	**20**	**100.00**	**20**	**100.00**

Existence of Human Resource Department

In both the hotels 100 per cent respondents said that their hotels have separate human resource department. It showed having a separate human resource department in the hotels reflect the soundness and higher levels of standard when it comes to giving 'state of best services to guests' and also high level of job satisfaction to employees. (Table 4.7)

Functions Performed by Human Resource Department

The respondents from Cambay and Inder Residency hotel were asked a question related to functions performed by human resource department by their hotel. Maximum numbers of respondents from both hotels considered all the HRD

Table 4.7: Existence of Human Resource Department

Existence of Separate Human Resource Department	Cambay		Inder Residency	
	N	%	N	%
Yes	20	100.00	20	100.00
No	0	0.00	0	0.00
Total	**20**	**100.00**	**20**	**100.00**

functions were performed by their hotels. When the above functions are compared, recruitment, selection and placement rank first in order of preference for respondents from both the hotels. Career planning and development was least performed by human resource department. (Table 4.8)

Table 4.8: Functions Performed by Human Resource Department in Hotels

Functions Performed by Human Resource Department	Cambay		Inder Residency	
	N	%	N	%
Recruitment, selection and Placement	4	20.00	9	45.00
Career Planning and Development	2	10.00	4	20.00
Training Programme	3	15.00	7	35.00
Performance Appraisal	2	10.00	5	25.00
Feedback and Counseling	3	15.00	3	15.00
All of the above	9	45.00	11	55.00

Recruitment in Hotels

Sources of Vacancy for Managers

The respondents in Cambay and Inder Residency hotel were asked question related to their sources of vacancy clearly indicated that every hotel adopts different methods for recruiting the new managers. In the Cambay, majority of mass *i.e.*, 35 per cent was coming through 'Placement Agency', 30

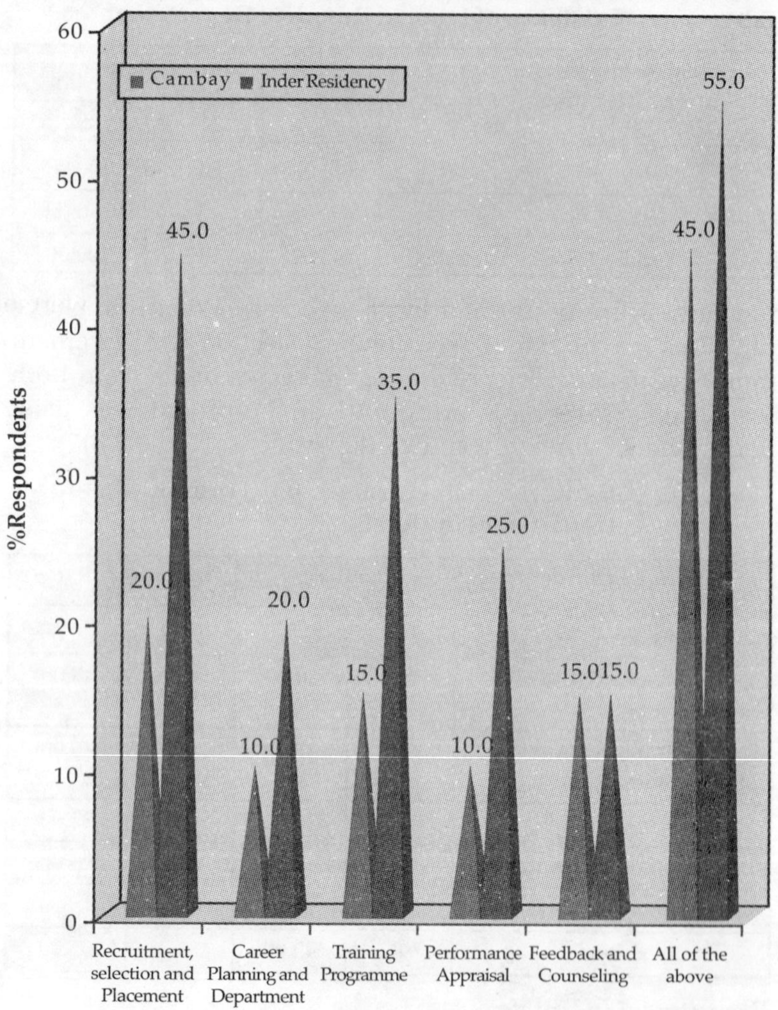

Fig. 4.1: Functions Performed by Human Resource Department in Hotels

per cent through 'Advertisement' and 20 per cent through 'Employment Exchange' whereas in Inder Residency majority of mass was coming through 'Advertisement' (55%), 'Placement Agency' (20%) and 'Employee referrals' (20%). (Table 4.9)

Table 4.9: Sources of Vacancy for Managers

Sources of Vacancy for Managers	Cambay		Inder Residency	
	N	%	N	%
Advertisement	6	30.00	11	55.00
Employment Exchange	4	20.00	0	0.00
Placement Agency	7	35.00	4	20.00
Reference	0	0.00	0	0.00
Employee referrals	2	10.00	4	20.00
Through Investigation	1	5.00	1	5.00
Total	**20**	**100.00**	**20**	**100.00**

Application of Chi Square Test

Test of association was applied to see whether sources of vacancy for managers were associated with sampled hotels or not. The above test result showed non significant association (χ^2 = 6.955, d.f = 4, NS) of sources of vacancy for managers and sampled hotels.

Chi Square	D.f	Result
6.955	4	NS

Best Method of Recruitment

In the opinion of respondents of Cambay 'Advertisement' (30%) and 'Placement Agency' (30%) was the best method for recruitment of managers while in the opinion of respondents of Inder Residency 'Reference' (40%) and 'Placement Agency' (25%) was the best method for recruitment of new manager. (Table 4.10)

Table 4.10: **Best Method of Recruitment**

Best Method of Recruitment	Cambay		Inder Residency	
	N	%	N	%
Advertisement	6	30.00	3	15.00
Employment Exchange	3	15.00	1	5.00
Placement Agency	6	30.00	5	25.00
Reference	3	15.00	8	40.00
Employee referrals	2	10.00	1	5.00
Through Investigation	0	0.00	2	10.00
Total	**20**	**100.00**	**20**	**100.00**

Application of Chi Square Test

To find out whether any significant difference exists between two hotels on the basis of best method of recruitment, chi sqr test was applied. The calculated value of chi sqr was 6.697 and the table value of chi sqr for 5 d.f at 5 per cent level of significance is 11.070. Since the calculated value of chi sqr is less than table value. It indicated that there was no significant difference between two hotels on the basis of best method of recruitment.

Chi Square	D.f	Result
6.697	5	NS

Worst Method of Recruitment

The respondents in both the hotels were asked question which is the worst method of recruitment in their opinion. Half of the respondents of Cambay felt that 'Reference' (50%) and 'Employment Exchange' (35%) was the worst method for recruitment while in Inder Residency manager's felt that 'Through Investigation' (35%) and 'Employment Exchange' (25%) was the worst method respectively. (Table 4.11)

Table 4.11: Worst Method of Recruitment

Worst Method of Recruitment	Cambay		Inder Residency	
	N	%	N	%
Advertisement	0	0.00	2	10.00
Employment Exchange	7	35.00	5	25.00
Placement Agency	0	0.00	1	5.00
Reference	10	50.00	3	15.00
Employee Referrals	3	15.00	2	10.00
Through Investigation	0	0.00	7	35.00
Total	**20**	**100.00**	**20**	**100.00**

Application of Chi Square Test

In order to test association between Cambay and Inder Residency hotels with worst method of recruitment, chi sqr test was applied. The above test results ($\chi^2 = 14.303$, d.f = 5, $p < 0.05$) showed the significant difference exists between two hotels on the basis of worst method of recruitment. The result showed that 'Reference' method was worst method of recruitment for managers in Cambay hotel whereas recruitment through investigation method was considering worst method by managers of Inder Residency.

Chi Square	D.f	Result
14.303	5	*

(* $p < 0.05$)

Factors Affecting Successful Recruitment

In both the hotels 40 per cent respondents have opinion that successful recruitment depended on "Public Image of an Organization" while 35 per cent respondents of both the hotels felt that "Available of skilled person in the market". Work culture of an organization was carried and radiated by the personnel working for the company so when it comes to successful recruitment "Public Image of an Organization" is the golden asset for current employees and the prospective candidates getting into the board of the organization.

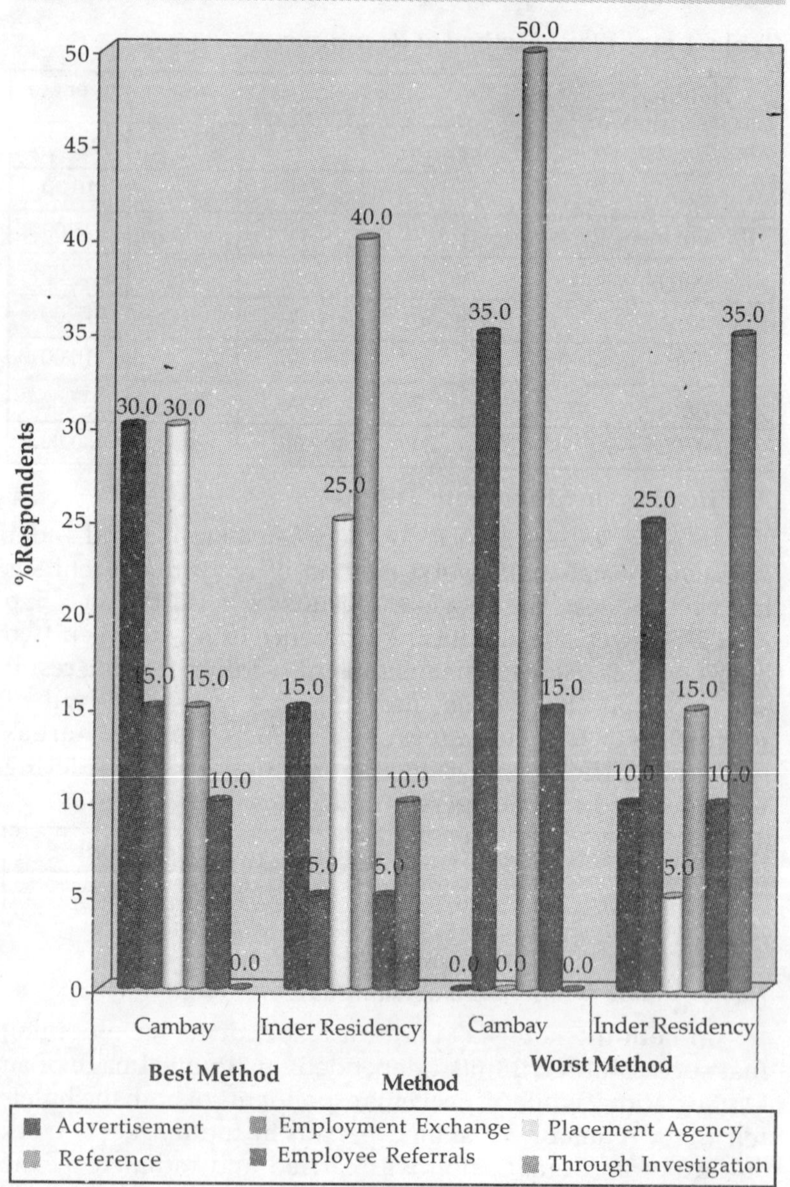

Fig. 4.2: Best and Worst Method of Recruitment

Table 4.12: Factors Affecting Successful Recruitment

Factors for Successful Recruitment	Cambay		Inder Residency	
	N	%	N	%
Public Image of Organization	8	40.00	8	40.00
Available of skilled person in the market	7	35.00	7	35.00
Method of recruitment followed by the organization	2	10.00	4	20.00
On salary and Perks	2	10.00	3	15.00

Selection in Hotels

Selection Process

Table 4.13 reveals that 60 per cent and 70 per cent respondents from Cambay and Inder Residency respectively selected through 'Interview' and 35 per cent of Cambay, respondents were goes for "Direct Appointment". Some managers of Inder Residency also selected by written test.

Table 4.13: Procedure for Selection of Managers

Selection Process	Cambay		Inder Residency	
	N	%	N	%
Direct appointment	7	35.00	0	0.00
Written test	0	0.00	2	10.00
Interview	12	60.00	14	70.00
Both written test and Interview	1	5.00	4	20.00
Total	**20**	**100.00**	**20**	**100.00**

Application of Chi Square Test

Test of association chi sqr was applied to find out whether any significant difference exists between sampled hotels and their selection process for managers or not. The value of chi sqr is 10.954 and table value is 7.815. Since calculated value is greater than table value. It indicated that there was a significant difference between sampled hotels on the basis of the selection process for their managers.

Chi Square	D.f	Result
10.954	3	*

(* $p < 0.05$)

Weightage given to Academic Qualification

Table 4.14: Weightage given to Academic Qualification in Selection of Managers

Weightage given to Academic Qualification	Cambay		Inder Residency	
	N	%	N	%
To great extent	9	45.00	7	35.00
To some extent	8	40.00	13	65.00
Irrelevant	3	15.00	0	0.00
Total	**20**	**100.00**	**20**	**100.00**

Application of Chi Square Test

Test of association chi sqr was applied to see whether weightage given to academic qualification is associated with sampled hotels or not. The test result showed the non significance association between sampled hotels and weightage given to academic qualification. (χ^2 = 4.440, d.f = 2, NS).

Chi Square	D.f	Result
4.440	2	NS

Weightage given to Experience

Table 4.14 and 4.15 depicts that Cambay hotel more focused on academic qualification of managers rather than experience in selection of managers while Inder Residency more focused on experience of managers compare to their academic qualification.

Table 4.15: Weightage given to Experience in Selection of Managers

Weightage given to Experience	Cambay		Inder Residency	
	N	%	N	%
To great extent	8	40.00	13	65.00
To some extent	9	45.00	7	35.00
Irrelevant	3	15.00	0	0.00
Total	**20**	**100.00**	**20**	**100.00**

Application of Chi Square Test

To find out whether any significant difference exists between two hotels and weightage given to experience or not, chi sqr test was conducted. The test result showed that there was non significant difference between two hotels and weightage given to experience. (χ^2 = 4.440, d.f = 2, NS).

Chi Square	D.f	Result
4.440	2	NS

Weightage given to Communication Skill and Smartness

Table 4.16 clearly indicated that more weightage given to communication skill and smartness of the managers of Cambay hotel as compare to managers of Inder Residency.

Table 4.16: Weightage given to Communication Skill and Smartness

Weightage given to Communication Skill	Cambay		Inder Residency	
	N	%	N	%
To great extent	11	55.00	7	35.00
To some extent	8	40.00	13	65.00
Irrelevant	1	5.00	0	0.00
Total	**20**	**100.00**	**20**	**100.00**

Application of Chi Square Test

Chi sqr was applied to find out whether any significant difference exists between two hotels and weightage given to communication skills are associated or not. The test result showed that there was no significant association between two hotels and weightage given to communication skills. ($\chi^2 = 3.079$, d.f = 2, NS).

Chi Square	D.f	Result
3.079	2	NS

Training Programme in Hotels

Training Facilities

Table 4.17 Clearly Indicated that Management of Inder Residency Hotel Provided more Training to their Managers Compare to Cambay Hotel.

Table 4.17: Adequate Training Facilities Provided by Hotels to their Managers

Training Facilities	Cambay		Inder Residency	
	N	%	N	%
Often	7	35.00	14	70.00
Normally	8	40.00	6	30.00
Rarely	5	25.00	0	0.00
Total	**20**	**100.00**	**20**	**100.00**

Application of Chi Square Test

Test of association chi sqr was applied to see whether frequency of training facilities is associated with sampled hotels or not. The test result showed the significant association between sampled hotels and frequency of training ($\chi^2 = 7.62$, d.f = 2, $p < 0.05$). The observation tables are observed it can be clearly seen that in Inder Residency, training are provided often wherever this percentage was just half for Cambay hotel.

Chi Square	D.f	Result
7.619	2	*

(* $p < 0.05$)

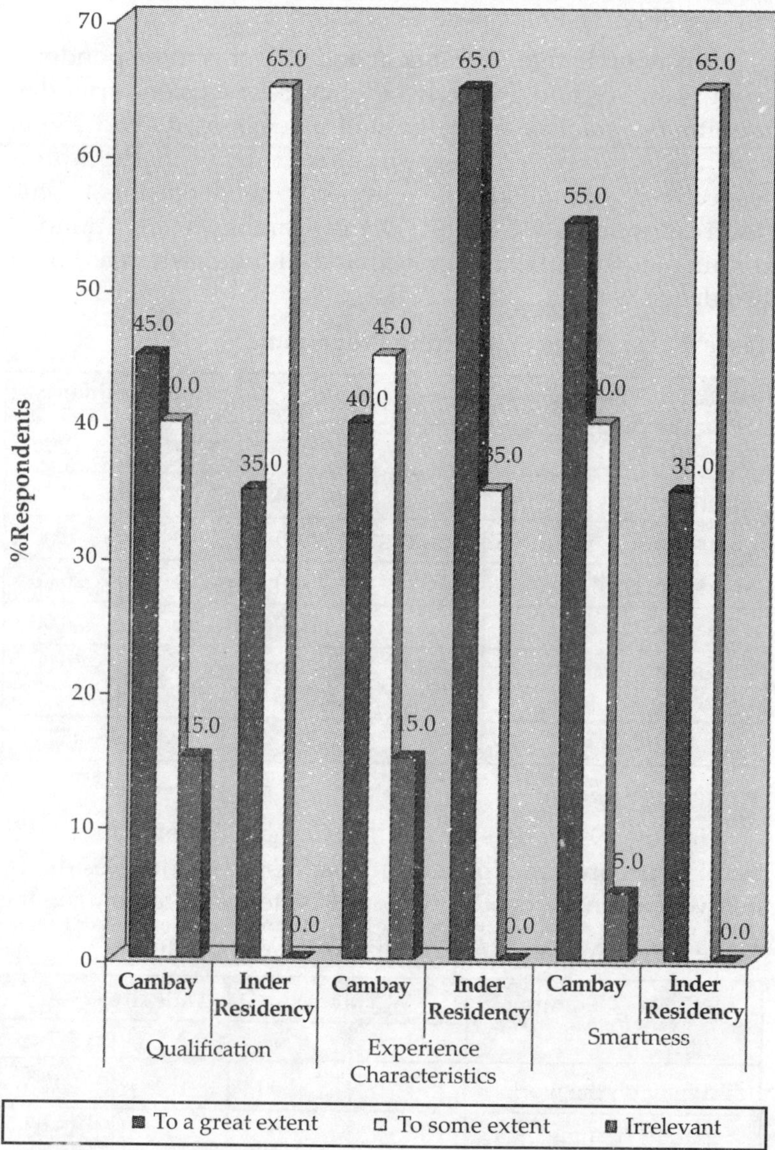

Fig. 4.3: Weightage given to Qualification, Experience and Smartness

Areas of Training Programme

It is notable that 45 per cent and 60 per cent respondents from Cambay and Inder Residency respectively attended training programme in the field of management. And 25 per cent and 20 per cent respondents from both the hotels respectively attended training in personnel department. Only few respondents (10% and 5%) of Cambay were attended training in the field of finance and IT field whereas Inder Residency was nil.

Table 4.18: Areas of Training Programme

Areas of Training Programme	Cambay		Inder Residency	
	N	%	N	%
Management	9	45.00	12	60.00
Marketing	0	0.00	0	0.00
Personnel	5	25.00	4	20.00
Finance	2	10.00	0	0.00
Information and Technology	1	5.00	0	0.00
All Above	4	20.00	9	45.00

Methods of Training

Table 4.19 clearly showed that Cambay followed separate training programme for their managers and Inder Residency followed training on the work for betterment for managers.

Table 4.19: Methods of Training Followed by Hotels

Methods of Training	Cambay		Inder Residency	
	N	%	N	%
Training on the work	1	5.00	15	75.00
Separate Training Programme	16	80.00	3	15.00
Both	3	15.00	2	10.00
Total	**20**	**100.00**	**20**	**100.00**

Application of Chi Square Test

The above results of chi sqr test shows the method of training are significantly associated with sampled hotels. ($\chi^2 = 21.345$, d.f = 2, $p < 0.001$). It can easily be seen from observation tables that in Inder Residency, training on work were preferred whereas in Cambay hotel, separate training programme given in priority.

Chi Square	D.f	Result
21.345	2	***

(*** $p < 0.001$)

Utility of Training Programme

Table 4.20 reflected that training programme helps managers for better performance, job satisfaction and promotion in hotel industries.

Table 4.20: Training Programme Helps Managers

Training Programme Helps Managers	Cambay		Inder Residency	
	N	%	N	%
Better Performance	17	85.00	20	100.00
Job Satisfaction	15	75.00	17	85.00
Promotion	17	85.00	13	65.00

Problems faced by Managers during Training Programme

In Cambay, managers faced the communication problems with trainee and problem of learning while Inder Residency, managers faced the communication problem with trainee and different level of trainees provided training together. (*See table 4.21 on next page*)

Application of Chi Square Test

Test of association chi sqr was applied to find out whether significant difference exists between two hotels and problems faced by managers during training programme. The calculated value of chi sqr is 9.092 and the table value for 3 d.f calculated at 5 per cent level of significance is 7.815. Since chi sqr value

Table 4.21: Problems faced by Managers from Employees During Training Programme

Problems faced by Managers during Training Programme	Cambay		Inder Residency	
	N	%	N	%
Communication problems with trainee	5	25.00	9	45.00
Different level of trainees	1	5.00	6	30.00
Difficult to learn	7	35.00	3	15.00
No Problem	7	35.00	2	10.00
Total	**20**	**100.00**	**20**	**100.00**

is greater than table value. It clearly indicated that there was significant difference between two hotels and problems faced by managers during training programme. The observed table indicated that communication problems with trainee more prevalent and different levels of trainees were in Inder Residency than Cambay hotel whereas difficult in learning was more found in Cambay than Inder Residency hotel.

Chi Square	D.f	Result
9.092	3	*

(* $p < 0.05$)

Salary, Bonus and Allowances in Hotels

Salary According to Nature of Job

More than ¾ respondents from both the hotels were agreed that adequate salary paid by management to their managers.

Table 4.22: Salary According to Nature of Job

Salary According to Nature of Job	Cambay		Inder Residency	
	N	%	N	%
Yes	15	75.00	18	90.00
No	5	25.00	2	10.00
Total	**20**	**100.00**	**20**	**100.00**

Application of Chi Square Test

The result of chi sqr test in the above table showed that there was no significant difference exists between two hotels and salary according to nature of job. ($\chi^2 = 1.558$, d.f = 1, NS).

Chi Square	D.f	Result
1.558	1	NS

Management Considers Manager's Qualifications an Expertise while Making Salaries and Allowances

Half of the managers from Cambay and 55 per cent managers from Inder Residency hotel reported that normally, the management considered manager's qualification and expertise while making salaries, allowances and pre-requisites. (Table 4.23)

Table 4.23: Management Considers Manager's Qualifications and Expertise while Making Salaries and Allowances

Management Considers Manager's Qualification	Cambay		Inder Residency	
	N	%	N	%
Always	7	35.00	2	10.00
Often	3	15.00	7	35.00
Normally	10	50.00	11	55.00
Total	**20**	**100.00**	**20**	**100.00**

Application of Chi Square Test

Test of association was applied to see whether any significance difference exists between two hotels and management consideration for manager's qualification or not. The test result showed that significant difference exists between two hotels and management consideration for manager's qualification. ($\chi^2 = 14.780$, d.f = 2, $p < 0.001$). The observation table indicated that in Cambay hotel, management always considered managers qualification whereas this percentage was less in Inder Residency.

Chi Square	D.f	Result
14.780	2	***

(*** $p < 0.001$)

Overtime Received by the Managers

Table 4.24 clearly indicates that in Cambay hotel, management generally gave overtime to their managers while Inder Residency rarely gives overtime to their managers.

Table 4.24: Overtime Received by the Managers

Overtime Received by the Managers	Cambay		Inder Residency	
	N	%	N	%
Often	9	45.00	3	15.00
Normally	7	35.00	1	5.00
Never	4	20.00	16	80.00
Total	**20**	**100.00**	**20**	**100.00**

Application of Chi Square Test

In order to test whether sampled hotels and overtime received by managers are associated with each other or not, chi sqr test was applied. The result clearly indicated that two hotels and overtime received by managers were significantly associated with each other. ($\chi^2 = 16.205$, d.f = 2, $p < 0.001$). The observation table clearly showed that overtime was often received by managers of Cambay hotel than Inder Residency.

Chi Square	D.f	Result
16.205	2	***

(*** $p < 0.001$)

Bonus Received by the Managers

Table 4.25 has been shown that Cambay hotel generally gave bonus to their managers while Inder Residency never gave bonus to their managers.

Table 4.25: Bonus Received by the Managers

Bonus Received by the Managers	Cambay		Inder Residency	
	N	%	N	%
Often	8	40.00	0	0.00
Normally	5	25.00	1	5.00
Never	7	35.00	19	95.00
Total	**20**	**100.00**	**20**	**100.00**

Allowances Received by the Managers

Table 4.26 visualized that 75 per cent and 65 per cent respondents from Cambay and Inder Residency respectively received the vehicle/petrol allowances while 55 per cent and 45 per cent received the telephone allowances. 45 per cent and 30 per cent respondents received medical benefits, 40 per cent and 20 per cent respondents received children education allowances and 20 per cent and 95 per cent respondents received other allowances like club, gym and sports, gaming zone, picnic and parties and swimming pool etc.

Table 4.26: Allowances Received by the Managers

Types of Allowances	Cambay		Inder Residency	
	N	%	N	%
Medical	9	45.00	6	30.00
Children Education	8	40.00	4	20.00
Vehicle/Petrol	15	75.00	13	65.00
Telephone	11	55.00	9	45.00
Entertainment	8	40.00	6	30.00
Other	4	20.00	19	95.00

Basis for Allowances Paid

Table 4.27 It was notable that In Cambay hotel, managers received maximum allowances *i.e.*, children education, vehicle/petrol allowances, telephone and entertainment allowances on fixed basis and only medical allowances received on actual basis while In Inder Residency, managers received medical, children education and entertainment allowances on fixed basis and vehicle/petrol and telephone allowances on actual basis.

Table 4.27: Basis for Allowances Paid

Allowances	Cambay				Inder Residency			
	Actual		Fixed		Actual		Fixed	
	N	%	N	%	N	%	N	%
Medical	14	70.00	0	0.00	0	00.00	7	35.00
Children Education	0	00.00	13	65.00	0	0.00	4	20.00
Vehicle/Petrol	0	00.00	17	85.00	13	65.00	0	00.00
Telephone	0	00.00	17	85.00	4	20.00	5	25.00
Entertainment	0	00.00	15	75.00	0	0.00	6	30.00

Basic Facilities Provided by Hotels to Managers

Accommodation Facilities

Maximum respondents from Cambay and Inder Residency were not getting accommodation facilities provided by the hotels. All managers from both the hotels received HRA in the absence of housing facility.

Table 4.28: Accommodation Facilities Provided to the Managers

Accommodation Facilities	Cambay		Inder Residency	
	N	%	N	%
Yes	1	05.00	1	05.00
No	19	95.00	19	95.00
Total	**20**	**100.00**	**20**	**100.00**

Transportation Facilities

In Cambay hotel, management provided transportation facility to their managers while Inder Residency, management not provided transportation facility to their managers.

Table 4.29: Transportation Facilities Provided by the Hotels

Transportation Facility	Cambay		Inder Residency	
	N	%	N	%
Yes	20	100.00	0	0.00
No	0	0.00	20	100.00
Total	**20**	**100.00**	**20**	**100.00**

Uniform in Hotels

All the respondents from both the hotels reported that uniform was compulsory in their respective department.

Table 4.30: Uniform is Compulsory in Hotels

Uniform is Compulsory	Cambay		Inder Residency	
	N	%	N	%
Yes	20	100.00	20	100.00
No	0	0.00	0	0.00
Total	**20**	**100.00**	**20**	**100.00**

Medical Facilities

Table 4.31 visualized that all managers were state that there was no hospital/dispensary facility available in hotel area. In Cambay hotel, management provided ESI facility to their managers for treatment while Inder Residency, management provided cash reimbursement for treatment to their managers.

Table 4.31: Dispensary/Hospital Facility Available in Hotels

Medical Facilities	Cambay		Inder Residency	
	N	%	N	%
Yes	0	00.00	0	00.00
No	20	100.00	20	100.00
Total	**20**	**100.00**	**20**	**100.00**

Other Welfare Facilities

Cambay hotel provided other welfare facilities like entertainment, club, gym and sports, transportation, fashion show, food festival, gaming zone, picnic and parties etc., to their managers while Inder Residency provided other welfare facilities like parties and picnic, recreation room, rest room, club, bar, swimming pool, gaming zone and gym etc. to their managers. The survey clearly showed that both the hotels were not provided the medical benefits to the manager's family members.

Motivation in Hotels

Motivation Method Adopted by Hotel Management

Table 4.32 depicted that in Cambay hotel, managers motivated by giving promotion (55%), encouragement (40%) and 35 per cent managers motivated by giving rewards and monetary benefits respectively while in Inder Residency most of the managers *i.e.*, 70 per cent motivated by encouragement method and 20 per cent managers motivated by promotion method.

Table 4.32: Motivation Method Adopted by Hotel Management for Increasing Productivity

Motivation Method	Cambay		Inder Residency	
	N	%	N	%
Giving reward	7	35.00	0	0.00
Monetary benefits	7	35.00	3	15.00
Promotion	11	55.00	4	20.00
Encouragement	8	40.00	14	70.00

Effect of Motivation on Productivity

Table 4.33 showed that 80 per cent and 95 per cent managers from Cambay and Inder Residency hotel respectively felt that motivation methods generally increased productivity.

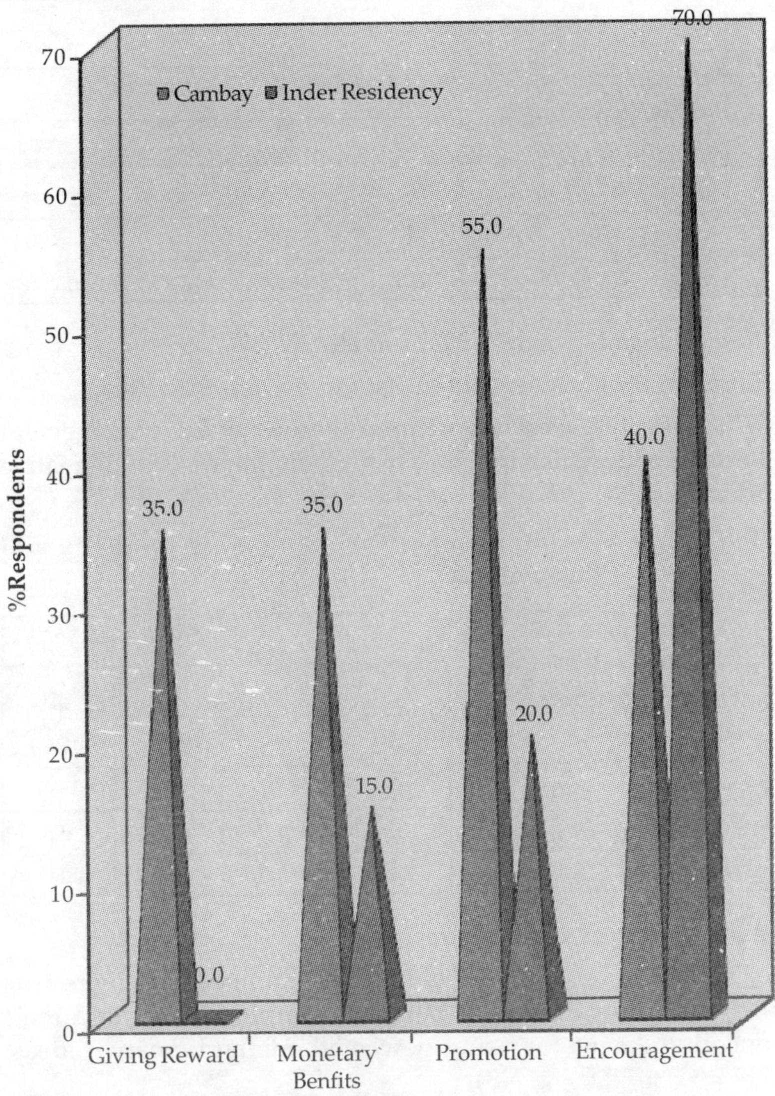

Fig. 4.4: Motivation Method Adopted by Hotel Management for Increasing Productivity

Table 4.33: Effect of Motivation on Productivity

Frequency of Increase Productivity	Cambay		Inder Residency	
	N	%	N	%
Often	16	80.00	19	95.00
Normally	4	20.00	1	5.00
Total	**20**	**100.00**	**20**	**100.00**

Rewards and Incentive Plans in Hotels

Encouragement for using New Methods and Creative Ideas

Table 4.34 clearly indicated that generally management encouraged to managers for using new methods and creative ideas.

Table 4.34: Encouragement for using New Methods and Creative Ideas

Encouragement for Applying New Methods and Creative Ideas	Cambay		Inder Residency	
	N	%	N	%
Often	10	50.00	9	45.00
Normally	3	15.00	9	45.00
Rarely	7	35.00	2	10.00
Total	**20**	**100.00**	**20**	**100.00**

Application of Chi Square Test

The above results of chi sqr test showed that there was no significant difference between sampled hotels and their encouragement for using new methods and creative ideas. (χ^2 = 5.830, d.f = 2, NS).

Chi Square	D.f	Result
5.830	2	NS

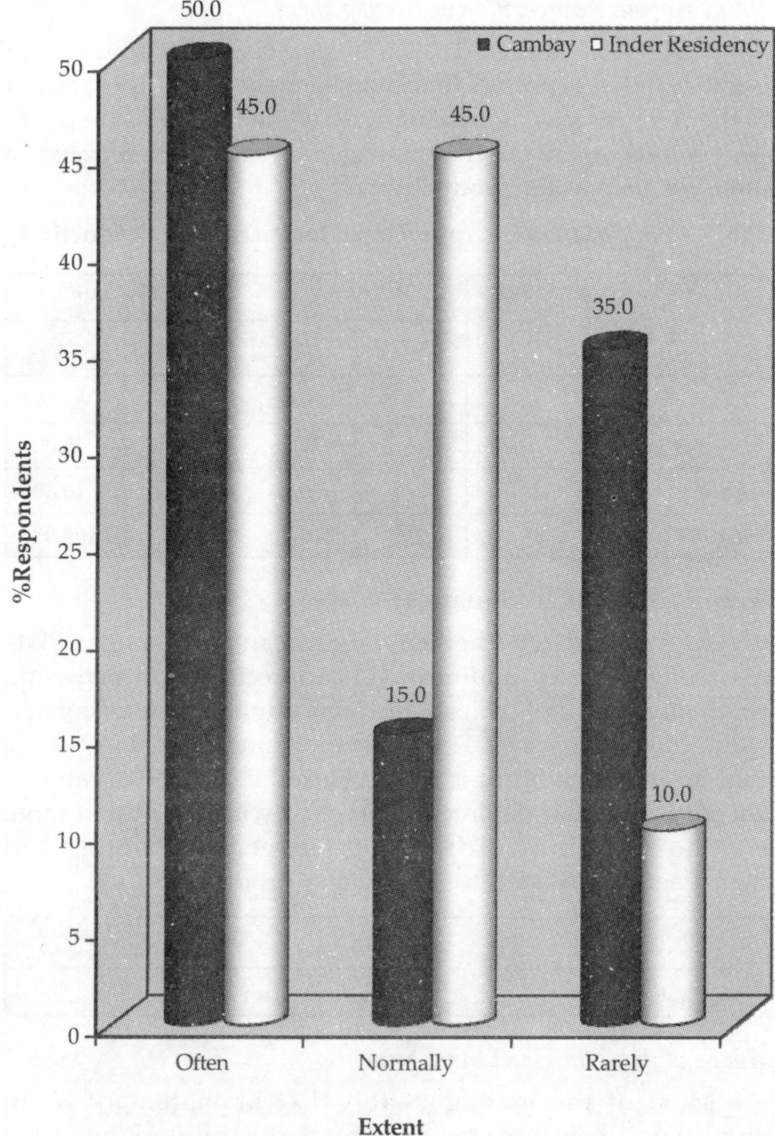

Fig. 4.5: Encouragement for using New Methods and Creative Ideas

Opinion about Appreciation by Management

Table 4.35 depicted that 50 per cent managers from Cambay hotel reported that management often appreciated to them for increasing productivity while Inder Residency 45 per cent managers felt that management often appreciated to them for increasing productivity.

Table 4.35: Managers Appreciated for Increasing Productivity

Managers Appreciated by Management	Cambay		Inder Residency	
	N	%	N	%
Often	10	50.00	9	45.00
Normally	6	30.00	9	45.00
Rarely	4	20.00	2	10.00
Total	**20**	**100.00**	**20**	**100.00**

Application of Chi Square Test

To find out whether any significant difference exists between two hotels and managers appreciated for increasing productivity or not, chi sqr test was applied. The calculated value of chi sqr was 1.319 and table value for 2 d.f at 5 per cent level of significant is 5.991. Since the calculated value of chi sqr is less than table value. It clearly indicated that there was no significant difference between two hotels and managers appreciated for increasing productivity.

Chi Square	D.f	Result
1.319	2	NS

Appreciated by the Hotel Management

Most of the managers felt that management often appreciates their honesty, sincerity and hard working of the managers.

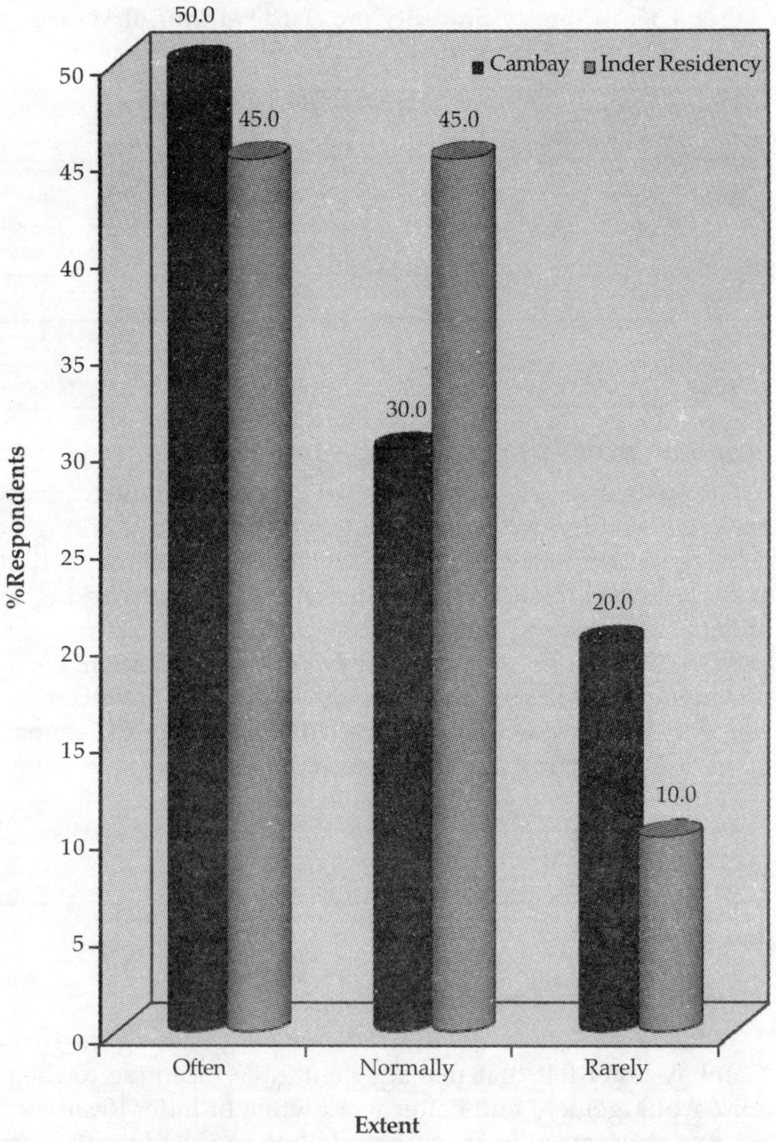

Fig. 4.6: Managers Appreciated for Increasing Productivity

Table 4.36: Honesty, Sincerity and Hard Working of Managers are Appreciated by the Hotel Management

Honesty, Sincerity and Hard Working of Managers are Appreciated	Cambay		Inder Residency	
	N	%	N	%
Often	11	55.00	13	65.00
Normally	3	15.00	6	30.00
Rarely	6	30.00	0	0.00
Total	**20**	**100.00**	**20**	**100.00**

Application of Chi Square Test

Chi sqr test was applied to see whether sampled hotels and appreciation for honesty, sincerity and hard working of managers are associated or not. The result showed that sampled hotels and honesty, sincerity and hard working of managers are significantly associated. ($\chi^2 = 7.146$, d.f = 2, $p < 0.05$). The observed table clearly indicated that in Inder Residency, managers were often appreciated for honesty, sincerity and hard working whereas the percentage of Cambay hotel in this regard was less than Inder Residency.

Chi Square	D.f	Result
7.146	2	*

(* $p < 0.05$)

Incentive Plan for Managers

Table 4.37 showed that 80 per cent managers from Cambay hotel felt that management gave incentive to them for encouragement and better work while In Inder Residency 60 per cent managers reported that management gave incentive to them for encouragement.

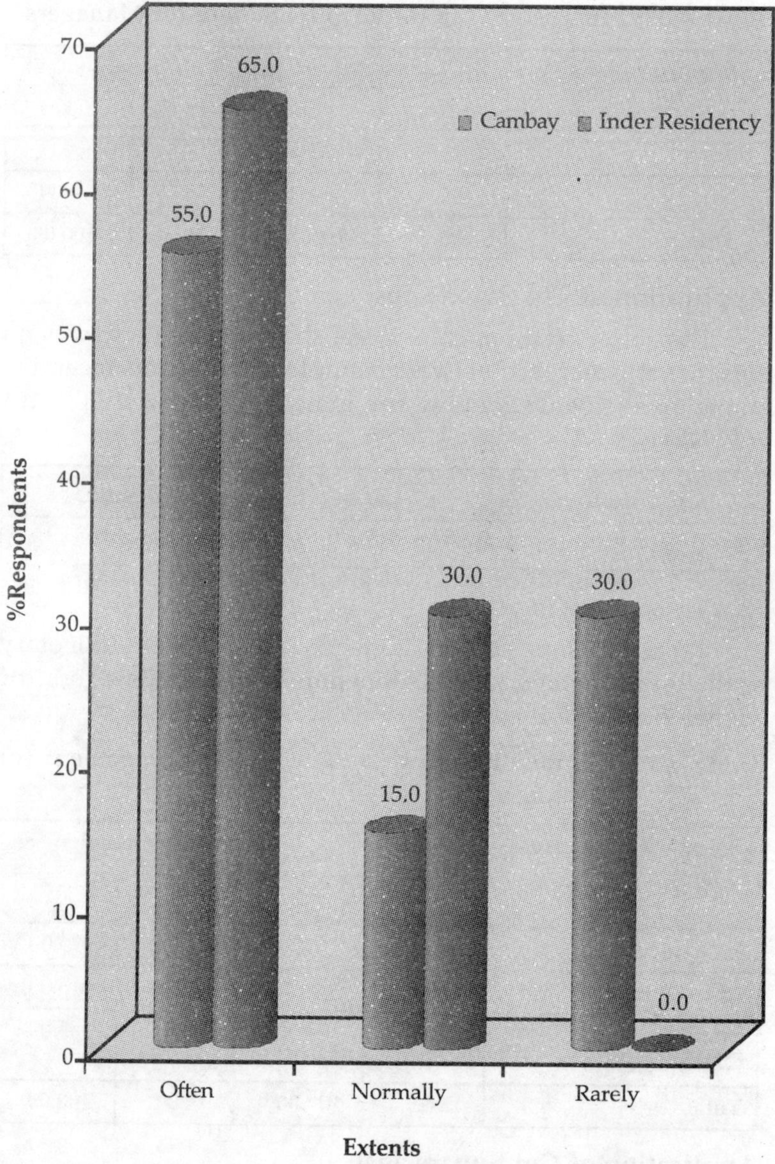

Fig. 4.7: Honesty, Sincerity and Hard Working of Managers are Appreciated by the Hotel Management

Table 4.37: Incentive Plan for Encouragement for Managers

Incentive Plans	Cambay		Inder Residency	
	N	%	N	%
Yes	16	80.00	12	60.00
No	4	20.00	8	40.00
Total	**20**	**100.00**	**20**	**100.00**

Application of Chi Square Test

The above result of chi sqr test showed that there was no significant difference between sampled hotels and incentive plans for encouragement for managers. (χ^2 = 1.905, d.f = 1, NS).

Chi Square	D.f	Result
1.905	1	NS

Kinds of Incentive Plan

Table 4.38 showed that management gave both monetary and non-monetary incentive benefits to the managers for higher productivity.

Table 4.38: Kinds of Incentive Plan for Encouragement for Managers

Kinds of Incentive Plan	Cambay		Inder Residency	
	N	%	N	%
Monetary	2	10.00	4	20.00
Non-Monetary	6	30.00	3	15.00
Monetary and Non-monetary	12	60.00	13	65.00
Total	**20**	**100.00**	**20**	**100.00**

Application of Chi Square Test

Test of association chi sqr was applied to see whether kinds of incentive plans are associated with sampled hotels or not. The test showed that there was no significant association between sampled hotels and kinds of incentive plan. ($\chi^2 = 1.707$, d.f = 2, NS).

Chi Square	D.f	Result
1.707	2	NS

Nature of Monetary Benefits

Table 4.39 revealed that, management gave monetary benefits to the managers. In Cambay Hotel 50 per cent managers reported that management gave individual bonus to mangers, 35 per cent said that hotel gave increment and 15 per cent said that management gave more allowances for encouragement while Inder Residency, 90 per cent managers said that management gave increment and 10 per cent felt that management gave more allowances for encouragement.

Table 4.39: Nature of Monetary Benefits

Monetary Benefits	Cambay		Inder Residency	
	N	%	N	%
Increment	7	35.00	18	90.00
More allowance	3	15.00	2	10.00
Individual bonus	10	50.00	0	0.00
Total	**20**	**100.00**	**20**	**100.00**

Application of Chi Square Test

To find out whether sampled hotels and monetary benefits are associated with each other or not, chi sqr test was applied. The above result showed that there was significant association between sampled hotels and monetary benefits. ($\chi^2 = 15.040$, d.f = 2, $p < 0.001$). The observation table indicated that in Inder Residency, increment was more preferred as monetary benefits whereas in Cambay, this percentage was half of the Inder Residency.

Chi Square	D.f	Result
15.040	2	***

(*** $p < 0.001$)

Nature of Non-monetary Benefits

Table 4.40 depicted that, management also gave non-monetary benefits to their managers. In Cambay Hotel 7 (35%) managers reported that management gave appreciation, 9 (45%) managers said that hotel gave more facilities and 4 (20%) managers said that management gave reward for encouragement to them while Inder Residency, 15 (75%) managers said that management gave appreciation and 2 (10%) managers felt that management gave more facilities and 3 (15%) managers said that management gave reward for encouragement.

Table 4.40: Nature of Non-monetary Benefits

Non-monetary Benefits	Cambay		Inder Residency	
	N	%	N	%
Appreciation	7	35.00	15	75.00
More facilities	9	45.00	2	10.00
Reward	4	20.00	3	15.00
Total	**20**	**100.00**	**20**	**100.00**

Application of Chi Square Test

The above result of chi sqr test showed that there was a significant association between sampled hotels and non-monetary benefits. ($\chi^2 = 7.506$, d.f = 2, $p < 0.05$). The observation table clearly indicated that appreciation as non-monetary benefits was more followed by Inder Residency than Cambay hotel.

Chi Square	D.f	Result
7.506	2	*

(* $p < 0.05$)

Promotion and Demotion Policy in Hotels

Basis of Promotion

65 per cent and 70 per cent managers from Cambay hotel and Inder Residency hotel reported that both seniority and merit basis was adopted for promotion by their management.

Table 4.41: Basis of Promotion

Basis of Promotion	Cambay		Inder Residency	
	N	%	N	%
Seniority	2	10.00	1	5.00
Merit basis	5	25.00	5	25.00
Seniority and Merit basis	13	65.00	14	70.00
Total	**20**	**100.00**	**20**	**100.00**

Application of Chi Square Test

The above test result showed that there was non-significance difference between the sampled hotels on the basis of promotion. ($\chi^2 = 0.370$, d.f = 2, NS).

Chi Square	D.f	Result
0.370	2	NS

Promotion on Due Time

Table 4.42 revealed that in Cambay hotel, 55 per cent manager's felt that they get promoted on due time and 45 per cent managers not getting promoted on due time while in Inder Residency, 80 per cent manager's felt that they get promoted on due time while 20 per cent managers not getting promoted on due time.

Table 4.42: Manager's Promotion on Due Time

Manager's Promoted on Due Time	Cambay		Inder Residency	
	N	%	N	%
Yes	11	55.00	16	80.00
No	9	45.00	4	20.00
Total	**20**	**100.00**	**20**	**100.00**

Application of Chi Square Test

To find out whether significance difference exists between the two hotels and managers promotion on due time, chi sqr test was applied. The calculated value of chi sqr was 2.849 and the table value for 1 d.f at 5 per cent level of significance is 3.841. Since the calculated chi sqr value is less than table value. Therefore no significance difference exists between the two hotels and managers promotion on due time.

Chi Square	D.f	Result
2.849	1	NS

Effect of Timely Promotion

Table 4.43 has been shown that most of the managers from both the hotels felt that timely promotion increase manager's efficiency, more responsibility with job and increases their monetary benefits.

Table 4.43: Effect of Timely Promotion on Managers.

Effect of Timely Promotion	Cambay		Inder Residency	
	N	%	N	%
Increased efficiency at work	9	45.00	6	30.00
More responsible with job	5	25.00	3	15.00
Increased monetary benefits	10	50.00	12	60.00

Reason for Delay in Promotion

Table 4.44 has been shown that in Cambay Hotel, 50 per cent managers stated that delay in manager's promotion due to lack of proper qualification for promoted post, while 25 per cent, 45 per cent and 15 per cent managers respectively reported that no vacancy at higher level, managers were not trained or skilled and not completed the probation period. On the other hand in Inder Residency hotel, 65 per cent managers said that they were not promoted due to not trained or skilled, 30 per cent felt that due to lack of proper qualification for promoted post and 15 per cent said that no vacancy at higher level.

Table 4.44: Reason for Delay in Promotion

Reason for Delay in Promotion	Cambay		Inder Residency	
	N	%	N	%
Not proper qualification for promoted post	10	50.00	6	30.00
No vacancy at higher level	5	25.00	3	15.00
Not trained or skilled	9	45.00	13	65.00
Not completed the probation period	3	15.00	2	10.00

Manager's Demotion in Hotels

Table 4.45 revealed that In Cambay hotel; managers generally get demoted by the management. On the contrary in Inder Residency, 75 per cent managers said that they never get demoted by the management.

Table 4.45: Manager's Demotion in Hotels

Manager gets Demotion	Cambay		Inder Residency	
	N	%	N	%
Often	12	60.00	0	0.00
Normally	4	20.00	5	25.00
Never	4	20.00	15	75.00
Total	**20**	**100.00**	**20**	**100.00**

Application of Chi Square Test

Test of association was applied to see whether manager's demotion was associated with sampled hotels or not. The test result showed that there was significant association between the sampled hotels and manager's demotion. ($\chi^2 = 18.480$, d.f = 2, $p < 0.001$).

Chi Square	D.f	Result
18.480	2	***

(*** $p < 0.001$)

Reasons for Manager's Demotion

All 20 managers were not promoted because of not maintain punctuality, improper working and misbehave with management. (Table 4.46)

Table 4.46: Reasons for Manager's Demotion

Reasons for Demotion	Cambay		Inder Residency	
	N	%	N	%
Not punctual	7	35.00	0	0.00
Improper working	9	45.00	17	85.00
Misbehave with management	4	20.00	3	15.00
Total	**20**	**100.00**	**20**	**100.00**

Application of Chi Square Test

In order to test association between sampled hotels and reason for demotion, chi sqr test was applied. The above result showed that calculated value of chi sqr is 9.604 and the table value for 2 d.f at 1 per cent level of significant is 9.210. Since the calculated value of chi sqr is greater than table value. It clearly showed that there was significant association between sampled hotels and reason for demotion. It can also be inferred from the observation table that in Inder Residency, improper working has been main reason for demotion whereas in Cambay, the percentage in this regard was very less than Inder Residency.

Chi Sqr	D.f	Result
9.604	2	**

(** $p < 0.01$)

Industrial Relation

Relation between Managers and Hotel Management

Table 4.47 depicted that 16 (80%) managers from Cambay and 17 (85%) managers from Inder Residency hotel felt that they have good relations with management.

Table 4.47: Relation between Managers and Hotel Management

Relation between Managers and Hotel Management	Cambay		Inder Residency	
	N	%	N	%
Excellent	1	5.00	6	30.00
Good	15	75.00	11	55.00
Normal	4	20.00	3	15.00
Total	**20**	**100.00**	**20**	**100.00**

Application of Chi Square Test

The above test result showed that there was no significant difference between the two hotels and relationship between managers and hotel management. (χ^2 = 4.330, d.f = 2, NS).

Chi Square	D.f	Result
4.330	2	NS

Dispute between Managers and Hotel Management

Table 4.48 has been showed that in Cambay hotel, managers generally faced dispute with management whereas on the contrary in Inder Residency hotel, 80 per cent managers felt that they never faced dispute with management.

Table 4.48: Dispute between Managers and Hotel Management

Dispute between Managers and Hotel Management	Cambay		Inder Residency	
	N	%	N	%
Often	9	45.00	2	10.00
Normally	8	40.00	2	10.00
Never	3	15.00	16	80.00
Total	**20**	**100.00**	**20**	**100.00**

Application of Chi Square Test

To find out whether significant difference exists between the two hotels and dispute between manager and hotel

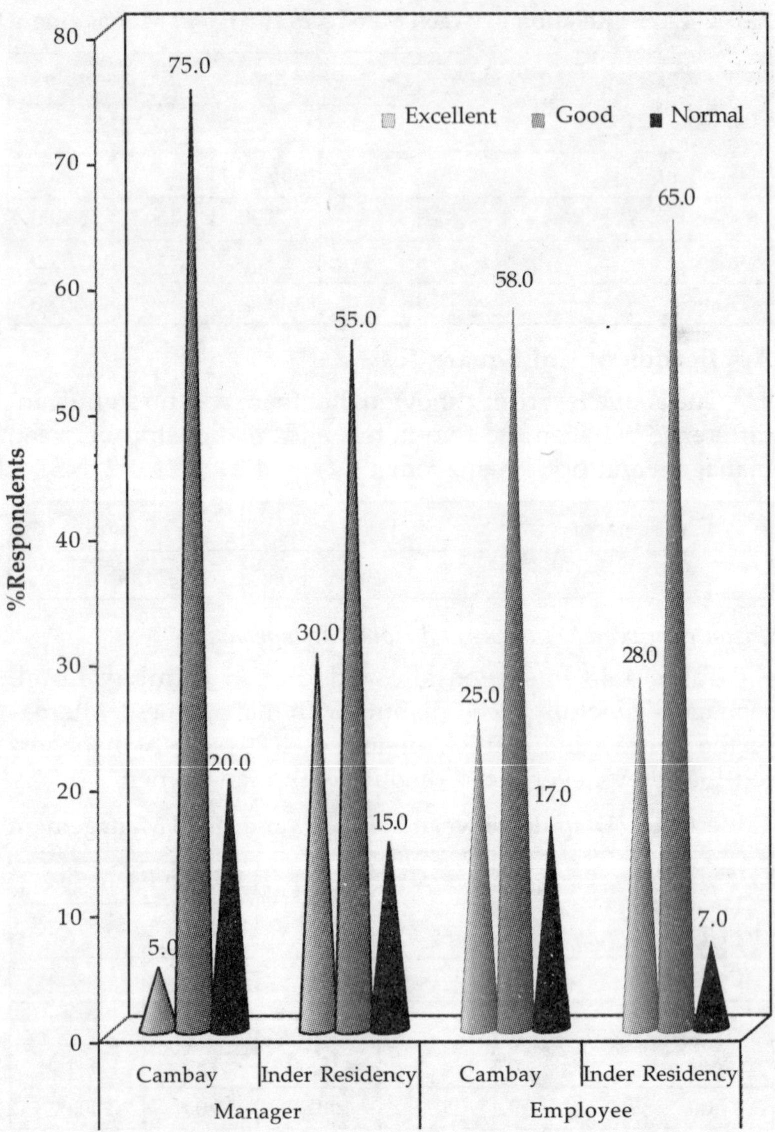

Fig. 4.8: Relation between Managers and Hotel Management

management, chi sqr test was conducted. The above test result showed that there was significant difference between the two hotels and dispute between manager and hotel management. ($\chi^2 = 16.944$, d.f = 2, $p < 0.001$). The observed table indicated that there was often dispute between managers and hotel management in Cambay hotel whereas in Inder Residency, the percentage in this regard was very less.

Chi Square	D.f	Result
16.944	2	***

(*** $p < 0.001$)

Grievance Handling Procedure

Table 4.49 clearly showed that in both the hotels, management has an effective grievance handling procedure for the managers.

Table 4.49: Management has an Effective Grievance Handling Procedure for the Managers

Effective Grievance Handling Procedure	Cambay		Inder Residency	
	N	%	N	%
Yes	15	75.00	16	80.00
No	5	25.00	4	20.00
Total	**20**	**100.00**	**20**	**100.00**

Application of Chi Square Test

To find out whether significant difference exists between the two hotels and grievance handling procedure for the managers, chi sqr test was conducted. The above test result showed that there was non significant difference between the two hotels and grievance handling procedure for the managers. ($\chi^2 = 0.143$, d.f = 1, NS).

Chi Square	D.f	Result
0.143	1	NS

Management Actively Involved in Solving Day to Day Problems for Managers

Table 4.50 described that through regular meetings and joint forums, generally management has actively involved in solving day to day problems for managers.

Table 4.50: Management Actively Involved in Solving Day to Day Problems for Managers

Management Actively Involved	Cambay		Inder Residency	
	N	%	N	%
Always	7	35.00	3	15.00
Often	6	30.00	10	50.00
Normally	7	35.00	7	35.00
Total	**20**	**100.00**	**20**	**100.00**

Application of Chi Square Test

Test of association chi sqr was applied to see whether management actively involved in solving day to day problems for managers are associated with sampled hotels or not. The test showed that there was no significant association between sampled hotels and management actively involved in solving day to day problems for managers. (χ^2 = 2.600, d.f = 2, NS).

Chi Sqr	D.f	Result
2.600	2	NS

Job Enrichment in Hotels

Career Development Plans for Managers

Table 4.51 showed that 85 per cent (17) managers from Cambay and 90 per cent (18) managers from Inder Residency hotel reported that management has definite plans for career development for them.

Table 4.51: Career Development Plans for Managers

Career Development Plans for Manager's	Cambay		Inder Residency	
	N	%	N	%
Yes	17	85.00	18	90.00
Normally	3	15.00	2	10.00
Total	**20**	**100.00**	**20**	**100.00**

Application of Chi Square Test

To find out whether significant difference exists between the two hotels and career development plans for the managers, chi sqr test was conducted. The above test result showed that there was non significant difference between the two hotels and career development plans for the managers. (χ^2 = 0.229, d.f = 1, NS).

Chi Sqr	D.f	Result
0.229	1	NS

Job Satisfaction in Hotels

Salaries, Allowances and Pre-requisites are Attractive Considering for Job Responsibilities

17 (85%) managers from Cambay and 9 (45%) managers from Inder Residency hotel felt that salaries, allowances and pre-requisites are attractive considering for job responsibilities whereas 15 per cent managers from Cambay and 55 per cent managers from Inder Residency reported that salaries, allowances and pre-requisites are average considering for job responsibilities. (*See table 4.52 on next page*)

Application of Chi Square Test

To find out whether significant difference exists between the two hotels and salaries, allowances and pre-requisities are attractive consideration for job responsibilities, chi sqr test was conducted. The above test result showed that the calculated value was 7.033 and table value 1 d.f at 1 per cent level of significance is 6.635. Since the calculated value is

Table 4.52: Salaries, Allowances and Pre-requisites are Attractive Considering for Job Responsibilities

Salaries, Allowances and Pre-requisites are Attractive Considering for Job Responsibilities	Cambay		Inder Residency	
	N	%	N	%
Attractive	17	85.00	9	45.00
Average	3	15.00	11	55.00
Unattractive	0	0.00	0	0.00
Total	**20**	**100.00**	**20**	**100.00**

greater than table value. It clearly shows that there is significant difference between the two hotels and salaries, allowances and pre-requisities are attractive consideration for job responsibilities. The observation table showed that salaries, allowances and pre-requisities are attractive in Cambay hotel whereas the percentage for the same was nearly half in Inder Residency than Cambay.

Chi Square	D.f	Result
7.033	1	**

(** $p < 0.01$)

Job Provides Enough Opportunities to Utilise the Manager's Skills and Abilities

Nearly 75 per cent managers from both the hotel said that job provides enough opportunities to utilise their skills and abilities up to some extent. (*See table 4.53 on next page*)

Application of Chi Square Test

Test of association chi sqr was applied to see whether job provides enough opportunities to utilise the manager's skills and abilities are associated with sampled hotels or not. The test showed that there was no significant association between sampled hotels and job provides enough opportunities to utilise the manager's skills and abilities. (χ^2 = 0.125, d.f = 1, NS).

Table 4.53: Job Provides Enough Opportunities to Utilise the Manager's Skills and Abilities

Job Provides Enough Opportunities to Utilise the Manager's Skills and Abilities	Cambay		Inder Residency	
	N	%	N	%
Fully	6	30.00	5	25.00
Up to some extent	14	70.00	15	75.00
Total	**20**	**100.00**	**20**	**100.00**

Chi Square	D.f	Result
0.125	1	NS

Working Conditions in Hotels

Table 4.54 showed that 15 (75%) managers from Cambay and 17 (85%) managers from Inder Residency hotel state that working environment was healthy and good and they were satisfied with the working conditions.

Table 4.54: Working Conditions in Hotels

Working Conditions are Good in Hotels	Cambay		Inder Residency	
	N	%	N	%
Yes	15	75.00	17	85.00
No	5	25.00	3	15.00
Total	**20**	**100.00**	**20**	**100.00**

Application of Chi Square Test

To find out whether any significant difference exists between the two hotels and working conditions, chi sqr test was conducted. The above test result showed that there is non significant difference between the two hotels and working conditions. (χ^2 = 0.625, d.f = 1, NS).

Chi Square	D.f	Result
0.625	1	NS

Social Security Facilities in Hotels

Table 4.55 clearly indicated that Cambay and Inder residency hotel management provided provident fund (P.F.) and gratuity to their managers and there was no pension scheme for the managers.

Table 4.55: Type of Social Security Facilities Provided by Hotel Management to their Managers

Social Security Facilities	Cambay		Inder Residency	
	N	%	N	%
Provident Fund	13	65.00	11	55.00
Pension	0	0.00	0	0.00
Gratuity	20	100.00	20	100.00

Analysis of Employee's Questionnaire

Profile of Sample Respondents

Distribution of Respondents

The sampling pattern has been shown in table 4.56. In this study we selected 200 employees, 100 employees each from Cambay hotel and Inder Residency hotel.

Table 4.56: Distribution of Respondents

Cambay		Inder Residency		Total	
N	%	N	%	N	%
100	50.00	100	50.00	200.00	100.00

Age-wise Distribution

Table 4.57 revealed the age wise distribution of respondents. It is notable that most of the respondents of Cambay (56%) and Inder Residency (49%) belonged to age up to 30; 39 per cent respondents and 46 per cent respondents from Cambay and Inder residency respectively belonged to the age group of 31-40. Young new generation given preference to increase productivity and profitability in hotel industry.

Only 5 per cent of respondents were 41-50 years of age from both the hotels. Whereas no respondents from Cambay and Inder Residency belonged to above 50 age group.

Table 4.57: Distribution of Respondents According to Age Group

Age Group	Cambay		Inder Residency	
	N	%	N	%
Up to 30	56	56.00	49	49.00
31 – 40	39	39.00	46	46.00
41 – 50	5	5.00	5	5.00
> 50	0	0.00	0	0.00
Total	**100**	**100.00**	**100**	**100.00**

Caste-wise Distribution

The caste-wise profile of the sample respondents is shown in table 4.58. 75 per cent respondents in Cambay and 84 per cent respondents from Inder Residency belonged to Hindu caste; it means the weightage of general caste employees is higher in both hotels. Only 10 per cent and 3 per cent respondents from Cambay and 9 per cent and 5 per cent respondents from Inder Residency respectively were Muslims and Christians. On the other hand 12 respondents from Cambay belonged to other caste (S.C, S.T and O.B.C) whereas percentage of other S.C, S.T and O.B.C category were very low in Inder Residency.

Table 4.58: Distribution of Respondents According to Caste

Caste	Cambay		Inder Residency	
	N	%	N	%
Hindu	75	75.00	84	84.00
Muslim	10	10.00	9	9.00
Christian	3	3.00	5	5.00
Others	12	12.00	2	2.00
Total	**100**	**100.00**	**100**	**100.00**

Educational Qualification-wise Distribution

Table 4.59 Distribution of respondents according to educational qualification depicted that 30 per cent employees in Cambay and 25 per cent employees in Inder Residency were Graduates while 17 per cent employees in Cambay and 16 per cent employees in Inder Residency were post graduate and 25 per cent and 27 per cent employees done MBA respectively from both hotels. Rest 23 per cent and 15 per cent employees from both hotels belonged to other category (MHRM, MIB, MTM, BE, ME etc.) This clearly indicated that most of respondents from both the hotels were graduates or MBA. It means they were highly efficient and knowledgeable.

Table 4.59: Distribution of Respondents According to Educational Qualification

Educational Qualification	Cambay		Inder Residency	
	N	%	N	%
Sr. Secondary	3	3.00	12	12.00
Graduation	30	30.00	25	25.00
Post Graduation	17	17.00	16	16.00
MBA	25	25.00	27	27.00
CA/CS	2	2.00	5	5.00
Other	23	23.00	15	15.00
Total	**100**	**100.00**	**100**	**100.00**

On the Basis of Length of Service

To study the sampled on the basis of length of service above categories were formed as shown in Table 4.60. The table showed that 74 per cent respondents from Cambay and 77 per cent respondents from Inder Residency were in the service since last one year. Only 26 respondents from Cambay and 23 respondents from Inder Residency were in the service of 2-5 years.

Table 4.60: Distribution of Respondents According to Length of Service

Length of Service	Cambay		Inder Residency	
	N	%	N	%
Upto 1 year	74	74.00	77	77.00
2-5 Years	26	26.00	23	23.00
6-10 years	0	0.00	0	0
>10 years	0	0.00	0	0
Total	**100**	**100.00**	**100**	**100.00**

It showed that majority of people have less sustainability from both hotels when they are fresher wherein as the tenure of service increases they are more stable. It is to be noticed that in both the hotels no one have experience more than five years of service in same hotels.

Application of Chi Square Test

Test of association chi sqr was applied to see whether distribution of respondents according to length of service is associated with sampled hotels or not. The test result showed that observed value of chi sqr is 0.243 and table value for 1 d.f at 5 per cent is 3.841. Since observed value of chi sqr is less than table value. There was non significance association between the sampled hotels length of service. The observation table also indicated that nearly equal per cent of employees were providing their services up to 1 and 2-5 years.

Chi Square	D.f	Result
0.243	1	NS

Designation-wise Distribution

On the basis of designation wise distribution, 54 per cent and 38 per cent respondents were executive category, 10 per cent and 16 per cent respondents were asst. managers and 36 per cent and 46 per cent respondents were from other category *i.e.,* Personnel Officer, Executive HR, Front Office Executive,

House Keeping Executive, Asst. Time Keeper, Security Guard, Bell Boy, Doormen, Durban, and Dispatch Clerks etc., respectively from Cambay and Inder Residency hotels.

Table 4.61: Distribution of Respondents According to Designation

Designation	Cambay		Inder Residency	
	N	%	N	%
Executive	54	54.00	38	38.00
Asst. Manager	10	10.00	16	16.00
Other	36	36.00	46	46.00
Total	**100**	**100.00**	**100**	**100.00**

Application of Chi Square Test

To find out the difference between the sampled hotels and designation of employees, chi sqr was applied. The above test result showed that there was non significance difference between sampled hotels and designation of employees. (χ^2 = 5.387, d.f = 2, NS)

Chi Square	D.f	Result
5.387	2	NS

Human Resource Development in Hotels

Essentiality of Separate Human Resource Department

The opinion of the employees about the human resource department was essential in hotels or not is shown in table 4.62. In both the hotels 100 per cent employees agreed that separate human resource department was essential in hotels. (*See table on next page*)

Existence of Human Resource Department

In both the hotels 100 per cent respondents said that their hotels have separate human resource department. It showed having a separate human resource department in the hotels reflect the soundness and higher levels of standard when it comes to giving "state of best services to guests" and also high level of job satisfaction to employees. (*See table 4.63 on next page*)

Table 4.62: Essentiality of Separate Human Resource Department in Hotels

Essentiality of Separate Human Resource Department	Cambay		Inder Residency	
	N	%	N	%
Yes	100	100.00	100	100.00
No	0	0.00	0	0.00
Total	**100**	**100.00**	**100**	**100.00**

Table 4.63: Existence of Human Resource Department

Existence of Separate Human Resource Department	Cambay		Inder Residency	
	N	%	N	%
Yes	100	100.00	100	100.00
No	0	0.00	0	0.00
Total	**100**	**100.00**	**100**	**100.00**

Functions Performed by Human Resource Department

The respondents from Cambay and Inder Residency hotel were asked a question related to functions performed by human resource department by their hotel. Maximum numbers of respondents from both hotels considered all the HRD functions were performed by their hotels. When the above functions are compared, recruitment, selection, placement and training rank first in order of preference for respondents from both the hotels. Feedback and counseling and career planning and development was least performed by human resource department. (*See table 4.64 on next page*)

Recruitment in Hotels

Sources of Vacancy for Employees

The respondents in Cambay and Inder Residency hotel were asked question related to their sources of vacancy clearly indicated that every hotel adopts different methods for recruiting the new employees. In the Cambay, majority of mass *i.e.*, 39 per cent was coming through 'Employee Referrals'

Table 4.64: Functions Performed by Human Resource Department in Hotels

Functions Performed by Human Resource Department	Cambay		Inder Residency	
	N	%	N	%
Recruitment, selection and Placement	1	1.00	27	27.00
Career Planning and Development	0	0	6	6.00
Training Programme	0	0	25	25.00
Performance Appraisal	1	1.00	9	9.00
Feedback and Counseling	0	0	4	4.00
All of the above	89	89.00	69	69.00

and 29 per cent through 'Placement Agency' whereas in Inder Residency majority of mass was coming through 'Placement Agency' (38%) and 'Advertisement' (31%). (Table 4.65)

Table 4.65: Sources of Vacancy for Employees

Sources of Vacancy for Employees	Cambay		Inder Residency	
	N	%	N	%
Advertisement	10	10.00	31	31.00
Employment Exchange	10	10.00	7	7.00
Placement Agency	29	29.00	38	38.00
Reference	7	7.00	10	10.00
Employee referrals	39	39.00	14	14.00
Through Investigation	5	5.00	0	0.00
Total	**100**	**100.00**	**100**	**100.00**

Application of Chi Square Test

Test of association was applied to see whether sources of vacancy for employees were associated with sampled hotels or not. The above test result showed the significant association ($\chi = 29.816$, d.f = 5, $p < 0.001$) of sources of vacancy

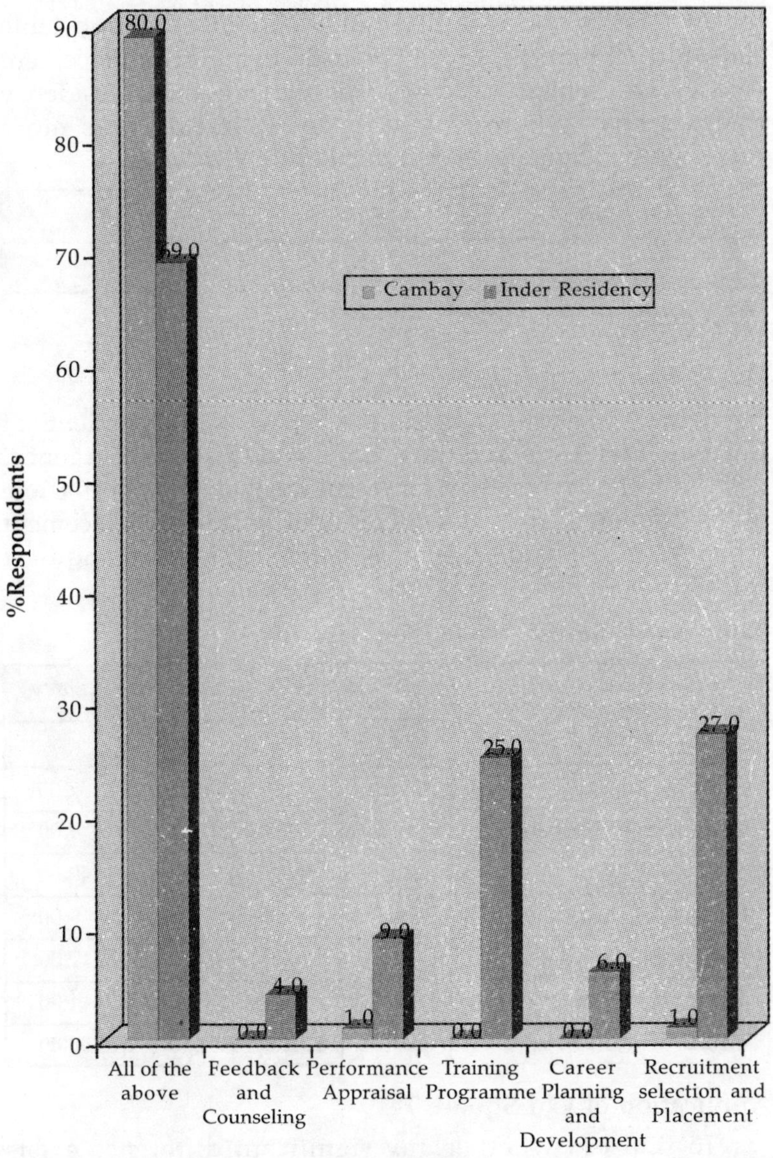

Fig. 4.9: Functions Performed by Human Resource Department in Hotels

for employees and sampled hotels. The observation table showed that percentage of 'Advertisement' and 'Placement Agency' as a source of vacancy was higher in Inder Residency than Cambay whereas 'Employees Referrals' was more preferred by Cambay than Inder Residency.

Chi Square	D.f	Result
29.816	5	***

(*** $p < 0.001$)

Best Method of Recruitment

Table 4.66 showed that in the opinion of respondents of Cambay 'Employee Referrals' (36%) and 'Placement Agency' (29%) was the best method for recruitment of employees while in the opinion of respondents of Inder Residency 'Placement Agency' (40%) and 'Advertisement' (32%) was the best method for recruitment of new employees.

Table 4.66: Best Method of Recruitment

Best Method of Recruitment	Cambay		Inder Residency	
	N	%	N	%
Advertisement	15	15.00	32	32.00
Employment Exchange	14	14.00	1	1.00
Placement Agency	29	29.00	40	40.00
Reference	4	4.00	9	9.00
Employee referrals	36	36.00	17	17.00
Through Investigation	2	2.00	1	1.00
Total	**100**	**100.00**	**100**	**100.00**

Application of Chi Square Test

To find out whether any significant difference exists between two hotels on the basis of best method of recruitment, chi sqr test was applied. The calculated value of chi sqr was 28.237 and the table value of χ for 1 d.f at 5 per cent level of significance is 3.841. Since the calculated value of chi sqr is greater than table value. It indicated that there was significant difference between two hotels on the basis of best method of recruitment.

Chi Square	D.f	Result
28.237	1	*

(* $p < 0.05$)

Worst Method of Recruitment

Table 4.67 showed that the respondents in both the hotels were asked question which is the worst method of recruitment in their opinion. The respondents of Cambay felt that 'Reference' (60%) and 'Through Investigation' (25%) was the worst method for recruitment while in Inder Residency employee's felt that 'Employment Exchange' (33%) and 'Reference' (25%) was the worst method.

Table 4.67: Worst Method of Recruitment

Worst Method of Recruitment	Cambay		Inder Residency	
	N	%	N	%
Advertisement	2	2.00	11	11.00
Employment Exchange	7	7.00	33	33.00
Placement Agency	4	4.00	10	10.00
Reference	60	60.00	25	25.00
Employee referrals	2	2.00	5	5.00
Through Investigation	25	25.00	16	16.00
Total	**100**	**100.00**	**100**	**100.00**

Application of Chi Square Test

In order to test association between Cambay and Inder Residency hotels with worst method of recruitment, chi sqr test was applied. The above test results ($\chi^2 = 43.375$, d.f = 5, $p < 0.001$) showed the significant difference exists between two hotels on the basis of worst method of recruitment.

Chi Square	D.f	Result
43.375	5	***

(*** $p < 0.001$)

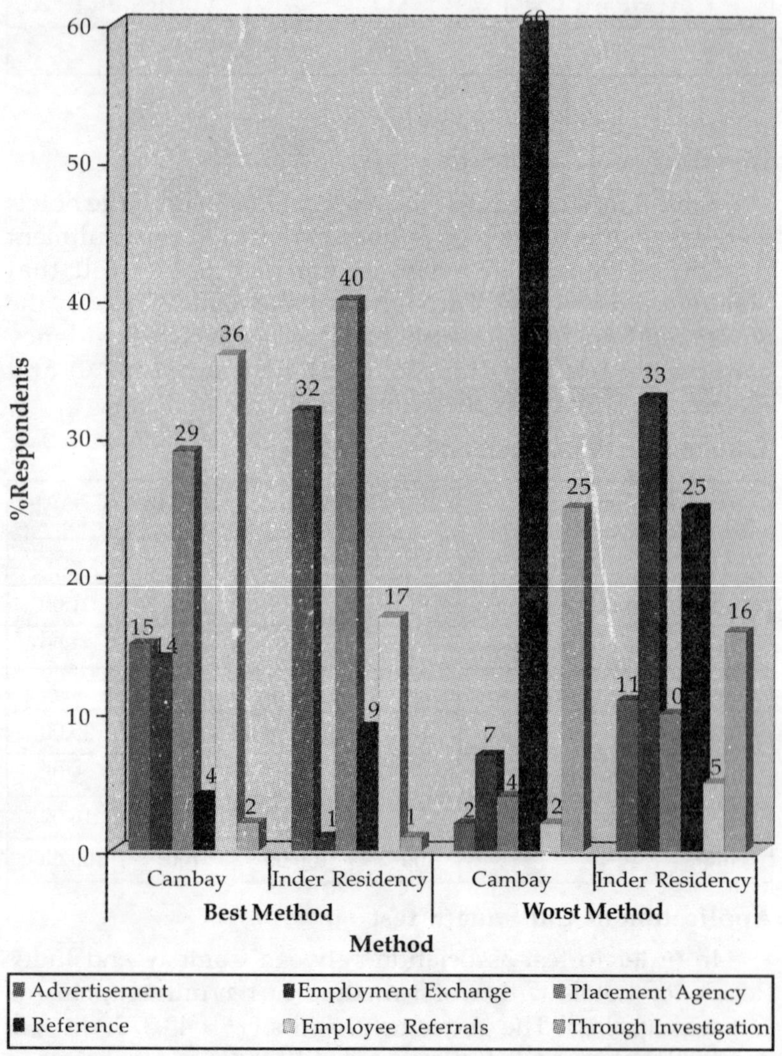

Fig. 4.10: Best and Worst Method of Recruitment

Selection in Hotels

Selection Process

Table 4.68 revealed that about ¾ th (70% and 71%) respondents from Cambay and Inder Residency respectively selected through 'Interview' and rest ¼ th (23% and 27%) respondents from both hotels were selected through "both written test and Interview".

Table 4.68: Procedure for Selection of Employees in Hotels

Selection Process	Cambay		Inder Residency	
	N	%	N	%
Direct appointment	6	6.00	0	0.00
Written test	1	1.00	2	2.00
Interview	70	70.00	71	71.00
Both written test and Interview	23	23.00	27	27.00
Total	**100**	**100.00**	**100**	**100.00**

Application of Chi Square Test

Test of association chi sqr was applied to find out whether any significant difference exists between sampled hotels and their selection process for employees or not. The value of chi sqr is 6.660 and table value is 7.815. Since calculated value is less than table value. It indicated that there was non significant difference between sampled hotels on the basis of the selection process for their employees.

Chi Square	D.f	Result
6.660	3	NS

Weightage given to Academic Qualification

Table 4.69: Weightage given to Academic Qualification in Selection of Employees

Weightage given to Academic Qualification	Cambay		Inder Residency	
	N	%	N	%
To great extent	59	59.00	43	43.00
To some extent	37	37.00	55	55.00
Irrelevant	4	4.00	2	2.00
Total	**100**	**100.00**	**100**	**100.00**

Application of Chi Square Test

Test of association chi sqr was applied to see whether weightage given to academic qualification was associated with sampled hotels or not. The test result showed the significance association between sampled hotels and weightage given to academic qualification. ($\chi^2 = 4.69$, d.f = 2, $p < 0.05$).

Chi Square	D.f	Result
4.69	2	*

(* $p < 0.05$)

Weightage given to Experience

Table 4.69 and 4.70 depicts that Cambay hotel more focus on academic qualification of employees rather than experience in selection of employees while Inder Residency more focus on experience of employees compare to their academic qualification.

Table 4.70: Weightage given to Experience in Selection of Employees

Weightage given to Experience	Cambay		Inder Residency	
	N	%	N	%
To great extent	41	41.00	60	60.00
To some extent	55	55.00	40	40.00
Irrelevant	4	4.00	0	0.00
Total	**100**	**100.00**	**100**	**100.00**

Application of Chi Square Test

To find out whether any significant difference exists between two hotels and weightage given to experience or not, chi sqr test was conducted. The test result showed the significant difference between two hotels and weightage given to experience. ($\chi = 9.943$, d.f = 2, $p < 0.01$). It can be inferred the observation table that percentage of weightage given to experience is high in Inder Residency hotel than Cambay hotel.

Chi Square	D.f	Result
9.943	2	**

(** $p < 0.01$)

Probation Period of Employees in the Hotel

Table 4.71 showed that maximum *i.e.,* 93 per cent and 80 per cent respondents from Cambay and Inder Residency hotels stated that employees have six month probation period at the time of joining.

Table 4.71: Probation Period of Employees in the Hotel

Probation Period	Cambay		Inder Residency	
	N	%	N	%
No Probation	4	4.00	8	8.00
Six month	93	93.00	80	80.00
Six month to one year	3	3.00	12	12.00
Total	**100**	**100.00**	**100**	**100.00**

Application of Chi Square Test

Chi sqr test was conducted in order to see whether there is any association between the sampled hotels and probation period. The above test result showed that calculated value of chi sqr is 7.710 whereas the table value for 2 d.f at 5 per cent level of significance is 5.991. Since the calculated value of chi sqr exceeds the table value. There was significant association

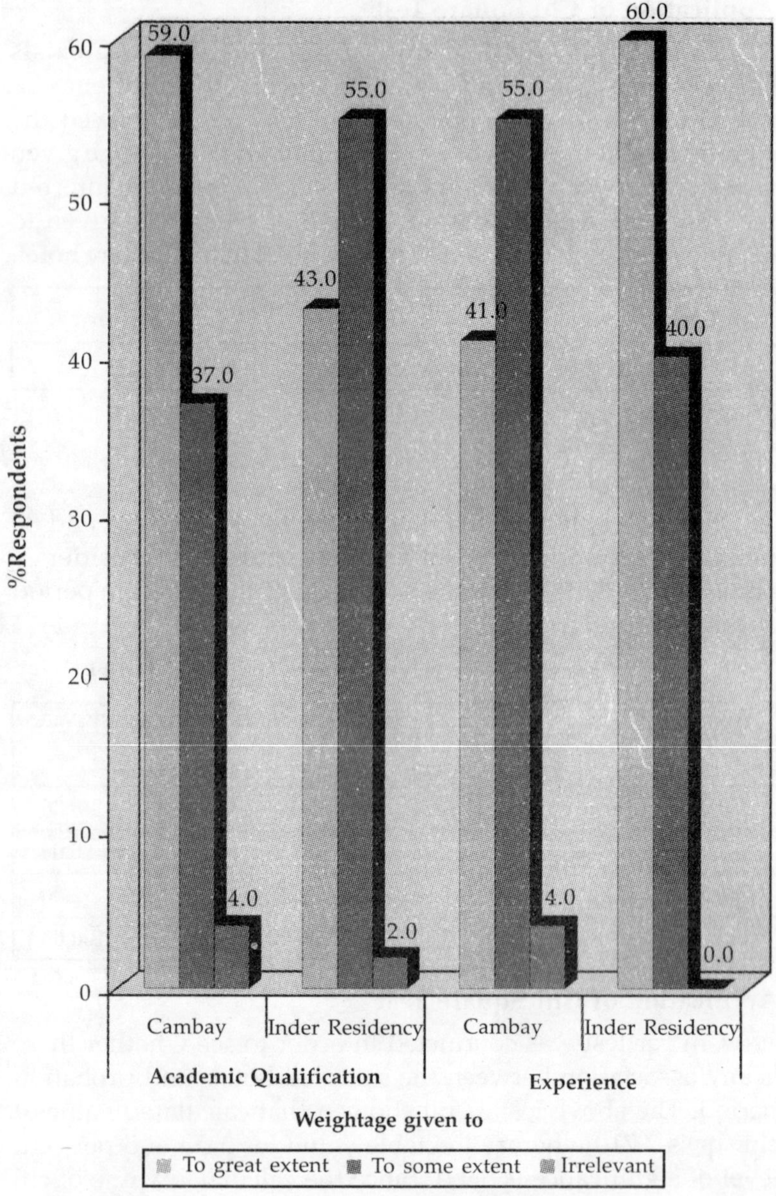

Fig. 4.11: Weightage given to Academic Qualification and Experience in Selection of Employees

between the sampled hotels and probation period. It can also be seen in the observation table that percentage of employees given no probation is just half in Cambay than Inder Residency.

Chi Square	D.f	Result
7.710	2	*

(* $p < 0.05$)

Training Programme in Hotels

Training Period in Hotels

Table 4.72 depicted that 59 per cent and 54 per cent respondent from Cambay and Inder Residency hotels Said that the hotel gives 1-3 months training to their employees at the time of appointment, 25 per cent and 35 per cent respondent from both the hotels said that there was no training provided to them in their respective department.

Table 4.72: Training Period at the Time of Appointment

Training Period	Cambay		Inder Residency	
	N	%	N	%
No Training	25	25.00	35	35.00
Upto 1 month	10	10.00	11	11.00
1-3 months	59	59.00	54	54.00
3-6 months	6	6.00	0	0.00
6 month - 1 year	0	0.00	0	0.00
Total	**100**	**100.00**	**100**	**100.00**

Application of Chi Square Test

Chi sqr test was applied to see whether there is any difference between the sampled hotels and training period at the time of appointment. The test result showed significant difference between the sampled hotels and training period at the time of appointment. ($\chi^2 = 7.936$, d.f = 3, $p < 0.05$). The observation tables indicated that percentage of employees given no training was less in Cambay than Inder Residency.

Chi Square	D.f	Result
7.936	3	*

(* $p < 0.05$)

Areas of Training Programme

Table 4.73 it is notable that maximum respondents from Cambay and Inder Residency respectively attended training programme to all respective area (Management, Marketing, Personnel, Finance, Information and Technology) and 17 per cent and 31 per cent respondents from both the hotels respectively attended training in management.

Table 4.73: Areas of Training Programme

Areas of Training Programme	Cambay		Inder Residency	
	N	%	N	%
Management	17	17.00	31	31.00
Marketing	6	6.00	16	16.00
Personnel	10	10.00	11	11.00
Finance	4	4.00	15	15.00
Information and Technology	7	7.00	11	11.00
All Above	50	50.00	37	37.00

Methods of Training

Table 4.74 clearly showed that Cambay followed separate training programme for their employees and Inder Residency followed training on the work for betterment for employees.

Table 4.74: Methods of Training followed by Hotels

Methods of Training	Cambay		Inder Residency	
	N	%	N	%
Training on the work	12	12.00	87	87.00
Separate Training Programme	78	78.00	10	10.00
Both	10	10.00	3	3.00
Total	**100**	**100.00**	**100**	**100.00**

Application of Chi Square Test

The above results of chi square test showed the method of training were significantly associated with sampled hotels. (χ = 113.133, d.f = 2, $p < 0.001$). It can easily be seen from observation tables that training on work was preferred in Inder Residency than Cambay. Whereas separate training programme was more prefer in Cambay than Inder Residency.

Chi Square	D.f	Result
113.133	2	***

(*** $p < 0.001$)

Utility of Training Programme

Table 4.75 reflected that training programme helps employees for better performance, job satisfaction and promotion in hotel industries.

Table 4.75: Training Programme Helps Employees

Training Programme Helps Employees	Cambay		Inder Residency	
	N	%	N	%
Better Performance	97	97.00	97	97.00
Job Satisfaction	94	94.00	61	61.00
Promotion	90	90.00	55	55.00

Satisfaction Level of Employee During the Training Programme

Table 4.76 indicated that 84 per cent and 90 per cent respondents from Cambay and Inder Residency hotels stated that they were satisfied with the training provided by their hotels. (*See table on next page*)

Application of Chi Square Test

To find out whether there was any association between sampled hotels and satisfaction level of employees, chi sqr test was applied. The above test result showed non significant association between sampled hotels and satisfaction level of employees. (χ^2 = 1.604, d.f = 2, NS).

Table 4.76: Satisfaction Level of Employee During the Training Programme

Satisfaction Level of Employee	Cambay		Inder Residency	
	N	%	N	%
To a great extent	19	19.00	21	21.00
To an extent	65	65.00	69	69.00
To a little extent	16	16.00	10	10.00
Total	**100**	**100.00**	**100**	**100.00**

Chi Square	D.f	Result
1.604	2	NS

Problems Faced by Employees During Training Programme

Table 4.77 revealed that in Cambay, 55 employees felt that management not gave adequate time for training to their employees and 39 employees stated that they have no problem during the training programme while Inder Residency, 64 employees doesn't have any problem during training and 21 respondents felt that poor guidance provided by management during training programme.

Table 4.77: Problems Faced by Employees During Training Programme

Problems Faced by Employees	Cambay		Inder Residency	
	N	%	N	%
Favoritism	4	4.00	6	6.00
Poor guidance	2	2.00	21	21.00
Inadequate time	55	55.00	9	9.00
No problem	39	39.00	64	64.00
Total	**100**	**100.00**	**100**	**100.00**

Application of Chi Square Test

Test of association chi sqr was applied to find out whether significant difference exists between two hotels and problems faced by employees during training programme. It indicated that there was significant difference between two hotels and problems faced by employees during training programme. ($\chi^2 = 55.226$, d.f = 3, $p < 0.001$). The observed table indicated that employees of Inder Residency faced problem of 'Poor Guidance' than employees of Cambay hotel. Whereas 'Inadequate Time' problem were more faced by employees of Cambay than Inder Residency.

Chi Square	D.f	Result
55.226	3	***

(*** $p < 0.001$)

Working Environment in Hotels

Working Department of Employees

Table 4.78 depicted that maximum respondents were from Front Office, F and B Service, F and B Production and Housekeeping department from both Cambay and Inder Residency hotel. It is to be notable that these were the main department of hotels. *(See table 4.78 on next page)*

Working Hours of Employees

Table 4.79 described that there were different timing in each department. 8 and 9 hour was for general administration and those employee who were working in main department (Front Office, F and B Service, F and B Production and Housekeeping), there timing was 10 or an above 10 hours in hotels. Generally 4 shifts were running *i.e.,* (6 AM to 2 PM, 2 PM to 10 PM, 10 PM to 6 AM, 8 AM to 5 PM or 9:30 AM to 6:30 PM) in the hotels. *(See table 4.79 on next page)*

Table 4.78: Working Department of Employees

Working Department of Employees	Cambay		Inder Residency	
	N	%	N	%
Purchase	1	1.00	1	1.00
Sales and Marketing	9	9.00	4	4.00
F and B Production	12	12.00	7	7.00
F and B Service	16	16.00	25	25.00
Accounts and Finance	6	6.00	5	5.00
HRD	1	1.00	3	3.00
General Administration	6	6.00	7	7.00
Information System	3	3.00	3	3.00
Personnel and Welfare	3	3.00	2	2.00
Front Office	18	18.00	14	14.00
Store	3	3.00	1	1.00
Security	2	2.00	4	4.00
Time Office	3	3.00	2	2.00
Engineering	4	4.00	5	5.00
House Keeping	7	7.00	13	13.00
Travel Desk	2	2.00	4	4.00
Other	4	4.00	0	0.00
Total	**100**	**100.00**	**100**	**100.00**

Table 4.79: Working Hours of Employee

Working Hours	Cambay		Inder Residency	
	N	%	N	%
Below 7 hours	0	0.00	0	0.00
7 hour	1	1.00	0	0.00
8 hour	14	14.00	25	25.00
9 hour	51	51.00	49	49.00
10 hour	4	4.00	10	10.00
Above 10 hour	30	30.00	16	16.00
Total	**100**	**100.00**	**100**	**100.00**

Working Conditions in Hotels

Table 4.80 revealed that 78 per cent employees from Cambay and 88 per cent employees from Inder Residency hotel stated that working environment was healthy and good and they were satisfied with the working conditions.

Table 4.80: Working Conditions in Hotels

Working Conditions are Good in Hotel's	Cambay		Inder Residency	
	N	%	N	%
Yes	78	78.00	88	88.00
No	22	22.00	12	12.00
Total	**100**	**100.00**	**100**	**100.00**

Application of Chi Square Test

Test of association was applied to see whether the sampled hotels were associated with good working conditions or not. The above test result showed non significant association between the sampled hotels and good working conditions. ($\chi^2 = 3.544$, d.f = 1, NS).

Chi Square	D.f	Result
3.544	1	NS

Satisfied with the Working Hours

Table 4.81 indicated that most of the employee from Cambay and Inder Residency hotel satisfied with the working hours. Only few employees *i.e.,* 10 per cent from Cambay and 13 per cent from Inder Residency were not satisfied with the working hours. (*See table 4.81 on next page*)

Application of Chi Square Test

To find out whether there was any difference between the sampled hotels and satisfaction with the working hours, chi sqr test was conducted. The result showed that calculated value of chi sqr is 4.195 and the table value for 3 d.f at 5 per cent level of significance is 7.815. Since the calculated value of

Table 4.81: Satisfied With the Working Hours

Satisfied with the Working Hours	Cambay		Inder Residency	
	N	%	N	%
Completely satisfied	21	21.00	22	22.00
Satisfied	69	69.00	65	65.00
Partially satisfied	10	10.00	9	9.00
Not Satisfied	0	0.00	4	4.00
Total	**100**	**100.00**	**100**	**100.00**

chi sqr is less than table value. It showed that there was non-significant difference between the sampled hotels and satisfaction with the working hours.

Chi Square	D.f	Result
4.195	3	NS

Salary, Bonus and Allowances in Hotels

Salary According to Nature of Job

Table 4.82 revealed that more than ¾ respondents from both the hotels were agreed that adequate salary paid by management to their employees.

Table 4.82: Salary According to Nature of Job

Salary According to Nature of Job	Cambay		Inder Residency	
	N	%	N	%
Yes	90	90.00	82	82.00
No	10	10.00	18	18.00
Total	**100**	**100.00**	**100**	**100.00**

Application of Chi Square Test

The result of chi sqr test in the above table showed that there was no significant difference exists between two hotels and salary according to nature of job. ($\chi^2 = 2.658$, d.f = 1, NS).

Chi Square	D.f	Result
2.658	1	NS

Management Considers Employee's Qualifications an Expertise while Deciding Salaries and Allowances

Table 4.83 showed that employees of Cambay and Inder Residency hotel reported that management considered employee's qualification and expertise while deciding salaries, allowances and pre-requisites.

Table 4.83: Management Considers Employee's Qualifications and Expertise while Deciding Salaries and Allowances

Management Considers Employee's Qualification	Cambay		Inder Residency	
	N	%	N	%
Always	25	25.00	10	10.00
Often	15	15.00	35	35.00
Normally	60	60.00	55	55.00
Total	**100**	**100.00**	**100**	**100.00**

Application of Chi Square Test

Test of association was applied to see whether any significance difference exists between two hotels and management consideration for employee's qualification or not. The test result showed that significant difference exists between two hotels and management consideration for employee's qualification. ($\chi^2 = 14.646$, d.f = 2, $p < 0.001$). The observation table indicated that in Cambay hotel, management always considers employee's qualification whereas this percentage was less in Inder Residency.

Chi Square	D.f	Result
14.646	2	***

(*** $p < 0.001$)

Overtime Received by the Employees

Table 4.84 clearly indicated that about half of the employees from Cambay and Inder Residency hotels got overtime and rest half were not receiving overtime. It is notable that excess workload in some department in hotels. So employees of some department getting overtime to fulfill the work load.

Table 4.84: Overtime Received by the Employees

Overtime Received by the Employees	Cambay		Inder Residency	
	N	%	N	%
Yes	45	45.00	49	49.00
No	55	55.00	51	51.00
Total	**100**	**100.00**	**100**	**100.00**

Application of Chi Square Test

In order to test whether sampled hotels and overtime received by employees were associated with each other or not, chi sqr test was applied. The result clearly indicated that there was non significant association between two hotels and overtime received by employees. (χ^2 = 0.321, d.f = 1, NS).

Chi Square	D.f	Result
0.321	1	NS

Bonus Received by the Employees

Table 4.85 has been shown that Cambay hotel generally gave bonus to their employees while Inder Residency never gave bonus to their employees.

Table 4.85: Bonus Received by the Employees

Bonus Received by the Employees	Cambay		Inder Residency	
	N	%	N	%
Normally	85	85.00	5	5.00
Never	15	15.00	95	95.00
Total	**100**	**100.00**	**100**	**100.00**

Application of Chi Square Test

Test of association was applied to see whether there was any association between the sampled hotels and bonus received by the employees or not. The result showed that there was significant association between the sampled hotels and bonus received by the employees. The observation table indicated that percentage of employees in Cambay hotel receiving bonus was high than percentage of employees receiving bonus in Inder Residency.

Chi Square	D.f	Result
129.293	1	***

(*** $p < 0.001$)

Allowances Received by the Employees

Table 4.86 visualized that 67 per cent and 53 per cent respondents from Cambay and Inder Residency respectively received the vehicle/petrol allowances while 74 per cent and 41 per cent received the telephone allowances. 8 per cent and 36 per cent respondents received medical benefits, 18 per cent and 6 per cent respondents received children education allowances and 56 per cent and 6 per cent respondents received Entertainment allowances.

Table 4.86: Allowances Received by the Employees

Types of Allowances	Cambay		Inder Residency	
	N	%	N	%
Medical	8	8.00	36	36.00
Children Education	18	18.00	6	6.00
Vehicle/Petrol	67	67.00	53	53.00
Telephone	74	74.00	41	41.00
Entertainment	56	56.00	6	6.00

Basis for Allowances Paid

Table 4.87 showed that it is notable that in Cambay hotel, employees received maximum allowances *i.e.*, children education, vehicle/petrol allowances, telephone and entertainment allowances on fixed basis and only medical allowances received on actual basis while in Inder Residency, employees received medical, children education and entertainment allowances on fixed basis and vehicle/petrol and telephone allowances on actual basis.

Table 4.87: Basis for Allowances Paid

Allowances	Cambay				Inder Residency			
	Actual		Fixed		Actual		Fixed	
	N	%	N	%	N	%	N	%
Medical	7	7.00	0	0.00	0	00.00	32	32.00
Children Education	0	00.00	18	18.00	0	0.00	4	4.00
Vehicle/Petrol	0	00.00	64	64.00	49	49.00	0	00.00
Telephone	0	00.00	72	72.00	34	34.00	0	00.00
Entertainment	0	00.00	54	54.00	0	0.00	3	3.00

Basic Facilities Provided by Hotels to Employees

Accommodation Facilities

Table 4.88 showed that nearly per cent respondents from Cambay and Inder Residency were not getting accommodation facilities provided by the hotels and all the employees from both the hotels received HRA in the absence of housing facility.

Table 4.88: Accommodation Facilities Provided to the Employees

Accommodation Facilities	Cambay		Inder Residency	
	N	%	N	%
Yes	4	4.00	1	1.00
No	96	96.00	99	99.00
Total	**100**	**100.00**	**100**	**100.00**

Transportation Facilities

Table 4.89 revealed that Cambay hotel, management provided transportation facilities to their employees while Inder Residency, management not providing transportation facilities to their employees.

Table 4.89: Transportation Facilities Provided by the Hotels

Transportation Facility	Cambay		Inder Residency	
	N	%	N	%
Yes	100	100.00	0	0.00
No	0	0.00	100	100.00
Total	**100**	**100.00**	**100**	**100.00**

Uniform in Hotels

Table 4.90 All the respondents from both the hotels reported that uniform was compulsory in their respective department.

Table 4.90: Uniform is Compulsory in Hotels

Uniform is Compulsory	Cambay		Inder Residency	
	N	%	N	%
Yes	100	100.00	100	100.00
No	0	0.00	0	0.00
Total	**100**	**100.00**	**100**	**100.00**

Medical Facilities

Table 4.91 visualized that all employees were stated that there was no hospital/dispensary facility available in hotel area. In Cambay hotel, management provided ESI facility to their employees for treatment while Inder Residency, management provided cash reimbursement for treatment to their employees. The survey also clearly showed that both the hotels were not provided the medical benefits to the employee's family members.

Table 4.91: Dispensary/Hospital Facility Available in Hotels

Medical Facilities	Cambay		Inder Residency	
	N	%	N	%
Yes	0	00.00	0	00.00
No	100	100.00	100	100.00
Total	**100**	**100.00**	**100**	**100.00**

Motivation Methods in Hotels

Motivation Method Adopted by Hotel Management

In the opinion of Cambay hotel management motivated employees by giving monetary benefits (51%), by promotion (25%) and management motivated employees by encouragement (14%) and by giving rewards (10%) while in Inder Residency management motivated by encouragement method (70%) and by giving reward (15%). (Table 4.92)

Table 4.92: Motivation Method Adopted by Hotel Management

Motivation Method	Cambay		Inder Residency	
	N	%	N	%
Giving reward	10	10.00	15	15.00
Monetary benefits	51	51.00	10	10.00
Promotion	25	25.00	5	5.00
Encouragement	14	14.00	70	70.00

Effect of Motivation on Productivity

Table 4.93 showed that 97 per cent and 90 per cent employees from Cambay and Inder Residency hotel respectively felt that motivation methods generally increased productivity. (*See table 4.93 on next page*)

Rewards and Incentive Plans in Hotels

Encouragement for using New Methods and Creative Ideas

Table 4.94 clearly indicated that generally management encourage to employees for using new methods and creative ideas. (*See table 4.94 on next page*)

Table 4.93: Effect of Motivation on Productivity

Frequency of Increase Productivity	Cambay		Inder Residency	
	N	%	N	%
Often	97	97.00	90	90.00
Normally	3	3.00	10	10.00
Total	**100**	**100.00**	**100**	**100.00**

Table 4.94: Encouragement for using New Methods and Creative Ideas

Encouragement for Applying New Methods and Creative Ideas	Cambay		Inder Residency	
	N	%	N	%
Often	64	64.00	49	49.00
Normally	31	31.00	40	40.00
Rarely	5	5.00	11	11.00
Total	**100**	**100.00**	**100**	**100.00**

Application of Chi Square Test

The above results of chi sqr test showed that there was no significant difference between sampled hotels and their encouragement for using new methods and creative ideas. (χ^2 = 5.382, d.f = 2, NS).

Chi Square	D.f	Result
5.382	2	NS

Opinion about Appreciation by Management

Table 4.95 66 per cent employees of Cambay hotel reported that management often appreciated to them for increasing productivity while 72 per cent employees of Inder Residency felt that management normally appreciated to them for increasing productivity.

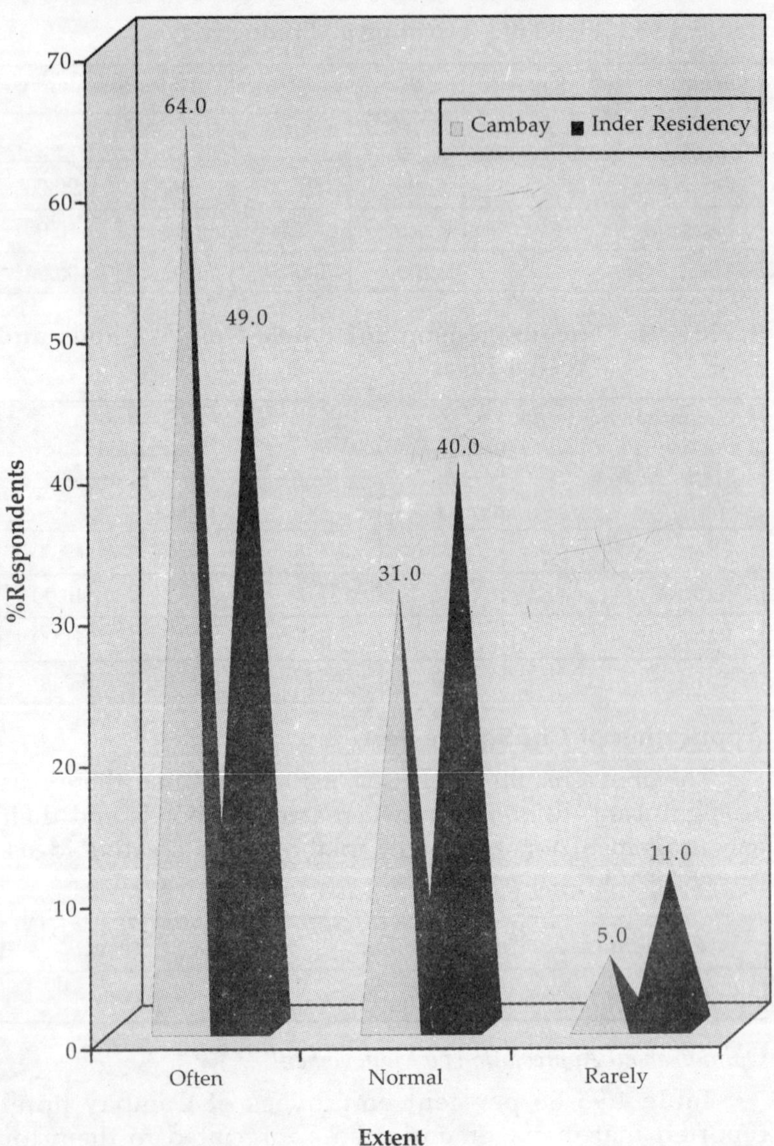

Fig. 4.12: Encouragement for using New Methods and Creative Ideas

Table 4.95: Employee's Appreciated for Increasing Productivity

Employee's Appreciated by Management	Cambay		Inder Residency	
	N	%	N	%
Often	66	66.00	22	22.00
Normally	25	25.00	72	72.00
Rarely	9	9.00	6	6.00
Total	**100**	**100.00**	**100**	**100.00**

Application of Chi Square Test

To find out whether any significant difference exists between two hotels and employees appreciated for increasing productivity or not, chi sqr test was applied. It clearly indicated that there was significant difference between two hotels and employees appreciated for increasing productivity. ($\chi^2 = 45.373$, d.f = 2, $p < 0.001$). The observation table showed that percentage of employees appreciated by management was higher in Cambay hotel than Inder Residency.

Chi Square	D.f	Result
45.373	2	***

(*** $p < 0.001$)

Table 4.96 shows that most of the respondent felt that management often appreciated their honesty, sincerity and hard working of the employees.

Table 4.96: Honesty, Sincerity and Hard Working of Employees are Appreciated by the Hotel Management

Honesty, Sincerity and Hard Working of Employees are Appreciated	Cambay		Inder Residency	
	N	%	N	%
Often	72	72.00	59	59.00
Normally	20	20.00	30	30.00
Rarely	8	8.00	11	11.00
Total	**100**	**100.00**	**100**	**100.00**

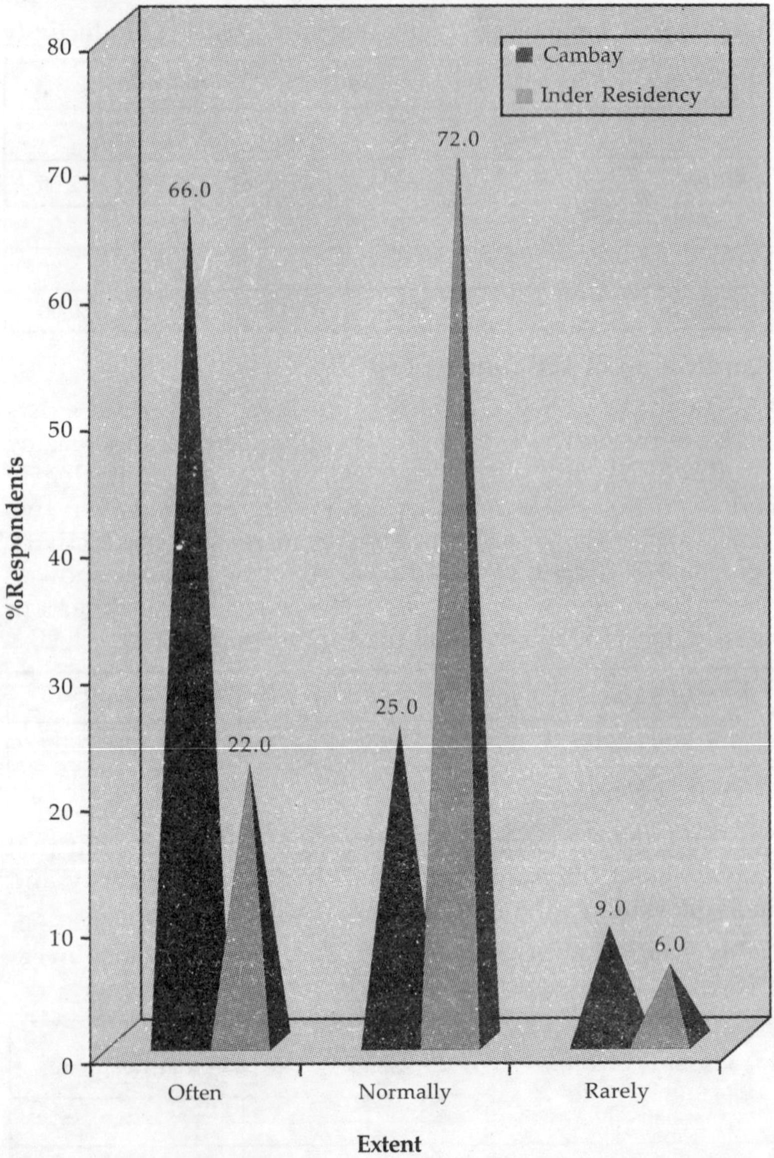

Cambay
Inder Residency

%Respondents
0
10
20
30
40
50
60
70
80

66.0
22.0
25.0
72.0
9.0
6.0

Often
Normally
Rarely

Extent

Fig. 4.13: Employees Appreciated for Increasing Productivity

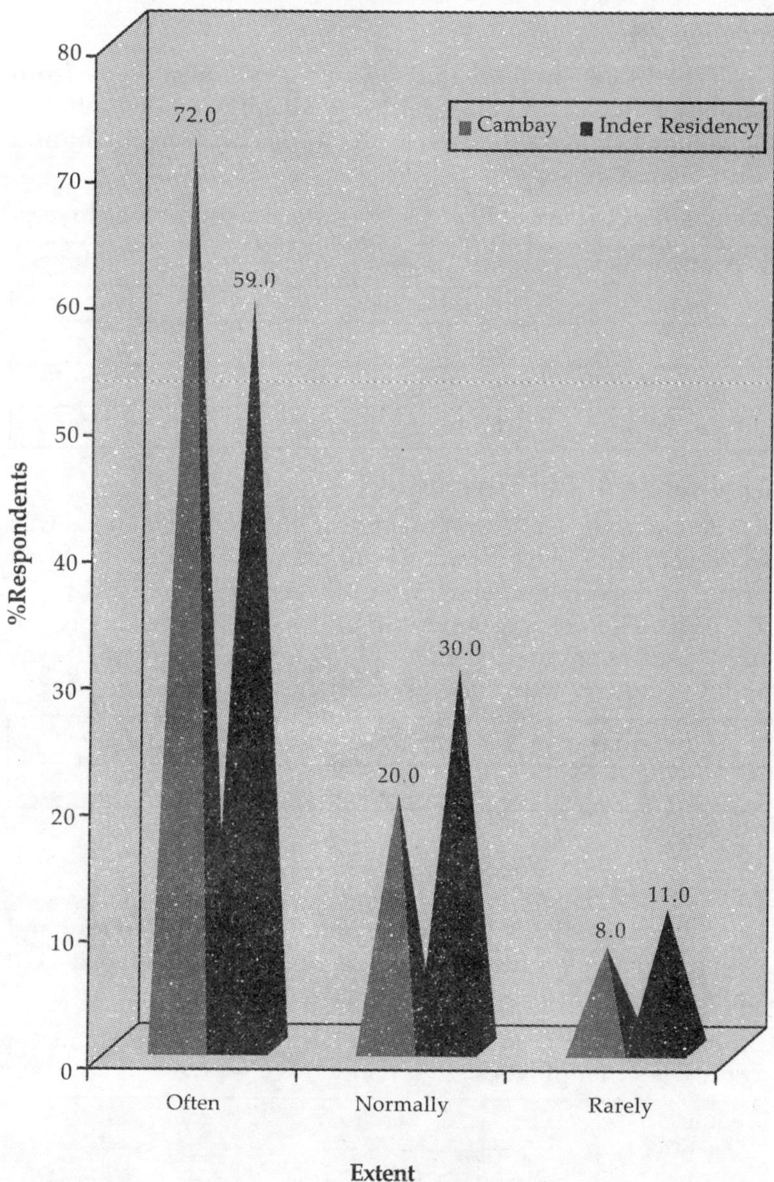

Fig. 4.14: Honesty, Sincerity and Hard Working of Employees are Appreciated by the Hotel Management

Incentive Plan for Employees

Table 4.97 showed that 85 per cent employees from Cambay hotel and 70 per cent Inder Residency hotel felt that management gave incentive to them for encouragement and better work.

Table 4.97: Incentive Plan for Encouragement for Employees

Incentive Plans	Cambay		Inder Residency	
	N	%	N	%
Yes	85	85.00	70	70.00
No	15	15.00	30	30.00
Total	**100**	**100.00**	**100**	**100.00**

Application of Chi Square Test

The above result of chi sqr test showed that there was significant difference between sampled hotels and incentive plans for encouragement for employees. ($\chi^2 = 6.452$, d.f = 1, $p < 0.05$). The observation table indicated that percentage of employees receiving incentive plans for encouragement was high in Cambay than Inder Residency.

Chi Square	D.f	Result
6.452	1	*

(* $p < 0.05$)

Kinds of Incentive Plan

Table 4.98 shows that 54 respondents from Cambay and 32 per cent respondent from Inder Residency said that management gave monetary benefits to them.

Table 4.98: Kinds of Incentive Plan for Encouragement for Employees

Kinds of Incentive Plan	Cambay		Inder Residency	
	N	%	N	%
Monetary	54	54.00	32	32.00
Non-Monetary	46	46.00	68	68.00
Total	100	100.00	100	100.00

Application of Chi Square Test

Test of association chi sqr was applied to see whether kinds of incentive plans were associated with sampled hotels or not. The test showed that there was significant association between sampled hotels and kinds of incentive plan. ($\chi^2 = 9.874$, d.f = 1, $p < 0.01$). Percentage of monetary rewards for encouragement of employees was preferred in Cambay hotel than Inder Residency whereas non-monetary rewards were preferred in Inder Residency hotel than Cambay hotel.

Chi Square	D.f	Result
9.874	1	**

(** $p < 0.01$)

Nature of Monetary Benefits

Table 4.99 reveals that, management gave monetary benefits to the employees. In Cambay Hotel 68 per cent employees reported that management gave increment to employees, 41 per cent said that hotel gave more allowance and 7 per cent said that management gave individual bonus for encouragement while Inder Residency, 92 per cent employees said that management gave increment and 12 per cent felt that management gave more allowances for encouragement.

Table 4.99: Nature of Monetary Benefits.

Monetary Benefits	Cambay		Inder Residency	
	N	%	N	%
Increment	68	68.00	92	92.00
More allowance	41	41.00	12	12.00
Individual bonus	7	7.00	4	4.00

Nature of Non-monetary Benefits

Table 4.100 depicts that, management also gave non-monetary benefits to their employees. In Cambay Hotel 71 per cent employees reported that management gave appreciation, 28 per cent employees said that hotel gave more facilities and 8 per cent employees said that management gave reward for encouragement to them while Inder Residency, 44 per cent employees said that management gave appreciation and 11 per cent employees felt that management gave more facilities and 4 per cent employees said that management gave reward for encouragement.

Table 4.100: Nature of Non-monetary Benefits.

Non-monetary Benefits	Cambay		Inder Residency	
	N	%	N	%
Appreciation	71	71.00	44	44.00
More facilities	28	28.00	11	11.00
Reward	8	8.00	4	4.00

Promotion and Demotion Policy in Hotels

Basis of Promotion

Table 4.101 shows that 87 per cent and 86 per cent employees from Cambay hotel and Inder Residency hotel respectively reported that both seniority and merit basis was adopted for promotion by their management.

Table 4.101: Basis of Promotion

Basis of Promotion	Cambay		Inder Residency	
	N	%	N	%
Seniority	4	4.00	6	6.00
Merit basis	9	9.00	8	8.00
Seniority and Merit basis	87	87.00	86	86.00
Total	**100**	**100.00**	**100**	**100.00**

Application of Chi Square Test

The above test result showed that there was non significance difference between the sampled hotels on the basis of promotion. ($\chi^2 = 0.465$, d.f = 2, NS)

Chi Square	D.f	Result
0.465	2	NS

Promotion on Due Time

Table 4.102 shows that 71 per cent employees of Cambay and 78 per cent employees of Inder Residency felt that they were not promoted on due time.

Table 4.102: Employee's Promotion on Due Time

Employee's Promoted on Due Time	Cambay		Inder Residency	
	N	%	N	%
Yes	29	29.00	22	22.00
No	71	71.00	78	78.00
Total	**100**	**100.00**	**100**	**100.00**

Application of Chi Square Test

To find out whether significance difference exists between the two hotels and employees promotion on due time, chi sqr test was applied. The calculated value of chi sqr was 1.291 and the table value for 1 d.f at 5 per cent level of significance is 3.841. Since the calculated chi sqr value is less than table value. Therefore no significance difference exists between the two hotels and employees promotion on due time.

Chi Square	D.f	Result
1.291	1	NS

Effect of Timely Promotion

Table 4.103 has been shown that most of the employees from both the hotels felt that timely promotion increase employee's efficiency, more responsibility with job and increases their monetary benefits.

Table 4.103: Effect of Timely Promotion on Employees

Effect of Timely Promotion	Cambay		Inder Residency	
	N	%	N	%
Increased efficiency at work	34	34.00	28	28.00
More responsible with job	30	30.00	23	23.00
Increased monetary benefits	28	28.00	44	44.00

Reason for Delay in Promotion

Table 4.104 has been shown that in Cambay Hotel, 25 per cent employees stated that delay in employee's promotion due to not completed the probation period, 17 per cent employees stated that they were not promoted due to head of department and 14 per cent employees stated that they were not trained or skilled. On the other hand in Inder Residency hotel, 34 per cent employees said that they were not promoted due to head of department, 23 per cent employees stated that no vacancy at higher level, 18 per cent employees stated that they were not trained or skilled.

Table 4.104: Reason for Delay in Promotion

Reason for Delay in Promotion	Cambay		Inder Residency	
	N	%	N	%
Head of Department	17	17.00	34	34.00
No vacancy at higher level	3	3.00	23	23.00
Not trained or skilled	14	14.00	18	18.00
Not completed the probation period	25	25.00	10	10.00

Employee's Demotion in Hotels

Table 4.105 revealed that 94 per cent and 97 per cent employees from both the hotels were not getting demoted by the management.

Table 4.105: Employee's Demotion in Hotels

Employee gets Demotion	Cambay		Inder Residency	
	N	%	N	%
Yes	6	6.00	3	3.00
No	94	94.00	97	97.00
Total	**100**	**100.00**	**100**	**100.00**

Reasons for Employee's Demotion

Table 4.106 revealed that only few employees were demoted due to not maintain punctuality, improper working and misbehave with management.

Table 4.106: Reasons for Employee's Demotion

Reasons for Demotion	Cambay		Inder Residency	
	N	%	N	%
Not punctual	3	3.00	1	1.00
Improper working	1	1.00	0	0.00
Misbehave with management	2	2.00	2	2.00

Industrial Relation

Relation between Employees and Hotel Management

Table 4.107 depicted that 83 per cent employees from Cambay and 93 per cent employees from Inder Residency hotel felt that they have good relations with their management.

Table 4.107: Relation between Employees and Hotel Management

Relation between Employees and Hotel Management	Cambay		Inder Residency	
	N	%	N	%
Excellent	25	25.00	28	28.00
Good	58	58.00	65	65.00
Normal	17	17.00	7	7.00
Total	**100**	**100.00**	**100**	**100.00**

Application of Chi Square Test

Test of association was applied to see relation between employees and hotel management is associated with sampled hotels or not. The test result showed that there was non significant association between the sampled hotels and relation between employees and hotel management. (χ^2 = 4.735, d.f = 2, NS).

Chi Square	D.f	Result
4.735	2	NS

Dispute between Employees and Hotel Management

Table 4.108 indicated that 58 per cent employees from Cambay and 71 per cent employees from Inder Residency hotel never faced dispute with their management.

Table 4.108: Dispute between Employees and Hotel Management

Dispute between Employees and Hotel Management	Cambay		Inder Residency	
	N	%	N	%
Often	14	14.00	10	10.00
Normally	28	28.00	19	19.00
Never	58	58.00	71	71.00
Total	**100**	**100.00**	**100**	**100.00**

Application of Chi Square Test

To find out whether significant difference exists between the two hotels and dispute between employee and hotel management, chi sqr test was conducted. The above test result showed that there was non significant difference between the two hotels and dispute between employee and hotel management. (χ^2 = 3.700, d.f = 2, NS).

Chi Square	D.f	Result
3.700	2	NS

Effective Grievance Handling Procedure

Table 4.109 clearly showed that Cambay and Inder Residency hotels, management have an effective grievance handling procedure for their employees.

Table 4.109: Management has an Effective Grievance Handling Procedure for the Employees

Effective Grievance Handling Procedure	Cambay		Inder Residency	
	N	%	N	%
Yes	79	79.00	86	86.00
No	21	21.00	14	14.00
Total	**100**	**100.00**	**100**	**100.00**

Application of Chi Square Test

To find out whether significant difference exists between the two hotels and grievance handling procedure for the employees, chi sqr test was conducted. The above test result showed that there was non significant difference between the two hotels and grievance handling procedure for the employees. (χ^2 = 1.697, d.f = 1, NS).

Chi Square	D.f	Result
1.697	1	NS

Manger's Behaviour towards Employees

Table 4.110 showed that normally manager's behaviour towards their employee was impartial.

Table 4.110: Manger's Impartial Behaviour toward Employees

Impartial Behaviour	Cambay		Inder Residency	
	N	%	N	%
Often	25	25.00	29	29.00
Normally	70	70.00	64	64.00
Rarely	5	5.00	7	7.00
Total	**100**	**100.00**	**100**	**100.00**

Application of Chi Square Test

Test of association was applied to see whether there was any association between the sampled hotels or manger's behaviour towards employees, chi sqr test was applied. The above test result showed that calculated value of chi sqr is 0.898 and table value for 2 d.f at 5 per cent level of significance is 5.991. Since the calculated value of chi sqr is less than table value. The above test result showed that there was non significant difference between the sampled hotels or manger's behaviour towards employees.

Chi Square	D.f	Result
0.898	2	NS

Job Enrichment in Hotels

Career Development Plans for Employees

Table 4.111 revealed that 79 per cent employees from Cambay and 86 per cent employees from Inder Residency hotel reported that management has definite plans for career development for them.

Table 4.111: Career Development Plans for Employees

Career Development Plans for Employees	Cambay		Inder Residency	
	N	%	N	%
Yes	79	79.00	86	86.00
No	21	21.00	14	14.00
Total	**20**	**100.00**	**20**	**100.00**

Application of Chi Square Test

To find out whether significant difference exists between the two hotels and career development plans for the employees, chi sqr test was conducted. The above test result showed that there was non significant difference between the two hotels and career development plans for the employees. ($\chi^2 = 1.697$, d.f = 1, NS).

Chi Square	D.f	Result
1.697	1	NS

Managers Sympathetic in Dealing with the Problems of Employees

Table 4.112 indicated that managers were generally very sympathetic in dealing day to day problems of employees.

Table 4.112: Managers Sympathetic in Dealing with the Problems of Employees

Manager's Sympathetic	Cambay		Inder Residency	
	N	%	N	%
Always	25	25.00	15	15.00
Often	65	65.00	60	60.00
Normally	10	10.00	25	25.00
Total	**100**	**100.00**	**100**	**100.00**

Application of Chi Square Test

The above result of chi sqr test shows that there was significant difference between sampled hotels and managers sympathetic in dealing with the problems of employees. ($\chi^2 = 8.981$, d.f = 2, $p < 0.05$). The observation table indicated that percentage of managers in Cambay hotel having sympathy in dealing with the problems of employees was higher than Inder Residency.

Chi Square	D.f	Result
8.981	2	*

(* $p < 0.05$)

Job Satisfaction in Hotels

Salaries, Allowances and Pre-requisites are Attractive Considering for Job Responsibilities

Table 4.113 revealed that 65 per cent employees from Cambay and 22 per cent employees from Inder Residency hotel felt that salaries, allowances and pre-requisites were attractive considering for job responsibilities whereas 28 per cent employees from Cambay 72 per cent employees from Inder Residency reported that salaries allowances and pre-requisites were average considering for job responsibilities.

Table 4.113: Salaries, Allowances and Pre-requisites are Attractive Considering for Job Responsibilities

Salaries, Allowances and Pre-requisites are Attractive Considering for Job Responsibilities	Cambay		Inder Residency	
	N	%	N	%
Attractive	65	65.00	22	22.00
Average	28	28.00	72	72.00
Unattractive	7	7.00	6	6.00
Total	**100**	**100.00**	**100**	**100.00**

Job Provides Enough Opportunities to Utilise the Manager's Skills and Abilities

Table 4.114 revealed that nearly 78 per cent employees from Cambay and 81 per cent employees from Inder Residency hotel said that job provides enough opportunities to utilise their skills and abilities up to some extent.

Table 4.114: Job Provides Enough Opportunities to Utilise the Manager's Skills and Abilities

Job Provides Enough Opportunities to Utilise the Manager's Skills and Abilities	Cambay		Inder Residency	
	N	%	N	%
Fully	22	22.00	19	19.00
Up to some extent	78	78.00	81	81.00
Total	**100**	**100.00**	**100**	**100.00**

Social Security Facilities in Hotels

Table 4.115 clearly indicated that Cambay and Inder residency hotel management provided provident fund (P.F.) and gratuity to their employees and there was no pension scheme for the employees.

Table 4.115: Types of Social Security Facilities Provided by Hotel Management to their Employees

Social Security Facilities	Cambay		Inder Residency	
	N	%	N	%
Provident Fund	65	65.00	87	87.00
Pension	0	0.00	0	0.00
Gratuity	80	80.00	20	20.00

CHAPTER

5 Research Findings and Suggestions

THE HOTEL INDUSTRY comprises a major part of the Tourism industry. The hotel and tourism industries are complementary and are also highly connected by the country's overall economic performance. There are many different sectors in the tourism industry, and one of these is the hotel industry. Without an adequate development of hotel resources, all the national scenery, all the climate virtues and all sporting and recreational facilities will not suffice to sustain a good volume of tourist's trade. The expansion of tourism will inevitably bring about the development of the hotel industry. Indian tourism and hospitality sector has reached new heights today. Travelers are taking new interests in the country which leads to the upgrading of hospitality sector. Indian tourism and hospitality sector has reached new heights today.

Growth and Development of Tourism and Hotel Industry

The development of hotel industry goes back to 19th century. Hotel industry also known as travel and tourism industry. The travel and tourism industry encompasses lodging operations, transport activities, F and B operations and retail stores. According to World Tourism Organization (WTO) Madrid, Tourism has now become the world's largest industry, ahead of automobiles and petroleum products. The hotel industry has a direct impact on rural development. The industry has encouraged cottage industries in many ways – handlooms for furnishing, carpets, handicrafts etc.

Tourism in the World

The world tourism has faced various ups and downs during 2006 to 2010. In past few years it was affected by outbreak of H_1N_1 influenza virus, terrorism attacks and natural disasters. Among top ten countries of the world in terms of growth rate of foreign tourist arrivals. France was recorded with 77.90 Mn. Foreign tourist arrivals and ranked first. France, USA, Spain and China were top four countries in 2010 with highest number of foreign tourist arrivals.

Tourism in the Country

Tourism has been one of the most profitable industries in the country. This industry contributes to substantial amount of foreign exchange also. Foreign tourist arrivals in Indian increased from 2.29 Mn. To 5.58 Mn. from 1996 to 2010. However the year 2009 shows decline in foreign tourist arrivals in India various reasons such as global slowdown, terrorism attacks and natural disasters etc.

Tourism in the Rajasthan State

Rajasthan is famous for textiles, semi-precious stones and handicrafts. The attractive designs of jewellery and clothes are eye-catching and invite shoppers. Rajasthani furniture has intricate carvings and bright colours. Rajasthani handicrafts are in demand due to the intricate work on them.

Rajasthan's almost 80 per cent of the places are regarded as the places of tourist interest; these are — Udaipur — the city of lakes, Jaipur — the Pink City, Ajmer — the white marble Baradari on the Anasagar lake is exquisite, Dilwara Temple of Mount Abu, Jain Temples, Ranakpur Temple, Kumbhalgarh, Haldi Gaati, Jantar Mantar, Chittorgarh Fort, Lake Palace, City Palaces, Jaisalmer Havelis are part of the true architectural heritage of India.

Major festivals in the state are Camel Festival of Bikaner, Nagaur Fair, Desert Festival of Jaisalmer, Elephant Festival of Jaipur, Gangaur and Teej Festival celebrated all over the state, Mewar Festival in Udaipur, Urs in Ajmer Sharif, Marwar Festival at Jodhpur and Camel and Cattle Fair of Pushkar; which attract domestic and foreign tourist.

The above attractive tourists destinations and culturally rich festivals are centre of attraction for tourists in Rajasthan state. Every year domestic as well as foreign tourists turn up

Rajasthan state to enjoy these beautiful places and festivals. Owing to tourist arrivals, demand of hotel industry increases and specially upper class and foreign tourists prefer luxurious environment which results in increased demand of five star hotel industry.

Growth and Development of Tourism in the State of Rajasthan

Rajasthan attracted 14 per cent of total foreign visitors during 2009-10 which is fourth highest in all states of India. It positioned fourth place also in Domestic tourist visitors. The rate of growth of tourism in Rajasthan has been sustained at around 5-7 per cent per annum in the last few years. Domestic tourist in Rajasthan increased from 73.70 Lac to 255 Lac from 2000 to 2010. Foreign tourists increased from 6.23 Lac to 13 Lac in the same period.

Tourism in the Gujarat State

Gujarat also known as the Manchester of the East was famous for textile industries from the medieval times is visited by numerous big and small business travelers to make trade; they form the bulk of the patrons in hotels. Gujarat has undertaken extensive efforts to develop tourism activities and to attract greater number of tourists. Gujarat has immense potential to become a major tourist destination. The state has many enchanting tourist places, memorable historic monuments and sacred pilgrimages, depicting the glorious cultural heritage, which can attract both Indian and international travelers. The state has important pilgrimage places like Dwarka, Somnath, Dakor, Ambaji, etc., for Hindus, Udwada, Navsari and Surat for Parsees, Palitana, Girnar, etc., for Jains. In Gujarat Ahmadabad, Ambaji, Dwarka and Somnath are the major tourist destinations accounting for over 33 per cent (47.41 lacs) of the total tourist flow in the state. Celebration of festivals Navaratri Mahotsav, Patangotsav, Sharadotsav and Rannotsav, Kite Flying Festival, Dance Festival — Modhera, Kutch Mahotsav and Bhadra Purnima are the most important festivals of Gujarat; which attract lot of tourist and increases development opportunities for hotel industry in Gujarat state.

Growth and Development of Tourism in the State of Gujarat

The State Government decided the year 2006 as 'Tourism year', keeping in view the importance of tourism industry as an important factor of the development process and generator of large scale employment. The number of tourist (Domestic and Foreign) who visited Gujarat in 2002-03 was only 66.69 lacs which increased by 85.84 lacs in 2003-04. No. of tourists increased from 121.48 lacs to 206.37 lacs during slab of 2005-06 to 2009-10.

Human Resource Development

Human Resource Development in hotel industries is a countrywide issue and the subject of human resource development is everlasting value. It has unending facets and one cannot say with certainty as to what ideal theme of developing of human resource. Human Resource Development is the frameworks for helping employees develop their personal and organizational skills, knowledge, and abilities. Human Resource Development includes such opportunities as employee training, employee career development, performance management and development, coaching, succession planning, key employee identification, tuition assistance, and organization development. The focus of all aspects of Human Resource Development is on developing the most superior workforce. According to the American Management Association, "Management is the process by which human and physical resource are guided into dynamic and viable organizational units that attain objectives to the satisfaction of those served, and with a high degree of morale and sense of attainment on the part of those providing the service."

Since hotel industry is one of the most important service industries of an economy, it requires efficient workforce to render quality services to its customer. Every customer expects quality of service and value of money he/she pays, it becomes crucial for hotel management to maintain cordial manpower to meet these expectations. To train, motivate and to develop competent and proficient manpower, human resource department is essential to hotel industry.

Hotel Industry

The Indian hotel industry was a slow-growing industry, but in recent years, the hotels sector has grown at a faster rate than GDP (Gross Domestic Product). Some countries have an official body with standard criteria for classifying hotels, but in many regions there are none. There have been attempts at unifying the classification system so that it becomes an internationally recognized and reliable standard but large differences exist in the quality of the accommodations within one category of hotel. Hotels in India are broadly classified into 7 categories (five star deluxe, five-star, four stars, and three stars, two star, and one-star and heritage hotels) by the Ministry of Tourism.

Star Hotels in Rajasthan State

Some of the five star hotels in Rajasthan are — Hotel Inder Residency, Taj Lake Palace, Country Inn, Rambagh Palace, Taj Jai Mahal Palace, Le Meridien, Taj Hari Mahal.

Star Hotels in Gujarat State

Some of the five star Hotels in Gujarat are — Cambay Grand, Hotel Taj Residency, Le Meridien, Holiday Inn, Fortune Landmark, The Pride.

The upper class family prefer to go star hotels, that's why this category of hotel give much emphasis on training and development of their employees as compare to other category of hotels; so we selected this topic "Human Resource Development in five star hotel industry" for our study. We selected two five star hotels — Hotel Inder Residency (Udaipur) and Hotel Cambay Grand (Ahmedabad).

Analysis of Field Work

The data for this investigation were collected from primary as well as secondary sources. For collection of primary data, the following two type of questionnaire were constructed and adopted.

(i) Questionnaire for management of hotel industries.

(ii) Questionnaire for employees of hotel industries.

The first questionnaire has been prepared to collect information relating to the managers of different categories (General Manager, Director Sales and Marketing, Financial Controller, Resident Manager, Personnel Director, F and B Controller, GM HR, Executive Chief, Front office Manager etc.). In this category, we prepared a list of 50 managers for each selected hotels, out of them we randomly selected 20 managers from Cambay hotel and 20 from Inder Residency hotel, so in all 40 managers were selected for this study.

The second questionnaire was prepared to collect information relating to employees of these categories (*i.e.*, Personnel Officer, Executive HR, Front Office Executive, House Keeping Executive, Asst. Time Keeper, Security Guard, Bell Boy, Doormen, Durban, and Dispatch Clerks etc.). We prepared a list of 200 employees for each hotel out of them we randomly selected 100 employees from Cambay and 100 employees from Inder Residency. Hence 200 employees were selected from both the hotels for this study.

Main Findings of the Field Study

On the basis of the observation and analysis of various aspects of human resource development in hotel Inder Residency and Cambay hotel, main finding are summarized as under:

Human Resource Development

On the basis of survey, there is an existence of H.R.D department in Cambay and Inder Residency hotel. And all managers and employees responded that all the HRD functions (Recruitment, Selection and Placement, Career Planning and Development, Training Programme, Performance Appraisal, Feedback and Counseling) were performed by their hotels. It was found that feedback and Counseling and Career Planning and Development was least performed by human resource department.

Recruitment

The respondents in Cambay and Inder Residency hotel were asked question related to their sources of vacancy clearly indicates that every hotel adopted different methods for recruiting the new manager's. In the Cambay, majority of manager's *i.e.*, 35 per cent was coming through 'Placement Agency', 30 per cent through 'Advertisement' whereas in Inder Residency majority of managers were coming through "Advertisement" (55%). The chi square test result showed that there was insignificant association between the sources of vacancy for managers and sampled hotels.

In the Cambay, 39 per cent employees were coming through 'Employee Referrals' and 29 per cent through 'Placement Agency' whereas in Inder Residency majority of employees were coming through 'Placement Agency' (38%) and 'Advertisement' (31%). Chi square test result revealed that both hotels adopt different methods for recruiting the new employees. It was observed that the percentage of 'Advertisement' and 'Placement Agency' as a source of vacancy was higher in Inder Residency than Cambay. Whereas 'Employees Referrals' was more preferred by Cambay than Inder Residency.

The research showed that nearly equal percentage of managers of Cambay responded that 'Advertisement' (30%) and "Placement Agency" (30%) was the best method for recruitment while in the opinion of managers of Inder Residency 'Reference' (40%) and 'Placement Agency' (25%) was the best method for recruitment. The chi square test result showed that there was no significance association between the two hotels on the basis of best method of recruitment.

In Cambay 'Employee Referrals' (36%) and 'Placement Agency' (29%) is the best method for recruitment of employees while in the opinion of employees of Inder Residency 'Placement Agency' (40%) and 'Advertisement' (32%) is the best method for recruitment. The chi square test result indicated that there was significance association between the two hotels on the basis of best method of recruitment.

Half of the managers of Cambay responded that 'Reference' (50%) and 'Employment Exchange' (35%) was the worst method for recruitment while in Inder Residency manager's state that 'Through Investigation' (35%) and 'Employment Exchange' (25%) was the worst method respectively. The chi square test results revealed the significant difference exists between two hotels on the basis of worst method of recruitment. The result showed that 'Reference' method was worst method of recruitment for managers in Cambay hotel whereas recruitment through investigation method was considering worst method by managers of Inder Residency.

The employees of Cambay responded that 'Reference' (60%) and 'Through Investigation' (25%) was the worst method for recruitment while in Inder Residency employees state that 'Employment Exchange' (33%) and 'Reference' (25%) was the worst method. The chi square test results showed the significant difference exists between two hotels on the basis of worst method of recruitment.

Selection

In Cambay and Inder Residency hotel, 40 per cent manager's have opinion that successful recruitment depended on "Public Image of an Organization" while 35 per cent manager's of both the hotels state that "Available of skilled person in the market". Work culture of an organization is carried and radiated by the personnel working for the company so when it comes to successful recruitment "Public Image of an Organization" is the golden asset for current employees and the prospective candidates getting into the board of the organization.

Most of the managers (45%) and employees (59%) from Cambay were given more importance on academic qualification than experience in their selection process, on the contrary in Inder Residency, more focus was given to managers (65%) and employees (60%) on experience rather than academic qualification. More weightage was given to communication skill and smartness of the managers of Cambay hotel (55%) as compared to managers of Inder Residency (35%). The chi square test result showed that there was no significant association between two hotels and weightage given to communication skills.

Training

70 per cent managers of Inder Residency hotel and 35 per cent managers of Cambay hotel responded that the management provided training facilities while half of the employees from Cambay (59%) and Inder Residency (54%) hotels state that the hotel management provided 1-3 months training to their employees at the time of appointment.

45 per cent and 60 per cent managers from Cambay and Inder Residency respectively attended training programme in the field of management. And 25 per cent and 20 per cent managers from both the hotels respectively attended training in personnel department. Only few managers (10% and 5%) of Cambay were attended training in the field of finance and IT field whereas managers from Inder Residency were nil. It was also notable that maximum employees from Cambay and Inder Residency respectively attended training programme in all respective area i.e. Management, Marketing, Personnel, Finance and Information and Technology.

80 per cent managers and 70 per cent employees of Cambay hotel stated that their hotel conducted 'Separate Training' programme while 75 per cent managers and 87 per cent employees of Inder Residency hotel stated that their hotel conducted 'Training on the work' programme. Managers and employees of both the hotels files training programme improve their performance, improve their level of satisfaction and opportunities for promotion.

84 per cent and 90 per cent employees from Cambay and Inder Residency hotels respectively stated that they were satisfied with the training provided by their hotels. The chi square test result showed non significant association between sampled hotels and satisfaction level of employees.

35 per cent of managers of Cambay hotel faced the problem of learning while 45 per cent managers of Inder Residency faced communication problem with trainee. The chi square test result also revealed that communication problems and different levels of trainees was more prevalent in Inder Residency than Cambay hotel whereas difficulty in

learning was more found in Cambay than Inder Residency hotel. It was also found that employees of Inder Residency (21%) faced problem of 'Poor Guidance' than employees of Cambay hotel. Whereas 'Inadequate Time' problem were more faced by employees of Cambay (55%) than Inder Residency.

Working Environment

Human Resource, Purchase, Sales and Marketing, Food and Beverage Production, Food and Beverage Service, Accounts and Finance, General Administration, Information System, Personal and Welfare, Front Office, Store, Security, Time Office, Engineering, House Keeping and Travel Desk are the main departments in both the hotels.

In Cambay hotel and Inder Residency hotel, there were four shifts in a day and nearly 50 per cent employees of Cambay and Inder Residency responded that they had nine hours of working in a day and nearly 90 per cent of the employees of Cambay and Inder Residency were satisfied with their working hours.

78 per cent and 88 per cent employees of Cambay and Inder Residency respectively reported that they had good working conditions in their hotels. Thus hotel are provided with secured, good and congenial working conditions.

Salary, Bonus and Allowances

More than ¾ managers and employees from Cambay and Inder Residency hotels were agree that adequate salary paid by management to them. Only 15 per cent managers of Inder Residency were paid overtime compare to 45 per cent managers of Cambay hotel. Chi square test result showed significant difference between managers paid overtime and sampled hotels. It also revealed that 45 per cent employees from Cambay and 49 per cent employees from Inder Residency hotel received over time. Only 5 per cent managers of Inder Residency were receiving bonus compare to 65 per cent managers of Cambay hotel. Similarly only 5 per cent employees of Inder Residency and 85 per cent employees of Cambay were receiving bonus by their management. Chi square test result revealed that employees and managers in

Cambay hotel were receiving more bonus compare to employees and managers in Inder Residency.

75 per cent and 65 per cent managers from Cambay and Inder Residency respectively received the vehicle/petrol allowances while 55 per cent and 45 per cent received the telephone allowances. 45 per cent and 30 per cent respondents received medical benefits, 40 per cent and 20 per cent respondents received children education allowances and 20 per cent and 95 per cent respondents received other allowances like club, gym and sports, gaming zone, picnic and parties and swimming pool etc. It showed that in Cambay hotel, managers received maximum allowances i.e. children education, vehicle/petrol allowances, telephone and entertainment allowances on fixed basis and only medical allowances received on actual basis while in Inder Residency, managers received medical, children education and entertainment allowances on fixed basis and vehicle/petrol and telephone allowances on actual basis.

Similarly 67 per cent and 53 per cent employees from Cambay and Inder Residency respectively received the vehicle/petrol allowances while 74 per cent and 41 per cent received the telephone allowances. 8 per cent and 36 per cent employees received medical benefits, 18 per cent and 6 per cent employees received children education allowances and 56 per cent and 6 per cent respondents received Entertainment allowances. It showed that in Cambay hotel, employees received maximum allowances i.e. children education, vehicle/petrol allowances, telephone and entertainment allowances on fixed basis and only medical allowances received on actual basis while in Inder Residency, employees received medical, children education and entertainment allowances on fixed basis and vehicle/petrol and telephone allowances on actual basis.

Basic Facilities

Accommodation Facilities

Nearly 5 per cent managers and employees of both the hotels were receiving accommodation facilities while 95 per cent managers and employees were received HRA in the absence of accommodation facility.

Transportation Facilities

Cambay hotel management provided transportation facilities to their managers and employees while Inder Residency hotel management not providing transportation facilities to their managers and employees.

Uniform

All the managers and employees from both the hotels reported that uniform is compulsory in their respective department.

Medical Facilities

The research also reveals that there is no hospital/ dispensary facility available in both the hotels. In Cambay hotel, management provides ESI facility to their managers and employees for treatment while Inder Residency, management provides cash reimbursement for treatment to their managers and employees. The survey clearly shows that both the hotels were not provided the medical benefits to the manager's and employee's family members.

Recreational Facilities

Cambay and Inder Residency hotel provides recreational facilities like entertainment, club, bar, gym, transportation, fashion show, food festival, gaming zone, recreation room, rest room, swimming pool, picnic and parties etc., to their managers and employees.

Motivation, Reward and Incentive Plan

In Cambay hotel, 55 per cent, 35 per cent and 35 per cent managers were motivated by 'Promotion', 'Giving Reward' and by 'Monetary Benefits' respectively. While in Inder Residency hotel 70 per cent managers motivated by 'Encouragement' and only 20 per cent managers motivated by 'Promotion'.

It was found that 51 per cent employees from Cambay hotel motivated by giving 'Monetary Benefits' on the other hand 70 per cent employees motivated by 'Encouragement' in Inder Residency. And it also observed that only 5 per cent of employees motivated through 'Promotion' in Inder Residency while 25 per cent employees motivated by 'Promotion' in Cambay hotel.

Nearly 90 per cent managers and employees from Cambay and Inder Residency hotel reported that management often appreciated to them for increasing productivity. Around 80 per cent managers and employees from Cambay hotel felt that management gives incentive to them for encouragement and better work while nearly 70 per cent managers and employees of Inder Residency reported that management gives incentive to them for encouragement. Generally management of Cambay and Inder Residency hotel encourage to managers and employees for using new methods and creative ideas. Chi square test result indicates that there was no significance difference between sampled hotels and their encouragement for using new methods and creative ideas.

The study reveals that management gave monetary benefits to the managers. In Cambay hotel 50 per cent managers reported that management gives individual bonus to them while Inder Residency, 90 per cent managers says that management give increment. The chi square test revealed that in Inder Residency, increment is more preferred as monetary benefits than Cambay. Management also gave non-monetary benefits to their managers. Only 35 per cent managers of Cambay hotel and 75 per cent managers of Inder Residency reported that management gives appreciation. The chi square test result showed that appreciation as non-monetary benefits is more followed by Inder Residency than Cambay hotel.

In Cambay hotel only 68 per cent employees reported that management offered increment to employees, while Inder Residency, 92 per cent employees stated the same. While management also offered non-monetary benefits to their employees. In Cambay hotel 71 per cent employees reported that management granted appreciation while in Inder Residency, only 44 per cent employees reported the same.

Appreciation as non-monetary benefit was more prevalent in Cambay than Inder Residency.

Promotion and Demotion

65 per cent and 70 per cent managers and 87 per cent and 86 per cent employees from Cambay hotel and Inder Residency hotel respectively reported that both seniority and merit basis was adopted for promotion by their management. The chi square test result showed that there was non significance difference between the sampled hotels on the basis of promotion.

In Cambay hotel, 55 per cent managers responded that they get promoted on due time while in Inder Residency 80 per cent managers stated that they get promoted on due time. Half of the managers of Cambay hotel were not promoted due to improper qualification for promoted post. 65 per cent managers of Inder Residency were not promoted due to they were not trained or skilled compared with 45 per cent managers of Cambay hotel. It revealed that promotion of managers of Cambay hotel was hindered by their improper qualification whereas lack of training and skills was problem for promotion of managers of Inder Residency.

71 per cent employees of Cambay and 78 per cent employees of Inder Residency responded that they were not promoted on due time. The chi square test result showed that there was no significant difference between the two hotels and managers promotion on due time. 25 per cent of employees of Cambay hotel were not promoted due to their incomplete the probation period compared with only 10 per cent employees of Inder Residency. 34 per cent of employees of Inder Residency were found to be not promoted due to resistance by their head of department compared with 17 per cent employees of Cambay hotel. It showed that incomplete probation period was main reason of delay in promotion in Cambay hotel whereas in Inder Residency resistance of head of department was main reason for delay in promotion.

Only few per cent managers and employees of Cambay and Inder Residency were demoted by their management. It was found that only few managers and employees from Cambay and Inder Residency were demoted due to not maintain punctuality, improper working and misbehave with management.

Industrial Relation

80 per cent managers and 83 per cent employees from Cambay and 85 per cent managers and 93 per cent employees from Inder Residency hotel felt that they have good relations with management.

It was observed that 15 per cent managers and 58 per cent employees from Cambay and 80 per cent managers and 71 per cent employees from Inder Residency hotel never faced dispute with management. In Cambay hotel, managers and employees generally faced dispute with management whereas on the contrary in Inder Residency hotel, managers and employees rarely faced dispute with management.

Nearly 75 per cent managers of Cambay and Inder Residency hotel agreed that their management had an effective grievance handling procedure for their managers. Similarly 79 per cent and 86 per cent employees of Cambay and Inder Residency hotel respectively agreed with the said statement.

Job Enrichment

More than ¾ managers and employees from Cambay and Inder Residency hotel responded that management has definite plans for career development for them. Hotel management was generally very sympathetic in dealing day to day problems of employees.

Job Satisfaction

85 per cent managers and 65 per cent employees from Cambay and only 45 per cent managers and 22 per cent employees from Inder Residency responded that salaries, allowances and pre-requisites are attractive considerations for job responsibilities. It showed that managers and employees of Cambay hotel were more in favour of salaries, allowances and pre-requisites compared to managers and employees of Inder Residency.

Nearly 75 per cent managers from both the hotel said that job provides enough opportunities to utilize their skills and abilities up to some extent. 75 per cent managers from Cambay and 85 per cent managers from Inder Residency hotel stated that working environment was healthy and good and they were satisfied with the working conditions.

Social Security Facilities

The research clearly indicates that Cambay and Inder residency hotel management provided provident fund (P.F.) and gratuity to their managers and employees and there was no pension scheme for the managers and employees.

Testing of Hypothesis

The hypotheses formulated for testing under this study are as follows:

Ha: 1 "Advertisement is the best method of recruitment than any other method of recruitment."

Hypothesis is rejected based on the following observation.

In Inder Residency, 40 per cent of managers responded that 'Reference' was the best method while only 15 per cent managers stated that 'Advertisement' was the best method of recruitment. Further 40 per cent employees said that 'Placement agency' was the best method compared with 32 per cent of employees stated that 'Advertisement' was the best method of recruitment. In Cambay hotel equal per cent (30%) of managers responded that 'Advertisement' and 'Placement Agency' was the best method of recruitment. While 36 per cent and 29 per cent employees favored 'Employee Referrals' and 'Placement Agency' respectively was the best method of recruitment. Only 15 per cent employee state that 'Advertisement' was best method of recruitment.

Since 'Placement Agency', 'Employee Referrals' and 'Reference' dominated as a method of recruitment than 'Advertisement'; therefore the above hypothesis is rejected.

Ha: 2 "Motivation method adopted by hotel management increases productivity in hotels."

Hypothesis is accepted based on the following observation.

80 per cent and 95 per cent managers from Cambay and Inder Residency hotel respectively responded that motivation methods often increased their productivity. Similarly 97 per cent and 90 per cent employees from both hotels stated that motivation methods often increased their productivity.

***Ha:* 3** "In Hotel Industry employees have less grievances and dispute with management."

Hypothesis is partially accepted based on the following observation.

In Cambay hotel, managers generally faced dispute with management whereas on the contrary in Inder Residency hotel, 80 per cent managers feels that they never faced dispute with management. The chi square test result shows that there was significant difference between the two hotels and dispute between managers and hotel management.

As 58 per cent and 71 per cent employees of Cambay and Inder Residency had never any dispute with hotel management. Only 42 per cent and 29 per cent employees from Cambay and Inder Residency respectively said that they had faced dispute with management. The chi square test result shows that there is no significant difference between the two hotels and dispute between employee and hotel management. Thus the above hypothesis can be partially accepted.

***Ha:* 4** "In Hotel Industries proper social security facilities have been provided by management to their employees."

Hypothesis is partially accepted based on the following observation.

As 65 per cent and 87 per cent employees of Cambay and Inder Residency stated that management provided P.F (Provident Fund) and 80 per cent and 20 per cent employees of both the hotels said that management provided gratuity. 65 per cent and 55 per cent managers of Cambay and Inder Residency hotel respectively stated that hotel management provided provident fund (P.F). All managers of both the hotel state that management provided gratuity. Out of these the hotels cannot provided to pension to their employees and managers.

Table 5.1: Testing of Hypothesis

Sr. No.	Hypotheses	Result
Ha : 1	"Advertisement is the best method of recruitment than any other method of recruitment."	Rejected
Ha : 2	"Motivation method adopted by hotel management increases productivity in hotels."	Accepted
Ha : 3	"In Hotel Industry employees have less grievances and dispute with management."	Partially Accepted
Ha : 4	"In Hotel Industries proper social security facilities have been provided by management to their employees."	Partially Accepted

Suggestions

As observed personally, as per procedures and administration of the hotels, it is clearly evinced that the hotels are managing its human resources efficiently. Most of the employees in hotel industries have enthusiastic, high level of patients, candid and good inter personal relationship. They have etiquette to deal with managers and top management. But at concluded by *Cerventes* in his famous novel Donquixote, there is "something good in bad of us and something bad in good of us", and with this concept it is always true that no system can be said to be perfect and ideal, and thus there is always some scope for improvement. Having studied, seen and observed the "Human Resource Development in Five Star Hotel Industry" in detail, the researcher is in a position to offer some tenable suggestions as under, which can go a long way in further ameliorating in developing of human resources in hotel industries. These suggestions can be implemented gradually and when facilities permit.

- According to 5 per cent of employees of Cambay and Inder Residency feedback and counseling and career planning and development was least performed by human resource department. Therefore it is suggested that human resource department of both the hotels should include feedback and counseling and career planning and development among their various functions. Career planning and development application can help employees in furthering their careers and also facilitate finding qualified internal employees for new job openings. Since these functions are backbone of successful human resource department, therefore due consideration should be given. Other suggestion to improve situation with career planning is to use more personal approach such as counseling employees by department's managers about the career development opportunities.
- Cambay hotel has given more emphasis on academic qualification than experience in selection process whereas Inder Residency more emphasized on experience than academic qualification in selection process. In Cambay hotel more weightage was given to communication skills and smartness in selection process compared to Inder Residency. So it is suggested that Inder Residency hotel should give more weightage to communication skills and smartness and both Cambay and Inder Residency hotel should consider experience as well as qualification for selecting the managers and employees.
- Percentage of managers of Cambay hotel (35%) provided with training facility was just half of percentage of managers of Inder Residency (70%). 25 per cent and 35 per cent employees from both the hotels responded that there was no training provided to them in their respective department. To improve the quality of training provided by both the hotels and to increase satisfaction it is suggested to introduce 'Train the Trainer' programme. 'Train – the – Trainer' programme is one of the easiest and most efficient ways to develop team of trained

managers. Both the hotels should also conduct seminars, conferences and workshops to train their employees.

- 25 per cent managers of Cambay hotel and 45 per cent managers of Inder Residency hotel faced communication problems with their trainees. Both the hotels should improve its communication problems with trainees by adopting 'open house communication'. Another way to improve communication between managers and their trainees is to introduce so called 'walking management' which can facilitate communication between managers and trainees by making it less formal.
- 55 per cent employees of Cambay hotel stated that they were not given adequate time for training. So it is suggested that Cambay hotel management should give enough time to train its employees. Cambay hotel should prefer 'on the job' method of training to overcome the time problem. Both the hotels should consider objective of training while selecting training method whether it is 'on the job' method or 'separate training'.
- Only 15 per cent of Inder Residency managers received overtime compared with 45 per cent managers of Cambay hotel. Nearly half of the employees of both Cambay and Inder Residency received overtime. For both the hotels it is suggested that if their managers and employees are working overtime it will generate more business and these hotels should share some part of this profit with their managers and employees by giving them overtime payment.
- 95 per cent and 35 per cent managers of Inder Residency and Cambay hotel respectively, did not receive bonus. Only 5 per cent employees of Inder Residency received bonus compared with 85 per cent employees of Cambay hotel. If hotels earn profit they should give bonus to their managers and employees to motivate them.
- In Cambay and Inder Residency, 71 per cent and 78 per cent employees respectively, were not promoted on due time. So it suggested that promotion policy should be

changed and promotion should be given to all employees on their due time.

- Both Cambay and Inder Residency do not provide accommodation and medical facilities to their managers and employees while Inder Residency does not provide transportation facility to its managers and employees. As these facilities increase productivity of managers and employees so both the hotels should provide accommodation and medical facilities to their managers, employees and their family members. Inder Residency should provide transportation facility to their managers and employees.
- There is no pension scheme in Cambay and Inder Residency hotel. So it is suggested that contributing pension scheme and leave encashment should be provided to all managers and employees at the time of retirement. These schemes will result in less leave and increased productivity.
- None of managers of Inder Residency was given reward for motivation while 35 per cent managers of Cambay were recorded in this category. It is suggested that an effective reward system should be established by both the hotels to facilitate the reconciliation of the interests of employees with the interests of the company. Rewards should be established objectively, based on agreed targets and indicators. The reward system should be transparent, clear and concise. Rewards must be aligned with individual goals, but also with collective goals, so as to encourage teamwork versus individualistic attitudes.
- Only 10 per cent and 20 per cent of managers of Cambay and Inder Residency respectively, were motivated through monetary benefits. And 54 per cent of employees of Cambay and 32 per cent employees of Inder Residency were motivated through monetary benefits. It revealed that monetary benefits were underestimated by both the hotels specially Inder Residency hotel. To fix this problem it is suggested to decrease importance of base salary,

increase importance of other income elements and introduce new income elements for managers and employees.

- 50 per cent managers of Cambay were delayed in their promotion due to improper qualification for concerned post whereas 65 per cent managers of Inder Residency were delayed in their promotion due to lack of skills. Hotels should provide enough opportunities of education for its managers for the required post and also conduct quarterly training programmes to improve their skills.
- 34 per cent employees of Inder Residency were delayed in their promotion due to resistance of their head of departments. So Inder Residency management should generate 'promotion policy' with specific guidelines to HOD's so that they follow "ethical practices" in promoting right person at right time.
- 45 per cent and 85 per cent managers from Cambay and Inder Residency respectively, were demoted due improper working. Further 20 per cent and 15 per cent managers from both the hotels were demoted for their misbehaviour with management. 35 per cent managers of Cambay were demoted due to not maintaining punctuality. During research it was observed that there are long working hours in hotels which creates frustration among managers and results into improper working, misbehaviour and unpunctuality. So it is suggested that rather than demoting managers, management should try to find out the causes of such problems and take corrective actions.

Bibliography

Books

Andrews Sudhir, House Keeping: A Training Manual, Tata Mc Graw Hill Education Pvt. Ltd., New Delhi.

Andrews Sudhir, Food and Beverage Service: A Training Manual, Tata Mc Graw, Hill Publications.

Armstrong, Michae, Hand Book of Personnel Management, Kogan Page Ltd., London, 1976.

Beckhard, Richard, Organization Development Strategies and Models, Addison Wesley Publishing Co., Readings, Mass, 1969.

Bagchi S. N., Anita Sharma, Food and Beverage Service, Aman Publications.

Bhagoliwal, T.N., Personnel Management and Industrial Relations, Sahitya Bhawan, Agra, 1986.

Bhatia, B.S. and Batra, G.S., Encyclopaedia of Business Management, Deep and Deep Publications, New Delhi, 1999.

Bhatia, B.S. and Verma, H.L., Studies in Human Resource development, Deep and Deep Publications, New Delhi, 1996.

Bhatia, S.K., Principles and Practice of Personal Management, Deep and Deep Publications, New Delhi, 1989.

Bhaya, Hiten, Methods and Techniques of Training Public Enterprises Managers, I.C.P.E., —, 1982.

Bolar Malati, Performance Appraisal – Readings, Case Studies and Surveys of Practices, Vikas Publishing House, New Delhi, 1978.

Burack, E. H. and Smith, R. D., Personal Management – A Human Resource Approach, John Wily and Sons, New York, 1982.

Carl Heyer (Ed.), The Encyclopedia of Management, Van Nostrand Reinhold Company, New York, 1973.

Chatterjee, N.N., Management of Personnel in Indian Enterprises, Allied Agency, Calcutta, 1986.

Craig, R.L., Training and Development Handbook – Guide to Human Resource Management, Mc Graw – Hill Publication, New York, 1976.

Donaidson, Les and Edward Scannel, Human Resource Development, Addison Wesely Publishing Co., Reading, Mass.

Douglas, Mc Gregor, The Human Side of Enterprises, Mc Graw Hill Book Co., New Delhi, 1960.

Egerts, Maejorie, Linda Brothers and Gisler, Careers in Travel, Tourism and Hospitality, Mc Graw Hill, 2005.

Ernest Dale, Management Theory and Practice, Mc Graw – Hill Book Company, New York, 1965.

Evans Nigel and Campbell, David, Strategic Management for Travel and Tourism, Licensing Agency Ltd., London, 2003.

Flippo, Edwin B, Personnel Management, Mc Graw – Hill, Koghakusha Ltd., Tokyo, 1980.

Gray, Dessler, Personal Management Modern Concept and Techinques Virginia Reston Publishing Co., 1978.

Holloran, Jack, Personnel and Human Resource Management, Prentice Hall, Englewood Cliffs, NJ, 1986.

Jayagopal, R, Human Resource Development Conceptual Analysis and Strategies, Sterling Publishers Pvt. Ltd., New Delhi, 1990.

J.O' Fallon, Michael and Rutherford, G. Denney, Hotel Management and Operations, John Wiley and Sons Publishing Co., Hoboken, New Jersey, 2011.

Kazmi, Azhar, Business Policy, Tata Mc Graw – Hill Publishing Company Ltd., New Delhi, 1992.

Khandelwal Anil, K., Human Resource Development Oxford and IBH Publishing Co., New Delhi, 1996.

Kohli, Uddesh and Vinayshil, Gotam, HRD – Global Changes Strategies and Planning Process in India, IJTD, New Delhi.

Laxminarain, M.L., Worker's Participation in Public Enterprises, Himalaya Publishing House, Bombay, 1986.

Ladler, Leonard, Corporate Human Resource Development, Van Nostrand Reinhold Co., New York, 1981.

Lillicrap Dennis and John Cousins, Food and Beverage Service, Published by Book Power/ELST Edition.

Lloyd, L, Byers and Leslie, W. Rue, Human Resources and Personnel Management, Richard B. Irvin, 1984.

Mary M.Go. Frank, Monachello Tom, Human Resource Management in the Hospitality Industry, 1996.

Megginson Leon C, Personnel and Human Resource administration, Richard D. Irwin Inc., Homewood, Illinois, 1977.

Mehta, Basant and Kothar, Kiran, Human Resource Development (Vol, 1,2), Discovery Publishing House Pvt. Ltd., New Delhi, 1999.

Mehta, Basant and Kanthalia, Shruti, Personnel Management in Banks, Discovery Publishing House Pvt. Ltd., New Delhi, 2008.

Michale J. Jucius, Personnel Management, D.B. Taraporavala Sons and Co. Pvt. Ltd., Bombay, 1977.

Mitra, Sudeep and Sinha, Kalpana, Team Building in a Public Sector Mining Organization in Aligning Human Resource Process, Tata Mc Graw Hill, 1995.

Morrison Alison and Rimmington Micheal, Entrepreneurship in Hospitality, Tourism and Leisure Industries, Elsevier Ltd., 1999.

Mohanty, Pragati, Hotel Industry and Tourism in India, S.B. Nangia, APH Publishing Co., New Delhi, 2008.

Parda, Jayanta Kumar and Jena, Rana Kanta, HRD – Concept and Mechanism in Management of Human assets, M.G. Rao, Discovery Publishing House, New Delhi, 1993.

Pareek, Udai and Rao, T.V., Designing and Managing Human Resource Systems, Oxford and IBH, New Delhi, 1981.

Pestonjee, D.M., Motivation and Job Satisfaction, Mc Millon India Ltd., New Delhi, 1991.

Pyo Sungsoo and Bouncken, B. Richard, Knowledge Management in Hospitality and Tourism, CRC Press, 2003.

Rao T.V., Reading in Human Resource Development, Oxford and IBH Publishing Co. Pvt. Ltd., New Delhi, 1991.

Rao, T.V., The HRD Missionary, Oxford and IBH Publishing Co. Pvt. Ltd. New Delhi, 1990.

Rao, V.K.R.V., Managerial Effectiveness, Mc Graw Hill, Koga Kusha Ltd., Tokyo, 1970.

Saiyadin, Mirza S., Human Resource Management, Tata Mc Graw Hill Publishing Co., New Delhi, 1988.

Sharma, G. D. and Sharma, K.K., Human Resource Management, Ramesh Book Depo, Jaipur, 2002.

Silvera, D.M., Human Resource Development – The Indian Experience, News India Publications, New Delhi, 1988.

Singh, N.K., Human Resource Development – The Indian Public Sector, Standing Conference of Public Sector, Standing Conference of Public Enterprises, New Delhi.

Steers, R.M. and Porter, L.W., Motivation and Work Behaviour, Mc Graw Hill Book Company, Singapore, 1991.

Subha Rao, P. and Rao, V.S.P., Personnel Human Resource Management, Konark Publishers Pvt. Ltd., New Delhi.

Subramaniam, C.V., Human Resource Management, S. Chand and Co., Delhi.

Saraswat Arvind, Professional Chef, Ubs Publishers Distributors Ltd.

Srivastav V.K., Hotel Accommodation: Operation and Management, Aman Publications, New Delhi.

Taylor Darrell Clifton, Hospitality Security, LLC, Boca Roton, 2012.

Tesone Dana and Pizam Abraham, Principles of Management for the Hospitality Industry, Linacre House, Jordon Hill, Oxford, UK, 2009.

Timothy J.Dallen, Teye B.Victor, Tourism and the Lodging Sector, Linacre House, Jordon Hill, Oxford, UK, 2009.

Articles

Wilson Mervyn D.J., "Training and Education in Contract Catering Management," *Journal of European Industrial Training Publisher*: MCB UP Ltd., ISSN: 0309-0590, (1977).

Smeral Egon, "The Impact of Globalization on Small and Medium Enterprises: New Challenges for Tourism Policies in European Countries," Volume 19, Issue 4, pp. 371-380, (1998).

Jithendran K. J., Baum Tom, "Human Resources Development and Sustainability — The Case of Indian tourism". *International Journal of Tourism Research,* Volume 2, Issue 6, pp. 403-421, (2000).

Olsen, Michael D; Chathoth, "Forces Driving Change in the Hospitality Industry in India" Prakash; Sharma, *Amit Journal of Services Research*, (2001).

Kuthiala, (S K), "Tourism and Hospitality Industry in India" *Journal of Services Research*, (2001).

Ciara Nolan, "Human Resource Development in the Irish Hotel Industry: The Case of the Small Firm *Journal of European Industrial Training*", Volume 26, Numbers 2-4, 2002, pp. 88-99, (2002).

Paul Hyland; Terry Sloan, "Learning to Compete: Post-graduate Training in an Ron Beckett Aerospace Company *Journal of European Industrial Training*", Volume 26, Numbers 2-4, 2002, pp. 100-108(9), (2002).

Sharon Kemp, "The Hidden Workforce: Volunteers' Learning in the Olympics *Journal of European Industrial Training*", Volume 26, Numbers 2-4, 2002, pp. 109-116(8), (2002).

Akama John S., "The Role of Government in the Development of Tourism in Kenya" *International Journal of Tourism Research,* Volume 4, Issue 1, pp. 1-14, (2002).

Jauhari Vinnie "Competencies for a Career in the Hospitality Industry: An Indian Perspective" www.emeraldinsight.com, (2006).

Rena Ravinder, "Education and Human Resource Development in Post-independent Eritrea: An Explanatory Note,"*International Journal of Education and Development* using Vol. 2, No. 4. (2006).

Wang Yu, "Strategic Employee Training And Development In Chinese Luxury Hotels" Tourismos: An *International Multidisciplinary Journal of Tourism,* ISSN: 17908418 EISSN: Volume: 1 Issue: 1 pp. 109-116, (2006).

Bauma Tom, and Szivas Edith, "HRD in Tourism: A Role for Government?" Volume 29, Issue 4, pp. 783-794, (2008).

Lye Philip "Human Resource Issues in the Hospitality Industry", www.biz-momentum.com (2007)

Gehrels, Sjoerd A., "How Hospitality Industry Managers' Characteristics Could Influence Hospitality Management Curricula" *The Electronic Journal of Business Research Methods,* Volume 5 Issue pp. 37-48, www.ejbrm.com, (2007).

Richard A. Swanson, "Demonstrating the Financial Benefit of Human Resource Development: Status and update on the Theory and Practice," *Journal of Human Resource Development Quarterly*, 9: 285-295. Doi: 10.1002/hrdq.3920090307, (2007).

Ian D. Clark, David A. Cahir, 'The Comfort of Strangers': Hospitality on the Victorian Goldfields, 1850-1860, *Journal of Hospitality and Tourism Management*, (2008).

Fujun Shen, Kenneth F.D. Hughey, "Connecting the Sustainable Livelihoods Approach and David G. Simmons Tourism: A Review of the Literature," *Journal of Hospitality and Tourism Management*, (2008).

Abel D Alonso and Alfred Ogle, "Exploring Design among Small Hospitality and Tourism Operations," *Journal of Retail and Leisure Property,* (2008) 7, 325-337; doi:10.1057/rlp.2008.23; (2008).

Dominique Keeffe, Rebekah Russell, "Customer Retaliation at the Rmployee-customer Bennett and Alastair Tombs, interface." ISSN: 1833-3672 Volume: 14 Issue: 4, pp. 438-450, (2008).

Greg G. Wang, Richard A. Swanson, "Economics and Human Resource Development: *A Rejoinder Human Resource Development Review*", Vol. 7, No. 3, pp. 358-36, (2008).

Lynn Perry Wooten, Erika Hayes James, "Linking Crisis Management and Leadership Competencies: The Role of Human Resource Development" *Advances in Developing Human Resources,* Vol. 10, No. 3, pp. 352-379, (2008).

Mary J. Fambrough, "Emotions in Leadership Development: A Critique of Emotional Intelligence Advances in Developing Human Resources", Vol. 10, No. 5, pp. 740-758, (2008).

Heisler, William J., "The Challenge of Causality: A Commentary on "Human Resource Systems in Kenya", *Cornell Hospitality Quarterly Journal,* (2008).

Grant Cairncross Stephen Kelly, Human Resource Development and 'Casualisation' in Hotels and Resorts in Eastern Australia. ISSN: 1833-3672 Volume: 14 Issue: pp. 367-385, (2008).

Abel D. Alonso and Alfred Ogle, "Impact of Daylight Savings on Small Hospitality and Tourism Businesses: A Western Australian Case Study" 314-324; doi:10.1057/thr.2009.16. (2008).

Oh, Juliana Kheng Mei Ms, "Human Resource Development in the Tourism Sector in Asia," Perspectives in Asian Leisure andTourism: Vol.1 :Iss.1, Article 7. http://scholarworks.umass.edu/palat/vol1/iss1/7. (2008).

Ahmed Naama, Claire Haven-Tang, "Human Resource Development Issues for the Hotel Sector in Eleri Jones

Libya: A Government Perspective." *International Journal of Tourism Research,* DOI: 10.1002/jtr.683Volume 10, Issue 5, pp. 481–492. (2008).

Daniel Edward Craig, "Online Reviews: The Bane of Hotels' Existence or an Unprecedented Opportunity?" www.danieledwardcraig.com (2009).

Dylan Tanner, "A New Standard for Sustainable Events and Tourism." http://ezinearticles.com. A--New--Standard--For--Sustainable--Events--and--Tourismandid=3355383, (2009).

Kini Mahima, "A Rewarding Career in Travel and Tourism Industry." http://ezinearticles.com. A--Rewarding--Career--in--Travel--and- Tourism--Industry&id=2408032. (2009).

Debpath, "New Horizon in Change Management – HRD Aspect" www.expertscolumn.com (2010)

Esther Hertzfeld, "PTACs are all about efficiency for hoteliers." (2010) Articles.com. 04 Feb, 2011. http://findarticles.com/p /articles/mi_m3072/is_14 _225/ai_n56737231.

Dawn M R Martin, "History of Vincent HRD." http://EzineArticles. com/?expert=Dawn_M_R_Martin. (2010)

Simon Waker Haughtone, "Human Resource Management — An Integral Part of Human Resource Development." http://EzineArticles.com/? expert=Simon_Waker_Haughtone. (2010),

Balu Rankonda, "Human Resource Development - How it Affects an Organization. "http://EzineArticles.com/?expert=Dawn_M_R_Martin. (2010),

Kaye (Kye-Sung) Chon, "Welcome to Hospitality 3e." ISBN-13: 9781439057377/ISBN-10:1439057370. www.http://edu.cengage.co.uk/ catalogue/product.aspx?isbn=1439057370, (2010)

Kathleenchester, "Benefits of Enterprise Resource Planning (erp) Systems." www.articlesnatch.com, (2011).

Fred Fish, "Restaurant Pos Software Is Provided by Expert." www.articlesnatch.com, (2011).

Emelia Ennin, "Boosting the Hospitality Industry." Ghana Business Guide. (2011).

Hotel Industries Publications

Annual Reports of Cambay Hotel

Annual Reports of Inder Residency Hotel

News Papers and Magazines

Economic Times of India

Financial Express

Business Standard

Times of India

Hotels and Caterers

Travel Express

Good House Keeping

Clean and Hygiene

Websites

www.hospitalitybizindia.com

www.financialexpress.com

www.expresshospitality.com

www.ezinearticles.com

www.bestwestern.com

www.fhrai.com

www.hospitalitybizz.com

www.multimediahr.com

www.pasosonline.org

www.gujarattourism.com

www.gujaratindia.com

Index